American Hebrew Literature

Judaic Traditions in Literature, Music, and Art
Harold Bloom *and* Ken Frieden, *Series Editors*

AMERICAN HEBREW
Literature

writing jewish
national identity
in the united states

MICHAEL
WEINGRAD

With a Foreword by ALAN MINTZ

SYRACUSE UNIVERSITY PRESS

We gratefully acknowledge the following for permission to quote from these sources: Arnold (Avraham) Band for *Hare'i bo'er ba'esh* by Arnold (Avraham) Band; Samuel Bavli for *Shirim* by Hillel Bavli; the Bialik Institute for *Aderet hashanim: Shirim* by Hillel Bavli; the Bialik Institute for *Al ha'i: Shirim* by Shimon Halkin; the Bialik Institute for *Be'ahalei Khush: Shirim* by Ephraim Lisitzky; the Bialik Institute for *Ner mul kokhavim* by Gabriel Preil; the Bialik Institute for *Asfan stavim, shirim 1972–1992* by Gabriel Preil; Chana (Annabelle) Farmelant for *Iyim bodedim: Sefer shirim* by Chana (Annabelle) Farmelant; Chana (Annabelle) Farmelant for *Pirhei zehut* by Chana (Annabelle) Farmelant; Tsiporah Porat for *Ad mashber* by Shimon Halkin; Jay Kleiman and Adina Kleiman for *Netafim: Shirim* by Chana (Anne) Kleiman; *Sunset Possibilities and Other Poems* © 1985 by Gabriel Priel, published by the Jewish Publication Society, with the permission of the publisher; Hakibutz Mameuchad for *Hamishim shir bamidbar* by Gabriel Priel; Sharona Tel-Oren for *Hakukot otiotayikh: Shirim* by Avraham Regelson; Rubin Mass for *Bein alimut uvein adishut* by Eisig Silberschlag; Commentary, Inc. for "The Last of the (Hebrew) Mohicans" by Michael Weingrad; Commentary, Inc. for "Review of Emma Lazarus" by Michael Weingrad; Prooftexts/Indiana University Press for "Lost Tribes: The Indian in American Hebrew Poetry" by Michael Weingrad.

Library of Congress Cataloging-in-Publication Data
Weingrad, Michael.
American Hebrew literature : writing Jewish national identity in the United States /
Michael Weingrad ; with a foreword by Alan Mintz. — 1st ed.
p. cm. — (Judaic traditions in literature, music, and art)
Includes bibliographical references and index.
ISBN 978-0-8156-3251-1 (cloth : alk. paper)
1. Hebrew literature, Modern—United States—History and criticism.
2. American literature—Jewish authors—History and criticism.   3. Hebrew literature, Modern—20th century—History and criticism.   4. Jews in literature.   5. Nationalism in literature.   6. Identity (Psychology) in literature.   I. Title.
PJ5049.U5.W45 2011
892.4'09973—dc22   2010046333

*For my parents, Barbara and Ronald Nelson
and
for my father, Leon Weingrad* ז״ל

מוֹנֶה מִסְפָּר לַכּוֹכָבִים, לְכֻלָּם שֵׁמוֹת יִקְרָא.

Anyone researching the intellectual and spiritual development of Jewish life in America will distort history if there is no attempt to describe the activity of those Jewish nationalists who dedicated their time and energy to the furtherance of Jewish education and communal life in their new country. Hundreds and thousands of these activists worked in their various cities and communities, yet they garnered neither respect nor recognition outside of their small circles, and some not even there because their accomplishments were named after the wealthy. These maskilim, the intelligentsia of our people, worked in a spirit of self-sacrifice, with no expectation of recompense beyond the satisfaction of their own consciences. These are our men of spirit, in whom every discerning person may take pride and say:

"May my portion be with them."

—ZVI SCHARFSTEIN. *Arba'im shanah ba'Amerikah* (Forty years in America)

We will seem to them like faceless Indians, like anonymous Aztecs,
We will seem to them like the tribes that were scattered and lost.

—GABRIEL PREIL. "Hamtanah lamahar ha'atomi" (Waiting for the atomic tomorrow)

MICHAEL WEINGRAD is professor of Judaic Studies at Portland State University. He lives in Oregon with his wife and three children.

Contents

Foreword

Alan Mintz

THE ASTONISHING POWER of the English language to absorb successive waves of immigrants from vastly disparate lands is one of the great sources of America's coherence as a society. Precisely because of that power, equally astonishing are the pockets of foreign-language culture that resisted linguistic integration and remained apart from or parallel to the rule of English. (There are more instances of this persistence than is generally realized, and *The Multilingual Anthology of American Literature*, edited by Werner Sollors and Marc Shell in 2000, is a good place to appreciate its diversity.) Yet even within this distinctive phenomenon, the cases of American Yiddish literature and American Hebrew literature stand out as unique. Most non-English American literature was written for immigrants who had not yet become English readers, or it was written by exiles who were sojourning in the United States with the hope of returning to their native country. On the other hand, serious Yiddish writers—as opposed to the journalists for the immigrant press—were creating an ambitious modern literature that they fully intended to transcend the immigrant experience. When it came to the Hebrew writers, the ambitions were even more idealized because there was virtually no such thing at the time as a native speaker of Hebrew. In fact, only a small minority of male immigrants possessed the competence to read Hebrew texts; nevertheless, the American Hebraists aimed to create an important Hebrew-language cultural center on these shores. The rule of English eventually proved overwhelming, but many fascinating and indelible Hebrew poems, short stories, and novels were written in the course of this effort, and the lessons of the legacy of American Hebraism have just now begun to be fully appreciated.

These ambitions must appear quixotic indeed in light of Hebrew's role today as the language of the State of Israel. Hebrew serves the communicative needs of a complex modern society at every level, and this mundane fact is a success story that even the most abandoned Zionist visionary could barely have imagined. Yet in the midst of unresolved conflict over territory in the Middle East, we often forget that the Zionist idea that took hold in the nineteenth century was rooted, like other European nationalisms, in both land *and* language. Although the idea of homeland could be carried in the national and religious imagination, its realization "on the ground" could be achieved only through conflict, diplomacy, and war. The Hebrew language, on the other hand, had been a portable and internally determined commodity for the thousands of years of the Jewish Diaspora. In modern times, even before the rise of the Zionist idea, Hebrew had become the banner of the Haskalah, the Hebrew Enlightenment in Eastern Europe, and was used for the first time to create all the appurtenances of a modern secular Jewish literature. It was no wonder then, when Hebrew was co-opted to become the national language of the envisioned Zionist homeland, that the advantage of its portability should prove similarly valuable.

And so Hebrew became a kind of portable homeland for the American Hebraists. They were Zionists, to be sure, and several of them eventually settled in Israel. But they believed, with their mentor Ahad Ha'am, that the challenges facing the Jewish people came not just from persecution and anti-Semitism but from an inner crisis: the collapse of the religious tradition in the face of modernity. In grappling with that crisis, they argued, Hebrew had a special role to play as a bridge between the ancient and the modern and between Diaspora Jewry and the growing national center in Palestine. If they had known about DNA at the time, I am sure they would have claimed that Hebrew is the cultural DNA of the Jewish people. For they believed that the very grammar and lexicon of a language create as well as convey the worldview of a nation. Hebrew was the right vehicle to bring Jews into modernity because it preserved an organic tie with the nation and, instead of jettisoning the disused religious values of the past, it stored them within the latent strata of linguistic memory.

With these beliefs as their fuel, the Hebraists set about creating educational institutions and a literary culture in America that were at their height between the two world wars. After these very young immigrants finished their schooling and wrote their early confessional lyric verse, they went on to discover America anew. They discovered the sagas of the Indians, the tales of the California gold rush, the transcendental vistas of the American landscape, small-town American life, the rhythms of jazz and African American spirituals and preaching, and the spectacle of New York City. This was a belated discovery of America, to be sure; but never before had this new world been encountered through Hebrew eyes, with all of the complex historical and national filaments that are wired into that lens. This is the fascinating encounter that is described with so much verve and intellectual excitement by Michael Weingrad in the pages that follow. His readings in the American Hebrew canon will open up their own new world for readers interested in American literature and the modern Jewish experience.

Acknowledgments

I AM GRATEFUL to the many people who in various ways enabled the completion of this book. Alan Mintz's advice and support have been invaluable throughout this project, and I am honored by his kind foreword to this book. I benefited greatly from a Harry Starr Fellowship at the Center for Jewish Studies at Harvard University in 2004, and thank the organizers Ruth Wisse and Avi Matalon, director Jay Harris, and the participants in the Starr seminar for their extremely helpful challenges and insights regarding my project. Stephen Katz, Philip Hollander, Avraham Novershtern, Dominic Williams, Yaron Peleg, Jill Aizenstein, and Shachar Pinsker read parts of the manuscript at various stages and aided me with their suggestions, knowledge, and warm collegiality. Naomi Sokoloff, Ross Posnock, Edward Alexander, Sidra Dekoven Ezrahi, David Biale, Raimonda Modiano, James Gibbons, and Dan Bridge encouraged many of the interests that would later become this book's passions. I thank Ken Frieden, Annelise Finegan, and the editors at Syracuse University Press for accepting this book into the wonderful Judaic Traditions series.

I want to thank the librarians at Canisius College; the Hebrew College of Newton, Massacussetts; and the incomparable Judaica collection at Harvard's Widener Library for their assistance. I am also indebted to Harold Schimmel for (among other things) telling me of a tiny used book store in Jerusalem in which he had seen a cache of books by the American Hebraists: two boxes that became my working library as I began this project. Cynthia Ozick, Nava Semel, and Chana Farmelant kindly answered my queries about their work, and Adina Kleiman about her mother's work. The friendship of Robert Whitehill has been an unexpected dividend of my research. I am grateful to Neal Kozodoy and the editors of *Commentary* for publishing my essay on the American Hebrew writers and allowing its revised appearance here. For a full list of credits, please see the copyright page.

Peter Cole, Edgar O'Hara, David Ehrlich, and Joe Butwin have been the most illuminating of literary guides and the most gracious of friends. My brother, Aaron Weingrad, has ever been my best coconspirator. My beloved teacher Richard Marcus taught me my aleph-bet.

My deepest gratitude is to my wife, Mel Berwin, and to our three children Lev, Nava, and Amirav, whose names are now the sweetest Hebrew words I know.

Introduction

OVER THE LAST HUNDRED YEARS, the story of Jews in the United States has been, by and large, one of successful and enthusiastic Americanization. Hundreds of thousands of Jews began the twentieth century as new arrivals to a foreign land, yet soon became shapers and definers of American culture itself. Among the most visible—and audible—expressions of this transformation has been the quick linguistic march of those immigrant Jews and their children from Yiddish to English.

This book presents a counterhistory of American Jewish culture, a road not taken by the majority yet that did not leave the majority untouched. It is about the literature written by a group of Jews whose core identity was neither American nor Jewish American but ardently and nationalistically Jewish, and whose overriding linguistic and cultural allegiance was neither to the Yiddish of their immigrant milieu nor to the English of their new country, but to the Hebrew language. This is a book about Hebrew literature in the United States.

The fact that a significant body of Hebrew literature has been written in the United States is not widely known, even among avid readers of Jewish literature. It is, as Alan Mintz has noted, "one of the best-kept secrets of Jewish American cultural history" (2003, 92). In the popular American imagination, certainly, Hebrew literature inhabits three domains, more or less: the ancient world of the Bible, the pious realm of synagogue and study house, and the contemporary vernacular of the State of Israel. The notion, then, of modern Hebrew fiction and poetry being written in the United States, let alone in such far-flung corners of the country as Louisiana or Texas, may seem surprising, even humorous, to many—producing something like the impression created by Mel Brooks's Yiddish-speaking Indians.[1]

Yet the presence of Hebrew writers in the United States reflects the history of modern Hebrew literature. From its beginnings in eighteenth-century Germany through its more elaborate development in Eastern Europe in the late nineteenth and early twentieth centuries, modern Hebrew literature was primarily a European and Diasporic phenomenon rather than a Middle Eastern one. And while in the interwar period the Land of Israel rapidly eclipsed these other centers of Hebrew literary production, Hebrew literature was nevertheless at that point still plotted on an international map, of which the United States was a part. The waves of mass migration that, beginning in the 1880s and continuing until the 1920s, brought two million Jews from what was then the heartland of

---

1. Consideration of American Hebrew literature in English-language scholarship, literary criticism, and anthologies is extremely rare. Even works dealing specifically with American Jewish literature tend to make no mention of the existence of literature in Hebrew. A. Mintz (2003) is a recent and welcome exception, as are A. Mintz (1993) and Spicehandler (1993). These are excellent introductions to the subject and begin to consider the question of the American identity of this literature, as does Katz (2009) in his erudite study of the representation of Native Americans and African Americans in American Hebrew literature, and Alan Mintz in a forthcoming study of some of the major American Hebrew poets. Chametzky et al. (2001) also breaks new ground by including brief selections from three of the immigrant Hebraists. Two excellent recent dissertations that analyze American Hebrew authors are Aizenstein (2008) and Hollander (2004). Other, mainly chapter-length works in English that deal with the American Hebraists as a group include Alter (1994), Kabakoff (1974), Lederhendler (1994), Shavit (1992), Silberschlag (1973), Wallenrod (1956), and Waxman (1941). The essays by Alter, Lederhendler, and Shavit are the most critically sophisticated; the others, written by Hebraists, are more useful for their information than for critical perspectives. Understandably, there has been more written in Hebrew scholarship, though this has been largely confined to a few prominent figures within American Hebrew literature, rather than a consideration of the literature as a whole or its relationship to American literature and culture. The exceptions are, by and large, written by the immigrant Hebraists themselves, e.g., the scholarship of Epstein and Kabakoff. Recently, the Israeli literary critic Benjamin Harshav gave considerable space to work by a number of the American Hebraists in his anthology of Hebrew Revival poetry (B. Harshav 2000). Gershon Shaked's discussion of American Hebrew prose in volume 3 of his study of Hebrew fiction is insightful.

modern Hebrew literature in Eastern Europe to the United States, therefore carried along a small minority of Hebraists. These were immigrant Jews passionately dedicated to the Hebrew language, rather than their Yiddish mother-tongue or a non-Jewish language such as English, as the medium for a modern, Jewish, national culture. By the end of the nineteenth century there were already a number of Hebrew writers in the United States including, for instance, the eccentric bohemian Naphtali Hertz Imber (1856–1909, in the United States from 1892), whose poem "Hatikvah" later became the Israeli national anthem; and Menahem Mendel Dolitzky (1856–1931, in the United States from 1892), championed by Judah Leib Gordon as the man who would bring the poetry of the Jewish Enlightenment to the United States.

These forerunners toiled in crushing obscurity. Nevertheless, by the First World War a small but critical mass of Hebraists had gathered in America and their efforts began to bear fruit. Although late-nineteenth-century American Hebrew publishing had minimal success, such early endeavors had helped to lay the technical foundation for twentieth-century projects, including progressively more ambitious though still short-lived journals such as *Shibolim* (1909) and *Hadror* (1911). A turning point was the appearance in 1913 of the inaugural issue of *Hatoren,* the most significant American Hebrew literary journal of its time. Two years later the monthly journal became a weekly under the editorship of Sholom Aleichem's son-in-law, the Hebrew writer Y. D. Berkowitz. Though it ceased publication in 1925, in the 1910s *Hatoren* represented a new center of gravity in the heretofore scattered world of American Hebraism, and it was the main forum in 1916 for calls to launch a united organization for the promotion of modern Hebrew culture. In February 1917 this newly formed Organization for Hebrew Culture (Hahistadrut ha'ivrit, hereafter referred to as the Histadrut) held its first congress with more than one hundred attendees, including a number of major cultural and Zionist figures then living in the United States due to the exigencies of the First World War. Participants included Zionist luminaries and Hebraist teachers, writers, and activists, such as David Ben-Gurion, Rabbi Meir Bar-Ilan, Shemarya Levin, Henrietta Szold, Yitzhak Ben-Tzvi, Eliezer Ben-Yehuda, Daniel Persky, Kalman Whiteman, Avraham Spicehandler, and Morris Levine. By the end of 1917, membership in the Histadrut was said to be as high as 1,200, including over two dozen different Hebrew cultural organizations from New York to San Francisco. Another important milestone was the launching of the journal *Hadoar* in 1921. *Hadoar* first appeared as a daily publication but did not last long in this form: its audience of Yiddish-speaking immigrants had little use for a Hebrew daily when they could get their news from Yiddish newspapers. Nevertheless, *Hadoar* was reorganized the following year as a weekly under the auspices of the Histadrut; in the years ahead it would become the longest-lasting Hebrew journal in the Diaspora and one of the longest-lasting journals in the history of Hebrew publishing. Throughout its many decades of existence, it was the central literary forum for Hebraism in America.[2]

The Hebraists were always a tiny minority among the Jewish immigrant population of the United States. As a point of comparison, the Yiddish daily press in the United States reached a peak circulation, during the First World War, of more than six hundred thousand; the daily *Hadoar* had a circulation of about nine thousand to twelve thousand. The Hebraists also differed culturally and sociologically from their fellow Jewish immigrants. As a rule, they were not the desperately poor and largely uneducated masses who took to peddling and sweatshop work. Nor were they socialist radicals bent on jettisoning the remnants of traditional Judaism along with the capitalist order. Instead, their backgrounds tended to be that of the Haskalah (Jewish Enlightenment)—that is, they came from traditional Jewish milieus where they received extensive religious educations, then found their way into Western modernity through the avid absorption of secular and university education, while retaining a deep commitment to Jewish national belonging. Practically and ideologically, Hebrew was the bridging medium for this process, fostering a deep connection with Jewish tradition yet providing a vehicle for the creation of a modern national culture. Many of the Hebraists were teachers, and a number worked in university and academic settings. Their Europe-to-America story is not so much that of Irving Howe's splendid and well-known *World of Our Fathers* as it

---

2. The most complete source of information on the Histadrut is Pelli (1998). Useful articles on the rise of the Hebraist movement are A. Mintz (1993) and Z. Shavit (1988).

is the Hebrew educator Zvi Scharfstein's rather less famous though delightful combination of personal memoir, ethnography, history, and biography *Arba'im shanah ba'Amerikah* (Forty years in America). Like Howe, albeit not with the same scope or detail, Scharfstein discusses the economic, sociological, and cultural transformations of the Eastern European Jews in the United States. Yet his emphases are rather different: not Yiddish theater or the history of the Labor movement, but the history of Jewish education and Zionist activism; not the Triangle Shirt Fire but Haim Nahman Bialik's visit to the United States; not the rise and fall of Yiddish but the attempt to preserve Hebrew.

The Hebraists' work was intertwined with that of other Jewish nationalist programs, institutions, and figures in the United States. They cooperated closely with and held positions of leadership in American Zionist organizations; they were colleagues of cultural nationalists such as the philosopher of Reconstructionism Mordecai Kaplan and the indefatigable impresario of Jewish education Samson Benderly. Nevertheless, they were ideologically and culturally distinct in their reverence for Hebrew, and they differed from other Zionists in their emphasis on Jewish national renewal through Hebrew culture more than political activism. Their concerns were often sidelined by Zionist and other Jewish nationalist organizations, and their backgrounds as immigrant products of the Eastern European Jewish Enlightenment marked them as different from many of these other Jewish activists and leaders.

Perhaps the most far-reaching impact the Hebraists had on American Jewish life was in the area of education. The ideological influence and efforts of Hebraist teachers, administrators, and educational theorists were key factors in the transformation of much of American Jewish religious and synagogal education for youth into what became known as the "Hebrew school," with its emphasis on secular-national culture rather than purely religious or liturgical instruction. This transformation was effected through a network of Jewish teachers colleges that trained Jewish educators and that were staffed and shaped by immigrant Hebraists. These centers of Hebraism included the Hebrew College of Boston, Gratz College in Philadelphia, the Hebrew College of Baltimore, and the Teachers Institute of the Jewish Theological Seminary in New York. Moreover, a number of today's prominent scholars in the field of Jewish studies, editors of important Jewish magazines such as *Commentary,* rabbis, teachers, community leaders, and intellectuals attended at one time or another the educational institutions, teachers colleges, and summer camps inspired wholly or in part by the Hebraist vision, suggesting that the Hebraists made a significant if still underappreciated contribution to the most substantive currents in American Jewish intellectual and scholarly life. Also, despite the overwhelmingly male provenance of the Hebraists, we may speculate upon the effect Hebraist education may have had in helping to foster a more egalitarian religious and scholarly climate within American Judaism. It is worth noting that the two women mentioned by Pamela Nadell, in her recent history of women's rabbinic ordination, as having been allowed to take courses in rabbinics at the Jewish Theological Seminary long before women in the Conservative movement were allowed to study for the rabbinate, were both daughters of Hebraists (Nadell 1998, 180–82).[3]

And there was literature. Hebrew writers in America produced lyric and epic poetry, short fiction and novels, essays, criticism, polemics, memoirs, and translations. They created journals and forums for literature and scholarship, from *Hatoren* and *Hadoar* to *Bitsaron* and the annual *Sefer hashanah lihudei Amerikah.* The writing of Hebrew belles lettres in the United States was but one aspect of the wider Hebraist enterprise and, on a practical level, a sharp distinction between Hebrew literature and the other facets of American Hebraism is impossible to maintain because most of the notable American Hebrew writers were also teachers, scholars, editors, and organizers. Nevertheless literature, and especially poetry, was considered absolutely central to the enterprise and ideology of Hebraism. The Hebraist ideal was fundamentally embodied in the figure of the writer, the one who

3. Henrietta Szold, the great Zionist leader, was influenced by her father's Hebraism. Ziona Maximon was the daughter of the Hebraist educator Shalom Baer Maximon. For chapters on Szold and Shalom Baer Maximon, see Scharfstein (1956). On the teachers colleges, see Ackerman (1993), Alter (1968), Band (1998), and the essays by Midge Decter and Gerson Cohen in Rosenberg and Goldstein (1982). Among many other intellectuals, the last two editors in chief of *Commentary,* Neal Kozodoy and Norman Podhoretz, both attended Hebraist institutions.

could, through the activity of literature, draw on the sources of tradition and reconfigure them as modern culture, bridging the Jewish past and the Jewish future.

And yet the literature and culture created by the Hebraists in America remain largely unknown. Indeed, for all the hard-won accomplishments of the Hebraists—their literary output, their impact on education, the islands of Hebrew culture they created and preserved and through which their American-born students passed—theirs was a brief flourishing, with a heyday from roughly 1915 to 1925 that was always based more on hopes and aspirations than on solidity and permanence. By the 1960s, most of the American Hebrew writers had died or moved to Israel. Moreover, the simple and obvious fact is that despite their best efforts, the Hebraists were always a marginal group that never succeeded in determining the values or agenda of the American Jewish mainstream. Their program of Jewish national rebirth through the Hebrew language found only limited linguistic and ideological acceptance among American Jewry, and throughout the twentieth century to the present the overwhelming majority of American Jews have been illiterate in Hebrew. The programmatic failure of the Hebraists is mirrored by their invisibility in American Jewish popular memory, in which the lost language of immigrant origins is Yiddish, whereas Hebrew is seen as a success story but not an American story.[4]

As this book shows, however, the marginality of the Hebraists to the American Jewish cultural mainstream was to a considerable extent a mutual phenomenon. That is, the Hebraists were Jewish nationalists, uninterested in and often vehemently opposed to the hybrid and highly Americanized forms of Jewish identity and culture that emerged in the course of the twentieth century. They could not avoid grappling with America and American identity, but they did so in ways that distinguished them from the American Jewish mainstream.

4. For an appraisal of the situation of American Hebrew literature in the late 1960s, see Kabakoff (1974). For a history of the Histadrut that runs through the mid-1990s, see Pelli (1998).

The main purpose of this book is therefore to explore the American identity of a literature that was the central expression of a Jewish culture opposed to Americanization. In the chapters that follow I discuss Hebrew literature in the United States, from the emergence of a group of writers connected with the organized Hebraist movement in the early twentieth century to the present, and I do so with special focus on this literature's difficult process of self-definition as American and as not American. I first discuss the sources of the Hebraists' deep ambivalence toward the United States and in particular their vexed literary relationship with New York City (chapter 1). I then show how the Hebraists' relationship with American identity was conditioned by their equally ambivalent relationship with literary modernism (chapter 2). Chapter 3 analyzes the prominent place of the American Indian in the Hebraist imagination, and chapter 4 discusses the surprising extent to which the Hebrew writers engaged rural and small-town Christian America in their literature. Through a comparative study of Hebrew and English literary works dealing with the early American Jewish nationalist Mordecai Manuel Noah, chapter 5 looks at the cultural and emotional reverberations of the Hebraist conception of America as a merely temporary refuge. A consideration of the two finest writers among the immigrant Hebraists, their divergent attitudes toward the United States, and the place of the Holocaust in their work makes up chapter 6. Finally, the conclusion meditates on the state of Hebrew literature in America today, discussing the "traces" of Hebrew found in Jewish-American writers such as Philip Roth and Cynthia Ozick, as well as the surprising career of the last of the American Hebrew writers.

This book does not deal with the culturally distinct phenomena of Israeli writers residing in the United States, the reception of Israeli literature in America, or Christian Hebraism in America. I define the category of American Hebrew writer in connection with the institutions and venues of the Hebraist movement on American soil. Therefore I do not treat, say, the Israeli author Amos Oz's novel *Fima,* much of which was written in the United States, nor do I discuss authors such as Ted Carmi, born in America but whose literary career was essentially Israeli. Nor do I deal exhaustively with every Hebrew writer in America; by some estimates, the number of Hebraists and maskilim who put pen to paper in the United States was well over a hundred. Rather, I have focused upon works by more than a dozen authors whose aesthetic achievement, influence within Hebraist circles, and framing of identity issues made them the most sensible and fruitful choices. Nevertheless, there are several significant authors, such as A. S. Schwartz and Lev Arieli-Orloff, whom I have not analyzed here, though studies of their work would complement my own.[5]

Also, as I indicate throughout, this was not a homogeneous group. The American Hebrew poets and the fiction writers differ significantly from each other, the former generally tending toward a more idealized romanticism, the latter toward a more sociologically acute realism. There are the palpable differences between different immigrant generations, their experiences and attitudes. In chapter 6, I discuss Gabriel Preil and Shimon Halkin, today the two most critically esteemed poets among the American Hebraists and yet who in certain ways are quite unrepresentative of the other writers. Harry Sackler, whom I deal with in chapters 4 and 5, was claimed by Hebraists and Yiddishists alike yet does not fit entirely in either camp. This is to say that, though commonalities and tendencies are real and important, we should at no point lose sight of the particularity of genre, literary work, and author.

I will not make fashionable claims about the transgression of disciplinary boundaries, but I have written this book with multiple audiences in mind. It is intended as much for scholars and students of American literature and culture as for those in the fields of Jewish and Hebrew studies, and for those with other interests as well. To some extent, this reflects my own scholarly career. I began and completed my graduate training in a department of English, where I focused primarily on American literature. Yet during that time the field that began to compel my attention, and has defined my career since, was that of Jewish studies. This project has therefore been a wonderful way of bringing these two facets together, albeit and perhaps ironically in a subject that finds them so mutually antagonistic. I have tried

5. For a study of Christian Hebraism in the United States, see Goldman (2004). On the reception of Israeli literature in America, see Alan Mintz, *Translating Israel: Contemporary Hebrew Literature and Its Reception in America* (Syracuse, N.Y.: Syracuse Univ. Press, 2001).

to make intelligible to all readers the cultural figures and terms from these different worlds that herein intersect. Of necessity, I have engaged in more plot exposition than would be the case when treating better-known literary works (many of these works are little known even to scholars of Hebrew literature), but I have tried to make this as natural and unobtrusive as possible.

Reading the American Hebraists entails a number of challenges. As with so many of the Hebrew writers of their time, they had and deployed for literary effect an intimacy with the Hebrew Bible and traditional Jewish texts matched by few contemporary readers. Moreover, their aesthetic practices and assumptions often fly in the face of the modernist developments that condition the reading instincts of most serious readers today, whether in the English or the Hebrew-speaking world. From an Israeli perspective, meanwhile, it is difficult not to reduce American Hebrew literature to a case study of the failure of Jewish culture in Diaspora, a literary center that stagnated and died because it lacked the rejuvenating linguistic and cultural dynamism of a Hebrew-speaking society. By the same token, it may be difficult for post-Zionists and postmodernists to resist projecting their own ideological valuations and celebrations of Diaspora and marginality onto this literature. On the other hand, given my own American background, I have wrestled throughout this project with the Hebraists' resistance to American identity, their self-marginalization, and the way in which many of their most serious efforts to forge a connection with the American environment were—at least in the case of the poets (the prose writers were more comfortable in this regard)—often the most tortured works in their *oeuvres*.

Yet their ambivalence is also one of the most fascinating dimensions of a body of work that, both in its aesthetic achievements and its probing of the limits of cultural separatism and American identity, is necessary for the fullest understanding of literary culture in the United States. A consideration of American Hebrew literature can be an illuminating part of contemporary critical discussions of American literature in all its ethnic and linguistic varieties, particularly when dealing with such issues as language and nationhood, immigrant experience and identity formation, constructions of nature and the city, secularism and religiosity. In this, the case of

American Hebrew literature amplifies and challenges both the important work on literatures of the United States associated with scholars such as Werner Sollors and Marc Shell, and any number of studies of Jewish American literature that elide Hebraist culture.

The literature of the Hebraists also illuminates the choices American Jews have made in the course of the twentieth century and continue to make today. The Hebraists' resistance to the embrace of America, their ambivalent and uneasy truce with the realities of Jewish life in the United States, forms a provocative juxtaposition with the main currents of Jewish life in this, the most open and accepting society Jews have encountered in their millennia-long Diaspora history. The alienation of the Hebraists may not be a viable or desirable model. Certainly the bounties of America have been manifold for Jews; and this book, authored by a third-generation American and son of fluent Yiddish-speakers, is of course written in English, yet one more testimony to the acceptance and integration known by Jews in the United States. Nevertheless, the example of the Hebraists poses sharp and ongoing questions for American Jews about the culture they have inherited and are able to transmit. As Robert Alter wrote in a 1968 essay about the already fading legacy of the immigrant Hebraists and their teachers colleges:

> I cannot believe that any Jewish culture, whether religious or secular, that subsists entirely or even primarily in translation, can provide lasting or meaningful continuity with the Jewish past. This is not by any means to suggest what some of the more ardent Hebraists maintain, that the only "authentic" kind of Jewishness, now or in the past, has used Hebrew as its medium; but Hebrew does remain the one, indispensable key to three thousand years of Jewish experience. It may be a futilely misplaced utopianism to entertain the old impelling idea of the teachers colleges that substantial Hebrew-speaking enclaves can exist in this country. Nevertheless, I would contend that we have little prospect for surviving as a distinctive community unless there are appreciable numbers of Jews—however strong their linguistic loyalty to English—who are capable of reading the Bible in its original language, who understand the Hebrew of the prayerbook and of rabbinic law and legend, and for whom the reborn language of Israel, if not always fully intelligible, is at least not a foreign tongue.

We are, by general standards, a highly educated community, but in regard to knowledge of Jewish culture, rank ignorance prevails, as much among Jewish Ph.D.s as among Jewish cabdrivers. At least something, I think, must be preserved of the vision of the European-style Hebraists, however much our world differs from theirs. (Alter 1968, 61–62)

I myself did not know the immigrant Hebraists firsthand. I learned my Hebrew as an adult, not in the Jewish teachers colleges but from American-born university teachers in Seattle and from Israelis in Jerusalem. Approaching the Hebraists was therefore to find my way into an initially somewhat abstracted and remote culture, though in recent years I spent some time at the Hebrew College of Boston (now Newton), whose attractive glass and brick campus—one of the "houses" the Hebraists helped build, so to speak—gave my imagination a more architecturally solid anchor. More fundamentally, however, it was my growing appreciation for these writers' enterprise and achievements that made their vanished world more real to me. While my approach to their efforts is not devoid of skepticism and critical distance, it is also informed by my admiration, both for their literary accomplishments and for the selflessness and passion with which they fought for their cultural and spiritual ideals.

Note: All translations are my own unless noted otherwise in the list of sources.

American Hebrew Literature

1

America Is My Cage

NEW YORK CITY AND THE HEBRAIST
ALIENATION FROM AMERICA

IN THE INTRODUCTION to his 1938 anthology of American Hebrew poetry, Menachem Ribalow (1895–1953), then the most influential Hebrew critic and editor in the United States, remarked on the failure of Hebrew writers to depict present-day America in their work. Of Naphtali Hertz Imber, the poet whose "Hatikvah" was set to music as the Israeli national anthem, and who lived in the United States from 1892 to 1910, Ribalow observed: "[t]he land through which he wandered disappeared beneath his feet. Views of reality dissolved. And this poet was better equipped than any of his predecessors to apprehend, understand, see, and know America. First, he was by nature something of an artist-bohemian, a wanderer and a seeker, and second, he wrote books in English. And for all that we find next to no fertile, creative connection between him and his surroundings" (1938, vi). Nor, according to Ribalow, was this blindness to American life confined to the poets who made their mark in the nineteenth century: "even in our new, modern poetry neither America nor 'Americanness' makes its appearance through the present or through reality, but rather through the past and the visionary" (x). Ribalow noted that, while Hebrew poets avoided representing the modern American city, Yiddish poets had successfully developed a contemporary, urban poetry. Moyshe-Leyb Halpern, for example, "was captured by the mad, stormy spirit of New York; and in his poems, as in the poems of others in his group, we hear new, daring voices of the new world." Yet, asserted Ribalow, "there is no such thing in the Hebrew poetry here" (x).

I

Ribalow was not the only critic to remark on the apparent detachment of the Hebraists from their American surroundings. Certainly, when comparing Hebrew literature in the United States with American Jewish literature in either Yiddish or English, one of the first and most striking impressions one has is of the sharply more oppositional stance of the Hebraists toward their adopted country. This characteristic was noted even outside of Hebrew literature, an important instance being Abraham Cahan's English-language novel, *The Rise of David Levinsky*, which captures, along with so much else in the sweep of American Jewish experience, the alienation from America that was so typical of the Hebrew writers and intellectuals. Published in 1917, the same year the Organization for Hebrew Culture held its first congress in New York City, Cahan's novel presents us with the type of the Hebrew writer in the character of Tevkin, who recites to the novel's protagonist a recent poem of his, paraphrased by Cahan as follows: "Most song-birds do not sing in captivity. I was once a song-bird, but America is my cage. It is not my home. My song is gone." In the encounter between Levinsky and Tevkin, Cahan has juxtaposed the enthusiasm of the Americanizing immigrant with the distaste for American life and culture that marked much of the Hebrew literature written in the United States. While Levinsky protests at "the idea of America being likened to a prison," Tevkin insists that, "for the spirit at least," America is inferior to Russia. For "even if our people do suffer appalling persecution" in Russia, there is nevertheless "more poetry there, more music, more feeling." In America, on the other hand, there is "too much materialism . . . too much hurry and too much prose, and—yes, too much machinery." In America, says Tevkin, it seems that even "the things of the spirit" are "machine-made" (Cahan 1960, 459).

This view of America as soulless, crass, and cruel was part of the cultural baggage the Hebraists brought with them from Europe, and it reflects the well-known catalogue of European prejudices against the New World, often a result of European anxieties about modernity and the modern city in particular. The Hebrew poet and scholar Eisig Silberschlag, who was by no means free of such sentiments himself, noted in 1958 that America was "a term of opprobrium in intellectual circles of European Jewry . . . as late as the First World War. America was synonymous with business, rudeness, heartlessness—with everything antithetical to civilized refinement" (1958, 336). Haim Nahman Bialik, the major Hebrew poet of the early twentieth century and the towering cultural figure in the Hebraist and Zionist movements of his time, admitted after his first and only trip to the United States in 1926 that he had gone to America "with considerable trepidation, traceable in the main to the general conception of the United States which obtains in the world. The name America immediately calls to mind noise, confusion, and hullabaloo which supposedly reign there in all aspects of life. America, we are told, is all bluff and business; everything is advertising, hollowness, inflatedness" (1968, 163).

To this familiar repertoire of European denigrations of the United States, the Hebraists added their dismay at what they found to be the lamentable state of Jewish learning and piety in the New World. With considerable justification, America was perceived among turn-of-the-century Jewish rabbinic and intellectual elites as a place that was hostile to traditional Jewish observance and backwards in terms of Jewish learning. Turning again to Cahan's novel, we note the horrified reaction of Reb Sender, one of Levinsky's fellow townsmen in Russia, when Cahan's protagonist confesses his intention to go to the United States. "'To America!' he said. 'Lord of the World! But one becomes a Gentile there'" (1960, 61). Not that this stopped the masses of Jewish immigrants who came to America in the late nineteenth and early twentieth centuries. As Arthur Hertzberg has pointed out, those who went to America tended to come from the least educated and most economically desperate segment of Eastern European Jewry, and were therefore the least concerned with the qualms of the elites regarding the quality of Jewish life in the United States (1989, 153–54).[1] The poet Zalman Shneur, who lived in America from 1941 to 1951, pointedly describes this sociology in the poem

1. Hertzberg observes that there was "a long tradition, of at least a century and a half [prior to the period of mass immigration] of rabbinic and intellectual distaste for the New World"; he mentions the Hebrew poets in the United States as epitomizing this distaste: "[a]lmost without exception the theme of these writers was their personal alienation in Jewish America, which they depicted as uncouth, money-mad, and destructive to the spirit" (1989, 154).

"Shir-mizmor la'Amerikah," published in 1934. In this poem, he writes that, at the beginning of the mass migration from Eastern Europe, the thought of going to America was entertained only by "the ignoramuses, the rabble, the wretched tailors and unskilled cobblers, those who had nothing to lose by leaving their place of origin with its many strictures and little sustenance" (Shneur 1934, 487). Though the poem is ultimately positive about Jewish life in America, Shneur describes their fellow Jews watching these emigrants leave for the United States, the way one would watch "sinners entering the mouth of hell, foot-soldiers going into the line of fire, or captured blacks going into abject slavery."[2] Although the Hebrew writers joined their fellow immigrants in the passage to America, they remained culturally distinct from them, being more typical products of the religious and intellectual institutions of Eastern Europe: educated at heders and yeshivas, sympathetic to the claims of traditional Judaism (even when not traditional in practice themselves), and steeped in the culture of the Jewish Enlightenment. They looked negatively on the state of Jewish life in America, and their writings frequently castigate American Jews for their ignorance of Judaism, their materialism and coarseness, and their assimilatory values.

This disdain for American Jewry was also fueled by the Hebraists' own sense of marginality. While Yiddish saw a heyday and English quickly became the dominant language of American Jewry, the Hebrew writers waited in vain for a substantial Hebrew readership to materialize on American soil. Theirs was an extreme minority position within American Jewry, which remained largely indifferent to the Hebraists' cultural and ideological passions. Typical were the sentiments of the poet Menahem Mendel Dolitzky, who saw his immigration to the United States in 1892 as a banishment into irrelevance:

---

2. Shneur then describes the subsequent American Jewish success story, likening the poor Jewish immigrants to a "new Joseph," i.e., the son who is sold into slavery in a far-off land but who then becomes a ruler able to provide for his starving brothers. Today, writes Shneur, "Bronx and Brooklyn are aflood with the flower of womanhood," beautiful young Jews who are the offspring of those once-destitute tailors and cobblers (1934, 487).

In Russia there were people one could fight—respectable enemies. We fought the battle of the Enlightenment and Zionism against our Orthodox brethren; but even the most fanatical of them were men of stature. We may have thought their opinions damaging, but we knew they were solid, stable. They had a tradition to fight for, and you had to respect them for fighting.

But here in America? If only we had some of those fanatics and reactionaries from the Old Country here! They at least were loyal and devout Jews. Here we have a pack of boors, ignoramuses, whose only thought is to "make a living," with nothing spiritual about them. And then there's no one to fight *with* you. The Jewish intellectuals? Heretic socialists, heroes of Yom Kippur and Tisha B'Av balls; or else professional careerists, uninterested in their own people. . . .

Then there's nothing to fight for. The Enlightenment and Zionism are disembodied spirits floating in chaos in this country—in the Old Country they were concrete ideas directly related to Jewish life and traditions. So there you are: in America, the Hebrew poet has no one to fight against, no one to fight with, and nothing to fight for. There's no place for him here—he's pushed aside into a corner. (Lisitzky 1959, 175–76)[3]

The poet and scholar Hillel Bavli referred to America as "a place where a Hebrew letter freezes in midair" (n.d., 88). His friend Shimon Halkin described the "acute uprootedness" of the Hebrew writer in America, his "miserable feeling that his environment has no use for his creations. . . . Pushed aside in the heartless surroundings of the noisy Jewish street and the cheap, counterfeit life there. . . . Is his loneliness not total?" (S. Halkin 1969, 1:84). Once again, Cahan's Tevkin is representative. Despite having published several celebrated volumes of poetry in Odessa, in America Tevkin has for the most part given up writing Hebrew poetry, contributing instead (though with little success) to the vastly more viable Yiddish press and working in real estate to support his family. "Can't a Hebrew writer make a living in New York?" Levinsky asks someone versed in the

3. It should be noted that this passage is not taken directly from Dolitzky, but from Ephraim Lisitzky's recollection of their meeting in his memoirs.

Lower East Side cultural scene. His informant "shook his head and smiled" (Cahan 1960, 453).

Of course, quite apart from any literary or cultural preoccupations, the experience of immigration itself could be traumatic enough to turn one's spirit against the New World. As with so many Jewish immigrants, the Hebraists' departure from Europe was not always a matter of choice. In America these writers were separated from their families, from their homes, from the landscape and culture and values familiar to them. They had to make their way, often young and alone, in an entirely new environment. Sometimes this was nothing short of terrifying, an ordeal marked by grinding fear and despair, and one recounted by many an immigrant, whether Jew, Hebraist, or not. In a poem written shortly after he arrived in the United States, Bavli, then around the age of nineteen, describes his migration to America as follows:

> I was like a sapling just beginning to bud,
> torn up before it had truly taken root;
> like a hatchling, wingless, abducted from its nest
> and brought to strange and distant lands.
>
> I was like a man forgotten by God,
> no brother, no friend among the multitudes around;
> alien skies above me, a strange people around,
> the gates locked and hearts sealed.
> (Bavli 1937–38, 1:4)

Bavli was actually among the most optimistic of the Hebrew writers in his depictions of the experience of immigration. Even in this melancholy poem he admits that "the day will come" when he will become familiar with his new surroundings, and when, despite his enduring homesickness, "the poetry of a strange people will also reside in my heart" (1937–38, 1:4). Few of the other Hebrew poets were this confident, so early after their arrival, that they would grow to feel an intimacy with their new culture.

We must consider, too, the contrast between these immigrants' typical places of origin—the small towns of Eastern Europe—and New York City, to which most of them decamped. The sheer difference in size and intensity of their new environment was enough to make them feel they had wandered into some nightmare world where life bore no resemblance to anything they knew. Kovno-born Shlomit Pflaum was not one of the American Hebraists—she was an educator and journalist, and only visited America to travel—but her impressions of her first encounter with New York City in 1920 encapsulate perfectly the reactions of most immigrant Hebrew writers (and a good many other arrivals to New York) when they first came to that overwhelming metropolis. "New York seemed to me like some fearsome and alien monster," wrote Pflaum. "Stone giants pressed upon my heart and brought me to despair. . . . How is it at all possible to live here?" Although during the course of her stay she came to appreciate America, she nevertheless writes in her memoirs: "all the while I stayed in New York I had to force myself constantly to fight against my feeling of bitterness and anger that churned in me against this exile. I felt myself alone among the massive crowds. I was perpetually oppressed by the awareness that, here I was, a superfluous creature, unimportant, insignificant, and solitary among millions" (quoted in Govrin 2003, 37).

Similarly, the Hebraist educator Zvi Scharfstein describes in his memoirs how, only a few days after his arrival in New York, he began "to quicken [his] step, to use [his] elbows, to push through the people." The "press and crowding" of New York, he reflects, "brought anger to people's faces and swelled their veins with rage; this was the spirit of worry and trouble and haste and nervousness, which assaulted the city dweller and made him a beast of war" (1956, 33).

The intellectual's alienation, the Jew's sorrow at the eroding of tradition, the artist's bitterness at the lack of an audience, the immigrant's loneliness and bewilderment in the big city—all contributed to the Hebrew writer's deep ambivalence toward America. Yet more than any of these factors, it was Hebraism itself, the worldview of which these writers partook and the values for which they stood, that prevented so many of them from ever feeling wholly part of America or at home within it. The Hebraists already had a Jewish national identity to which they were fiercely committed, leaving little room for any interest in an American national identity. Moreover, this national identity, or "Hebrew idea," as it took shape in the United States, included as one of its important components a willful resistance to Americanization and a sharply critical attitude toward the assimilatory currents in American Jewish life. As we shall see, there were certainly exceptions to the Hebraist ambivalence toward America, and a number of these writers revised their attitudes and notions over time. Nevertheless, this ideological alienation characterized most of the Hebrew writers in the United States.

Certainly, the Hebraists tended to be deeply unsympathetic to the melting pot ideal. Recalling the fierce debate at the 1917 Hebraist congress over the proposal that Hebrew be made a requirement for Jewish students in American public schools, Scharfstein noted that the idea would never work because in America "everyone comes willingly to be melted in one pot. The arriving nationalities march to their cultural sacrifice [*akedah*] with songs of praise and thanks, and everyone is united in one new and mighty nation" (1956, 184). Whether or not Scharfstein had in mind actual pageants such as the 1916 graduation ceremonies at the Ford Motor Company's English school, in which foreign-born workers literally marched from a mock steamship into a massive cauldron to the cheers of several thousand spectators (Sollors 1986, 89–91), the arch quality in his description of cultural affairs in America is signaled most strikingly by his reference to the melting pot as an *akedah,* a word that refers to Abraham's binding of Isaac for sacrifice. Similarly, in the publication announcing the founding of the Tarbut school, a Hebrew teachers college set up by the Histadrut in 1920, we read that the goal of the school was "to educate teachers from among our American-born children so that their Americanness will not suppress their Jewishness," and to keep these young Jews from "losing themselves and their people in the sweatshops or the melting pot" (quoted in Pelli 1998, 88). If for Scharfstein the melting pot could be likened to cultural child-sacrifice, here it is paired with the sweatshop as a devourer of Jewish peoplehood.

And yet, although the Hebraists rejected the melting pot, they cannot be subsumed within the cultural pluralist or "transnationalist" critiques of the melting pot, associated with their American contemporaries Horace Kallen and Randolph Bourne. Kallen's famous 1915 essay, "Democracy versus the Melting-Pot," advocated not a melting pot but a symphony, in which each ethnic group would be an instrument contributing its own

distinctive timbre. Yet, as John Higham observes, Kallen's cultural pluralism was still a proposal for an *American* national identity. It is itself "one
of the products of the melting pot," attractive precisely to those "confident
enough to visualize themselves at the center rather than the periphery of
American life," that is, "to people who were already largely assimilated"
(Higham 1993, 213). It was Harvard-educated Kallen, raised in Boston
since the age of five, who formulated cultural pluralism as a model for Jewish identity in America. The historian Ben Halpern concurs, juxtaposing
cultural pluralism with the ideology of the immigrant Zionists—and his
remarks certainly apply here to the Hebraist camp as well: "[t]he doctrine
of cultural pluralism which these Americans defended, and which was most
explicitly argued by Horace Kallen, was pale and bloodless in comparison to the full-blooded Diaspora nationalism" advocated by the immigrant
Zionists and Hebraists. Only "Black nationalists and Hispano-Americans
in our own times," wrote Halpern in 1979, "produced a close, albeit more
violent, American equivalent" (1996, 329).

The nationalism of the Hebraists was even more distant from Bourne's
"transnationalist" critique of the melting pot. In the 1916 essay "Trans-
National America," Bourne argued that America was to be a "federation of
cultures" (Bourne 1964, 115); and in "The Jew and Trans-National America," published the same year, Bourne even claimed that Zionism was, or
should be, the quintessence of the "new spiritual internationalism" (128) he
was advocating. Bourne asserted that, despite the Jew's "racial and religious
egoism . . . the Jewish State which Zionists are building is a non-military,
non-chauvinistic State. Palestine is to be built as a Jewish centre on purely
religious and cultural foundations" (129). As with many left-wing intellectuals, the definition of Zionism that Bourne sanctions here is mainly an
expression of his own antinationalism, pacifism, and socialism. This was
not, however, the ideal of the Hebraists, whose allegiance to Zion was,
if not primarily political, certainly much more than what Bourne means
by "purely religious and cultural." It was a national allegiance because it
stemmed from their allegiance to the Jewish people—conceived not as an
American ethnic group, but as a distinct, independent nation.

Indeed, we may ask the question: to what extent is Hebrew literature in
the United States an "ethnic literature"? Werner Sollors's now classic study,

Beyond Ethnicity: Consent and Descent in American Culture, shows with dialectical elegance how "ethnic literature provides us with the central codes of Americanness" (1986, 8), complicating notions of ethnic literature within a sophisticated understanding of American culture. Sollors's work on other immigrant and ethnic literatures is helpful in offering a framework and sensibility for seeing how American Hebrew literature participates in the wider dynamics of American culture. (The Hebraists' use of Indian motifs, the subject of chapter 3, is a clear instance.) Yet there are also cases in which Sollors's discussions point up the ways in which the Hebraists did not share in those "central codes of Americanness."

To take one example, Sollors shows the extent to which the American identity of various ethnic groups, whatever their apparent cultural distance from America's first English settlers, has been informed by the biblical tropes elaborated by the Puritans. The Puritans' theological understanding of their migration provided "a compelling set of codes and images" through which subsequent immigrant and ethnic groups have understood and dramatized their own experience of immigration and peoplehood, creating through biblical typology "a continued new exodus from Egyptian-old-world bondage to the shores of the American promised land" (43).

The Hebraists, on the other hand, could not present America as a promised land because the actual land of Israel existed for these Jewish nationalists as a real and longed-for place, and not as a literary antetype for America. When they did use biblical tropes to depict America, they chose not the promised land but the wilderness (for example, as in the title of Scharfstein's memoirs, mentioned previously, or in the poet Gabriel Preil's collection, *Fifty Poems from the Wilderness*); or the edge of the world that was biblical Tarshish; or the often degenerate, oppressive realms of Egypt, Babylon, and Nineveh; or even the *tohu vavohu*—the formless chaos preceding biblical creation. The Hebraists retained much of the traditional Jewish conception of exile, and America, unique and welcoming as it could be, was simply one facet of this exile. Equally important, the Hebraists' relation to the Bible was not simply narrative and thematic—i.e., typological, in the sense described by Sollors—but was more intricately linguistic. In Hebrew, certainly to the ears of the immigrant Hebraists, single words, grammatical structures, even prepositions can allude to the Bible.

Typological uses of the Bible would therefore seem a weakly imitative kind of art in their literary system. As we will see later in this study, the Hebraists' connection to America via the Bible was sometimes expressed through their sense of themselves as the original representatives of a biblical tradition and Jewish national saga that other American groups—New England Puritans, African Americans, rural Christians, Mormons, and others—were getting at second hand.

Sollors describes "the central drama in American culture" (6) as the ongoing tension between "descent" and "consent"—the former comprising race- and blood-based allegiances and conceptions and identity, usually associated with ethnic origins and birth; the latter manifest in volitional, contractual, constructed forms of identity. This useful framework for speaking about ethnic and American identities may not, however, accurately describe Hebraist culture and identity. Hebraism and Jewish nationalism are obviously marked by elements of descent, concerns with race and blood connections. Yet we must remember that Hebraism (like Zionism in this sense) was a chosen cultural program—a form of consent. Almost no Jews grew up speaking Hebrew as their first language during the period in which the Hebraists came of age. Their language, Hebrew, was conceived of as national and was often the object of metaphysical reverence on their part—yet it was not an ethnic language in the sense of being their mother tongue or the language of their place of origin. For all its autochthonous and biblical elements, to speak and write modern Hebrew was to some extent an act of self-creation.

CITY OF MOLOCH

Given the Hebraists' conflicted encounter with the United States, Ribalow's characterization of the Hebrew poets as being reluctant to engage modern, urban America becomes quite understandable. Nevertheless, there were efforts by Hebrew writers to grapple with the realities of contemporary New York City. Prose fiction writers were the most successful in this regard, and they produced a literature, similar to immigrant literatures in Yiddish and English, dealing with Jewish life in New York and the trials of dislocation and acculturation, albeit with a greater sense of anxiety about

Jewish identity in America. Among the poets, however, the ambivalence about the urban environment was far sharper and the presentation of New York City far darker. To explore the nature of this ambivalence and the way it reflects the conflicted national identity of the Hebraists in America, I want to look at three works by the poet Shimon Ginzburg (1890–1944).

Born in the Ukrainian village of Lipniki, Ginzburg received a traditional heder and yeshiva education before making his way to Odessa, where he was in contact with major writers such as Mendele Moykher-Sforim and Bialik. He published his first poems in *Hashiloah*, the most important Hebrew literary forum of the time. In his early twenties Ginzburg left Russia for the United States, where he was an enthusiastic participant in Hebraist groups, such as the Organization for Hebrew Culture, and where he served as an editor of the Hebrew monthly *Hatoren*, founded the short-lived annual *Luah Ahiever*, was active at the journal *Miklat*, and helped to found the Hebrew PEN Club. In addition to writing poetry and criticism, Ginzburg also made a significant contribution to scholarship by editing and writing about the works of the eighteenth-century poet, kabbalist, and thinker Moses Hayim Luzzato. In 1933 he immigrated to Palestine, but he returned in 1939 as the emissary of the Hebrew Writers Association to the United States, where he died. Ginzburg's three long poems, "Bamigdal" (In the tower), "Behar beit Kolombiyah" (On the temple mount of Columbia), and "No-York" (New York), all written in the 1910s, are among the first attempts to contend with the American city in Hebrew poetry, and are fascinating instances of how emotionally and ideologically fraught such an enterprise was.[4]

The first of these poems, "Bamigdal," was written in 1912, the year of Ginzburg's arrival in the United States, and was first published the following year in *Hashiloah*. The subject of the poem is Ginzburg's immigration to America and his attempt to hold on to the faith that God will somehow console him for all he has lost in coming to the New World. This consolation, however, is not to be found in America, which manifests itself in the

---

4. For biographical information on Ginzburg, see Ben-Or (1965).

poem as a realm that contradicts the very notion of a benign, meaningful universe. Instead, Ginzburg's consolation consists of a vision he is vouchsafed of the Land of Israel. The tower of the poem's title represents the fundamental dichotomy of the poem. It is, on the one hand, the American city, called a "tower of Satan" (1931b, 204) and often embodied by factory towers. On the other hand, it is the Zion that continues to give his life meaning, emblematized by the Tower of David in Jerusalem and visible to the despairing immigrant from atop "the tower of [his] dreams" (210).

The poem begins with the young poet's desolation at having to leave Russia, "the land of all I hold precious" (199). Bereft "of any hope for happiness," he compares himself to the Jewish exiles forced to leave Spain in 1492. The ship that bears him across the ocean is like "a gigantic, sharp-taloned bird" with "its prey in its mouth," and in the course of the spectacular and frightening sea voyage he is repeatedly tormented by the sense of living in a meaningless world. Gazing on the endless expanse of ocean, he hears the skies laugh mindlessly and the waves declare that "there is no God" (201). Throughout the voyage, however, his thoughts turn constantly to the Land of Israel, both as his source of meaning and as an absence that gnaws at him. When the ship stops briefly in Germany, the fertile farmlands he sees there make him think of the Holy Land. Later, after a moment of despair on the open sea, he senses God's presence, the Shekhinah "that has been exiled with me," and he hears a voice telling him: "Your God still lives, / and He is in Canaan. / There the secret life-stores of your God are in the fields of sun— / for their sake, live!" (202). The Land of Israel is again the locus of life and meaning and is what enables him to possess hope—even as he travels in the opposite direction from it, to America. Now he sees "the spirit of God hovering on the waters," which are "no longer formlessness and chaos" but lie placidly under the "yoke of heaven." And yet, just as his sense of divine order is restored through his meditation on the Land of Israel, he sights the coast of the United States in the distance, a "sparkling tower of light" which he pointedly notes is "not the tower of David" (202).

To Ginzburg, the Statue of Liberty presiding over the New York harbor seems a foreboding Fortuna, raising not a torch but (in the first published version of the poem) "a clenched fist" (1913, 70), promising anything and nothing to the arriving refugees:

> Come to me, all who are hungry, for bread, or for justice,
> or who yearn to breathe the air of freedom. Die here of hunger
> like a stray dog, or rise up and rule overnight!
> (Ginzburg 1931b, 203)

Although his reference to "the air of freedom" inevitably puts one in mind of the "huddled masses yearning to breathe free" in Emma Lazarus's sonnet, "The New Colossus," Ginzburg's confusion about what the statue is holding—much like Kafka, who in the novel *Amerika* (1927) has it lifting a sword—suggests that he was not familiar with that most famous of poems on the "mighty woman with a torch" (Lazarus 1982, 48). Nor was this unfamiliarity out of the ordinary, since Lazarus's poem did not become widely known or popularly associated with the statue until the 1940s. The main reference here is instead Ginzburg's alteration of the traditional Passover invocation ("Let all who are hungry, come and eat"), thereby turning Jewish hospitality into New York City indifference, and again reminding the reader of Ginzburg's exile and his hope: the Passover liturgy continues, "This year we are here; next year, in the land of Israel."

Disembarking, the speaker describes America as a "Moloch," an alien god to which the arriving immigrants bring their "sacrifices": one sacrifices "his youth," another "her happy smile," another "his phylacteries and beard," and many "their God" (Ginzburg 1931b, 203). New York itself is an asphyxiating jungle of iron, populated by teeming, faceless masses of exploited workers. Whereas the poet remembers the lovely dawn over "the fields of the Ukraine," in America daybreak is announced with "the blast of the profane horn" from "Satan's tower," which sends "tens of thousands of ant-people" scurrying to the subway (204). In the evening he sees thousands of soot-covered, exhausted workers, "slaves of the city" that pacifies them at night with the bread-and-circus entrancements of electric lights and "the witchcraft of its women." The air is choked with wires, exhaust, and noise. As for the Jews in America, Ginzburg is disgusted by their irreligiousness, coarseness, and ignorance. He denigrates those Jews whose "sabbath is Sunday," and who prefer "the rite of muscles and the game of baseball" to "the writing of God" and "the flame of the law" (204–5), and he describes a Reform high holiday synagogue service, which scandalizes him with its organ music, clean-shaven rabbi, and mixed seating.

Ginzburg's sorrow at being in America is expressed above all in the fact that, although the poem's ostensible subject is his immigration to the United States, the final section of the poem—which is nearly half of the poem's total length—appears to depart from America entirely, consisting instead of a compensatory vision of the Land of Israel. Midway into the poem, the young immigrant yearns for his parents and sister back in Russia, and he achingly wonders to himself if there is a paradise that can restore his sense of cosmic order, so damaged by his expulsion to the ends of the earth. In answer, he receives the dream-vision that serves, for the last time in the poem, to counter the loneliness and despair of the immigrant in New York with the imagination of the land of his forefathers. The Land of Israel in this vision is marked by everything that New York, for Ginzburg, is not. It is Jewishly observant: before the sabbath, the people bathe in the river Jordan, don clean clothes, and gather around the sabbath table. In implicit contrast to the Jewishly ignorant children of America, Ginzburg sees children preserving the chain of tradition, listening intently and respectfully to a sabbath melody that has been passed down the generations, for example, and he even senses the spirits of their forefathers present at the table as well. Unlike the horrid urban environment of New York, with its workers struggling to eke out a living, Ginzburg's Zion is an agrarian and self-sufficient land of peaceful villages and vineyards, fields swelling with produce, and children playing by a river. The sabbath too is contrasted to the hated city: "electric light does not vie" with the "modest glow" of the sabbath candles, and "no city tumult" spoils "the heart's meditation" (213).

Ginzburg's use of the vision has roots in several sources, from Hasidic-mystical narratives of the soul's ascent to the upper worlds to the device of the dream-vision in Hibat Tsion poetry, to the literary romanticism, received primarily through Bialik, that finds in childhood the surest example of the link between the individual and God. (In the vision, writes Ginzburg, his soul goes "to seek what it lost long ago . . . in the dawn of childhood" [211].) The content of the vision is primarily pastoral, particularly as the poem shifts from sabbath eve and its traditional images of

family piety to a sabbath morning that, far from taking place in any synagogue, consists of a sensual, idealized involvement with nature. A woman
named Shulamit—the biblical embodiment of Jewish feminine beauty—
dallies in a rose garden with a male figure, a suitor or groom who, as in
Psalm 19, is closely identified with the sun. She "abandons her cheeks" to
his kisses—whether the sun's or the lover's is not certain—"and striving
with the sweet heat opens her heart / to him" (214). The pastoral elements
reach their apex when

> the daughters of Zion
> idling among the corn
> in garlands of forget-me-nots, azure-eyed,
> still moist with dew—go out to the vineyards
> and to the dances.
>   (215)

They are glimpsed through the foliage by "ruddy" young men with "teeth
whiter than milk" (216), who leap into the vineyard, take the girls in their
arms, and kiss them. Obviously, many of these tropes of sensuality, nature,
and youth derive from the Song of Songs. They may also be inspired by
Moses Hayim Luzzato's eighteenth-century pastoral verse-drama, *Migdal
oz* (the title of Ginzburg's poem nods to this work), which Ginzburg would
later praise as "the opening page of modern Hebrew literature" (1931a,
103), and which was directly influenced by Italian pastoral drama.

On the face of it, Ginzburg's pastoral of the Land of Israel leaves America
behind entirely, functioning as an imaginative repudiation of the satanic
city of New York. Nevertheless, the penultimate section of the poem suggests that these two spheres—the America of Ginzburg's waking nightmare
and the Zion of his dreams—are not as distinct as they might initially
appear. Following the vineyard frolics of the daughters of Zion and their
lovers, Ginzburg depicts Shulamit and her groom entering a kind of
museum, in order to escape the noonday heat. This mausoleum-like store-
house contains Egyptian, Greek, and Christian artifacts: there is a "pharaoh" (1931b, 216) enclosed in a glass case, a host of Greek statues, and
images of "the man of Nazareth / and Mary Magdalene" (217). These relics

are objects of fascination, as well as part of an implicitly triumphal vision of Jews in the Land of Israel standing alive over the passive relics of their departed civilizational rivals. Furthermore, Ginzburg seems to use this episode to distinguish between the healthy, natural eros of the Jewish national awakening and the alternately morbid and rampant eros represented by the Egyptian mummy, the Greek satyrs who "flit like birds to every lovely breast and rosy mound," and the figures of Jesus and Mary Magdalene, whose gaze is like "fine, dismal death" (217). As the sun—here linked with the healthy sensuality and national ascendance of the Jews—penetrates the tombs, the bride and groom turn pointedly away from these relics, and leave the museum to wander among living flowers.

Despite this measure of symbolic logic, however, one cannot help but wonder what a museum, with its mummy and Greek statuary and Christian religious paintings, is doing in this poem. The images are odd, to say the least, and surely out of place among the vineyards and sabbath tables of a pastoral of Zion. There were of course no such museums in Palestine at the time. What we have here, rather, is an importation from the reality of New York City—specifically, the Metropolitan Museum of Art, which by the end of the nineteenth century already had, in addition to its classical and European art, a collection of Egyptian antiquities that was the envy of the world and the pride of its patron, J. Pierpont Morgan. Just as Ginzburg describes the pharaoh's sandals in one display room and its owner in another, so do the museum guidebooks of the time.[5] Moreover, the flowers on which Shulamit and her companion subsequently gaze appear to be in a botanical garden: "Like a crystal palace is the conservatory," writes Ginzburg, "all glass / and all illuminated with light" (217). The couple look at rare tropical flora, including such specimens as the Panama hat plant (the original publication of the poem is even more specific, including a footnote with the Latin name of one of the floral species), and then exit

5. One late nineteenth-century museum guidebook lists "Ancient Egyptian sandles" [sic] as part of the collection (Handbook Number Ten n.d., 12); and a guidebook from the 1920s refers to "a pair of sandals" belonging to the mummified Egyptian nobleman Wah, who was also on display (Metropolitan Museum of Art 1927, 27).

the conservatory to stand by a pool of water lilies. Once again, although this is presented as part of the Zion of Ginzburg's imaginings, the site is taken from New York. When Ginzburg wrote his poem there was an elegant glass botanical conservatory in Central Park, a short walk from the Metropolitan Museum, and it featured tropical plants. (The conservatory was torn down in 1934, and today it is the site of the open-air Conservatory Garden.) Ginzburg might also have been inspired by the magnificent glass conservatory and water lily pools at the New York Botanical Garden in the Bronx, "but a short distance from the terminus of the Third Avenue Elevated Railroad" (*Bulletin of the New York Botanical Garden* 1909, 3) as an early twentieth-century description notes.

This intermixing of the real and the pastoral indicates the level of ideological ambivalence that shaped Ginzburg's portrayal of the American city. Plainly, Ginzburg was not averse to all aspects of New York. Some of the achievements of the modern American city—the spectacular museum and the botanical garden, both affordable to the public and accessible by mass transit—elicit Ginzburg's curiosity and admiration. "Like a spring in the sea they forget themselves" (216), writes Ginzburg when the couple enters the cool shadowy halls of the museum, showing how overwhelmed and fascinated Ginzburg could be by the cultural delights and serene spaces provided by New York. Yet Ginzburg does not present these aspects as part of New York. He detaches them from the real urban environment, effaces their origins, and makes them part of the pastoral Zion that he presents as a counter to America. What becomes the American city in Ginzburg's poem are those elements that he deplores.

Ginzburg's "Behar beit Kolombiyah" (written in 1916) also swerves from the reality of America to a dream-vision of the Land of Israel. Moreover, it demonstrates with even greater clarity how the Hebrew poet's relationship to America and American identity was mediated through his own Jewish national identity. Nevertheless, "On The Temple Mount of Columbia" differs considerably from "Bamigdal." First published in *Hatoren* in 1917, four years after "Bamigdal," the poem is not written in the prophetic, free-verse mode of the earlier poem, but rather in rhymed dactylic tetrameters. The rhyme playfully undercuts any vatic stance, seeming instead to savor

the non-Jewishness of the university milieu in which it is set, as Ginzburg
rhymes Hebrew words with foreign proper nouns such as "Calcutta" and
"Pestalozzi." Rather than the anguish and desperation of "Bamigdal,"
Ginzburg exhibits an often wry combination of wariness and curiosity
about the American scene he describes. And at the conclusion of this poem,
the speaker wakes from his dream-vision of Zion, sad to find himself still in
his New York exile, yet in so doing displaying a greater resignation to and
acceptance of his American home.

The first half of the poem is set at Columbia University, where Ginzburg attended the Teachers College under the tutelage of John Dewey. The
poem expresses Ginzburg's amazement at the university, the knowledge it
offers and the power it represents. "In respectful silence I approach the palace" (1931b, 94), he writes of his arrival at the campus. Entering the library,
this new "house of study," he is "swallowed among the waves of the sea
of books," and dazzled by the fields of psychology, astronomy, sociology,
and engineering, described in Ginzburg's flowery Hebrew as "the secret
wisdom of the human soul, the secret wisdom of the planetary routes, / the
secret wisdom of the forces hidden in society, in bridges" (95). At the same
time, however, he feels adrift and desolate in a world so foreign to Jewish
traditions of learning, one that has no place among the busts of Byron and
Pestalozzi for rabbinic sages such as Hillel or Ben-Zakai, and that drowns
out his "soul's prayer" with "the logic of the mighty" (95).

However, this poem is not simply about the individual Jewish immigrant's encounter with modern university education. Instead, national
consciousness is the central theme of the poem. It is not merely that the
university impresses, bewilders, and sometimes alienates the more traditional Jewish speaker in the poem, but that the speaker gives expression
to the sense of displacement and cultural inadequacy of the Jewish nation
as a whole before the ascendant power of the American nation, a nation of
which he is not a part. Education in this poem is not represented as a melting pot in which people can shed their national allegiances. Instead, the
university is a site for interactions between students who maintain and are
identified precisely by their nationality. Ginzburg marvels at the collection
of students who have come to this American temple of knowledge: "up the
marble stairs hurries a daughter of Calcutta; / and after her, a Japanese, a

Negro, / a young man from Jaffa in Judea, and myself" (95). These different nationalities (and race here is a form of national identity) do not fall away in the pursuit of education, but remain the operative identifiers of most all the figures in the poem.

Thus, on the library steps the speaker gazes, not simply at the university architecture, emblems of universal enlightenment, but rather at the American flag, "the flag of a people of great deeds." Moreover, rather than focusing his attention on the flag itself, he directs his gaze to the eagle atop the flagpole, a more imperial figure than the stars and stripes, and to which he bows his head in submission. "You have conquered me," he thinks, "you, the rich, and I, the poor." By this he refers neither to his individual situation as a poor immigrant or a knowledge-hungry maskil, but to his identification as a member of the Jewish nation, in whose homeland "in Zion the mount of God does not rise." Because of the present politically and culturally impoverished condition of the Jewish nation, Ginzburg is forced to turn to America. Altering the prophet's praise of Zion, he confesses that "from you [America] goes forth Torah" (95). Here, as in the title, Ginzburg indicates that Columbia University is America's Temple, both a counterpart to the ruined temple in the Holy Land and a substitute for it, in a much more literal and forlorn way than Cahan's David Levinsky when he refers to the City College of New York as "my American Temple" (Cahan 1960, 215).

Inevitably, the First World War is the context for all these meditations on nationalism. The university, so beautiful in the sunlight, and so admirable in its educational offerings to the students, simultaneously glowers for Ginzburg with the dark possibilities of war, imperial ambition, and all the risks and dangers of modernity. He wonders whether the generation being educated here will be the "Huns of the future," who will use "the sword of science" to oppress "weak peoples" (Ginzburg 1931b, 94). The question of national reawakening and the horrors of imperial war is again taken up in his description of a Japanese friend, "whose country has sent him to bring back light," that is, to learn modernity from the West, a project in which Jewish maskilim were likewise engaged. Yet the Japanese student asserts that while the Japanese are at present "still the students of other peoples, / the day will come when we will teach them and be victorious" (96). The poet discerns in this boast "the arrogant dream" of Japan's imperial ambitions, and questions what will happen when "the imperial sun rises" (97).

Such concern does not mean Ginzburg is opposed to national identity. Implicit in the poem is, instead, the idea that other nationalisms such as the Japanese are fallen versions of the only benign one, which is Jewish (that is, Hebrew) nationalism. Thus, following the speaker's conversation with his Japanese friend, he is greeted in Hebrew by a pair of Jewish students. "The soul of our people," the poet thinks to himself as they pass by, "buried alive, now breaks forth / and rises from the sound of your word" (97). There is no anxiety or censure here, indicating that Ginzburg intends to juxtapose the warlike national awakening of the Japanese with the spiritual-cultural nationalism of the Hebraists.

In America, however, the Jews are losing their national identity. In the second half of the poem, the speaker moves from the university to a park bench, from which he eavesdrops on an argument between the two Jewish students who had greeted him at the university and a third Jewish student from Palestine. To the poet's dismay, only the latter is exercised by the Jewish national awakening; when he tells the other two that they should use their education to contribute to the Jewish homeland, they profess their allegiance to America, replying: "*This* is our homeland, her language is our language, we even suffer her pain" (emphasis in original). To them, the Jewish national idea, the "commandment of the dead forefathers," is nothing but "dreams" (98).

Appropriately, then, Ginzburg's conception of Jewish national identity and its relationship with America is distilled in a dream the poet has that night. In the dream he sees a "mighty ship" flying the flags of both the United States and of Israel, "in joyful fellowship waving" (99). On the deck are "many young figures," presumably Jews from the United States going to build up the Land of Israel. The port of Jaffa is thronged with ships bearing all manner of "flags of people and nations." When the pioneers disembark, "they pass through the formless wilderness like angels of God" and "sow there a springtime like nothing before." Then the speaker sees the "temple of the nation," rebuilt and rededicated, inspiring the Jewish people to "remember the most precious of its hopes" as the exiled divine presence returns "and dwells in the temple of God" (100). At the front of the temple is "a flag, white with blue," emphasizing that Ginzburg's dream of religious restoration is simultaneously a national dream. The flag is described as the emblem of the "peace of the all-powerful God" and of the vitality of "pure nature." Yet it is above all a national symbol, the banner of "a tiny, luminous people" (100), a people connected inalterably with the land that forged them.

Just before he wakes, the poet dreams of a message of blessing and thanks sent from Israel to the president of the United States. Thus, the excoriation of America that we saw in "Bamigdal" is largely absent in this poem. The Jewish stance here is one of friendship and gratitude toward the United States. Yet—and this is the essence of Ginzburg's position here—it is a stance based on Jewish nationhood, equal to but not part of America. In this dialectic of American sympathy and Jewish nationalism, Ginzburg's dream resembles Zvi Scharfstein's description of a boat trip he took, just a year before Ginzburg's poem was written, with a group of Jewish activists on their way from New York to the Zionist congress in Boston. (Indeed, Ginzburg may very well have been on that boat and was almost certainly at the congress.) On this boat, thronged with Jewish nationalists speaking in Yiddish and Hebrew, Scharfstein felt he had suddenly "returned to his native milieu" (1956, 125). Ironically, however, it was when the captain of the ship agreed to raise the blue and white Zionist flag, and the passengers, singing the Zionist anthem, were most overcome by feelings of Jewish "national pride and joy," that Scharfstein became most effusive about America:

> And a feeling of love then stirred in my heart for America, this generous, democratic country, neither resentful of people nor seeking to suppress their emotions. She is secure in her power and lets others live their chosen lives as they wish. This sentiment increased in me when we arrived at the grand, deluxe hotel in Boston where I was staying along with many of the other delegates. In the entrance was hung a large sign, "Welcome Zionists," and the same greeting waved on long banners in the large shops as well. We then passed by City Hall and there too waved the flag of Zion!
> Blessed be America! (Scharfstein 1956, 125–26)

Scharfstein's memoirs are generally quite positive toward America, certainly in the Hebraist context, yet it is still striking that in this episode he felt most enthusiastic about the United States precisely when he felt the greatest freedom as a Jewish nationalist.

Similarly, Ginzburg's sympathy for America in "Bamigdal" and "Behar beit Kolombiyah" depends upon his national separateness from it, not his participation in it. The multinational imagery of the dream consists of Jews from all countries, leaving those countries and returning to their true home. At the poem's Chaplinesque conclusion, Ginzburg is woken by a policeman who has found him asleep on a park bench. As the poet rubs his eyes and rises to go, he thinks sorrowfully of "the exilic Jewish masses" in America, "slaves, without a sovereign dream" (Ginzburg 1931b, 101).

In the final poem of our trilogy, "No-York" (written in 1917), Ginzburg does not seek to escape from America to the Land of Israel. In contrast to "Bamigdal," in which Ginzburg did not even mention the name "New York" outside of a single footnote, he devotes the whole of this long poem (over two dozen pages in its original publication) to an attempt to render the spirit and reality of New York City, that "divine and satanic poem, mighty and fearsome, written in free verse" (1931b, 263). Yet precisely because this time Ginzburg does not allow himself a poetic flight into his visionary Zion, his poem is more antagonistic and despairing of New York, not less. "New York terrifies me, swallows me," he writes, "as I wander tired and dejected day after day, overwhelmed by its size, oppressed, confused" (267). Although he tries to fight his deep aversion to the city and hold to some sort of neutrality—"not knowing whether to curse the city or to bless it"—he soon assumes the role of a prophet decrying its evils and hoping for deliverance.

Particularly striking is the poem's phantasmagoric vision of New York nightlife. The illuminated signs on Broadway are "mystic letters of fire"; in a concert hall the listeners "grasp the marble columns" so as not to be swept away "on the waves of the paradise-symphony"; in the movie theaters "shadows jump upon the screen as if at the command of a wizard's hand," conjuring a "dance of stormy desires in a world . . . full of splendor and fear" (1931b, 266). The poet wanders, terrified and fascinated, through an increasingly infernal tableau of decadence, deprivation, and danger, a Dante passing by (though never entering) the degenerate haunts of billiard hall, nightclub, and brothel, gazing at the sinners, "night-owls," and mid-night revelers, caught up in the confusion of sensations:

> And I stand before the giant window: there a girl with legs
>   exposed, as if she is drunk, dances a lewd dance,
> And attendants with white napkins flit about among the lines
>   of guests dressed in black,
> The sound of forks and glasses mixing with the flash of bright
>   tablecloths, and the bubbling whisper of beer with the
>   crashing of cymbals.
>   (268)[6]

He describes an underworld extending from the mansions of wealthy Riverside, in which "the decadent, rotting in their wealth" commit "deeds of Sodom," to Chinatown where "like a priest in the Holy of Holies, men and women offer up the incense of opium to a god of death" (269). Indeed, with its expansive cataloguing of the degenerate landscape of New York, the poem seems uncannily like a forgotten precursor to Allen Ginsberg's "Howl."

This resemblance derives not least from the fact that Ginzburg's New York, like that of his Beatnik namesake, is ruled by an evil figure called "Moloch." This powerful, demonic being—also referred to as "Satan" and the "City Lord"[7]—embodies all the exploitation and hardship Ginzburg sees in the city, and it is the source of the vulnerability and insignificance Ginzburg feels as a lonely immigrant in an indifferent land. This figure allows Ginzburg to personify everything contemptible and threatening about life in the American city, to create a devil responsible for the poet's sense of abandonment and impotence. Gazing up at the "palace-towers" of Wall Street, the poet asks: "is this the house of *Moloch* . . . ? Is this the

---

6. My translation of "No-York" is intentionally unfaithful to Ginzburg's hexameters, instead using free verse units based on Whitman's *Leaves of Grass,* which somehow feels more faithful to Ginzburg's intentions and in any case produces a more pleasing result in English.

7. *Sar hakrakh* can also be translated as "mayor," yet Ginzburg emphasizes the imperial and supernatural meanings of *sar* as angel, supernal power, governor, lord.

house of the creator of the ropes of gold and sin, / and the chains of iron, and the oppression that fills the wide world?" (270; emphasis in original). Elsewhere, Moloch is depicted as a factory owner and likened to the biblical pharaoh ruling over the slaves of a sweatshop. The language of class warfare is evident here, yet, like the other Hebraists, and in contrast to many of the Yiddish poets, Ginzburg's anticapitalism is more a reflection of his antipathy for urban life than of any actual socialist politics. Ginzburg's description of Moloch and his factory emphasizes the infernal machinery, whose "gigantic wheels grind and turn" (275), more than it does the downtrodden workers. Indeed, the central anxiety of the episode is not social or political, but sexual. The "slaves [who] wait upon the machine" expose "their hairy chests," while Moloch "passes among the lines of his female servants, crowded by the hundreds at their worktables, / and his eyes linger on the beautiful and well-formed." The factory then heats up to an unbearable degree, leading to an eruption of the phallic smokestacks, which "spit their ash into the face of the heavens" (275).

Yet neither are the concerns with national identity that we saw in "Bamigdal" and "Behar beit Kolombiyah" absent in this poem. Most striking, Ginzburg provides here a dark parody of the melting pot in his description of the crush of bodies in crowded New York subway cars. Instead of the forging of national unity through the fusion of peoples, Ginzburg depicts a crowd in the subway being "crushed together in a single mass." The melting pot's blending of ethnicities is portrayed as a grotesque mixing of categories, as "the scoundrel presses his flesh against the body of the innocent girl . . . / And a young beauty is thrown into the arms of a seated old man, / And an Italian pushes himself between the knees of a Jewish girl" (277). As this happens, Ginzburg has the city bridges themselves taunt: "O children of the city, gathered together from peoples so different, so numerous, come to the melting pot, and be melted within it, melted!" (278). Thus, the melting pot is identified with the American city's assault on innocence and flagrant crossing of boundaries.

In the same subway car we also find the Shekhinah, the divine presence that in "Bamigdal" accompanied the immigrant into exile, and who now cries out: "A day will come—Moloch! City!—when you will be overthrown." Whereas in the earlier two poems Ginzburg imagined the Land of Israel as a deliverance from New York, here, by confronting New York exclusively and refusing that escape, he must instead imagine the abolition of the city itself—its destruction and transfiguration. New York must be redeemed, in the apocalyptic sense. Although Ginzburg does turn several times to Nature as a counter to New York in the way that Zion is in the other poems—a thunderstorm and a snowstorm are described as attempts by Nature to reconquer the perverse domain of the city—Nature's powers are shown to be no match for the metropolis, and these attempts fail. Deliverance from the city must await the coming of the Messiah.

Ginzburg imagines this messianic conquest of the city near the end of the poem. A procession of humanity, with the Messiah at its head, marches through the city to defeat the City Lord and to realize "a new heaven and a new earth" (284). The revolutionary-socialist dimension of this vision is most in evidence in the poem's first publication in 1918, a year after the Russian Revolution. Ginzburg describes the throngs of people pouring out into the city streets in "a celebration of the working masses" and marching to a "final war with the tyrannical lord of the factory" (Ginzburg 1918, 26). A workers' revolution seemed to offer Ginzburg a deliverance, or at least an image of deliverance, from his urban nightmare in a manner recalling the passage from Michael Gold's *Jews Without Money:* "O, workers' Revolution, you brought hope to me, a lonely suicidal boy. You are the true Messiah. You will destroy the East Side when you come, and build there a garden for the human spirit" (Gold 1984, 309). However, the second publication of the poem, in Ginzburg's collected poems from 1931, minimizes references to political revolution, shifting the emphasis from the masses to the messiah figure. Ginzburg seems, then, to have transferred his redemptive hopes back to Jewish tradition. It is significant in this regard that the one entirely new section in the poem's 1931 version describes a group of Jewish schoolchildren in whose "innocent eyes" one detects "the dream of the messiah, / Which in one of [their] souls will catch flame at the end of days and illuminate the world" (Ginzburg 1931b, 280). It is the dedication of these children to Jewish study in the Talmud Torah, the Jewish supplemental school, despite all the corruptions and blandishments of America, that "will take the people of the city from their exile, from enslavement to Moloch" and "bring them into the kingdom of beauty"

(281). The messianic dream, whether of Ginzburg's end of days or of the Jewish fidelity seen in the Talmud Torah, functions in this poem as Zion does in the earlier two, providing a Jewish antidote to the American exile.

At the very end of the poem, Ginzburg appears to hold out hope for a more positive relation to America, in which New York itself can be the instrument of human redemption. Riding over the Williamsburg Bridge at night, he looks out at the multitude of lights in the darkness, signs of other people also traveling through the great night of the city. Gazing at these souls, all somehow interconnected, the poet experiences a sudden and profound sense of human communion and of God's enduring presence and goodness. A renewed "hymn of trust" replaces the bitter "prophecy of New York"; and the next morning, when Ginzburg again gazes on the bridges of New York, the same that earlier had so cruelly called for the melting of peoples, they now appear as "divine harps . . . waiting confidently for the unknown player who will come, / To play upon them the great song of the future" (284–85). Rather than the apocalyptic-messianic destruction of the city, Ginzburg offers a more private and mystical model of redemption. As Eli Lederhendler has observed, Ginzburg's imagery of the lights in the darkness and the "divine secret" they contain derives from kabbalistic redemption myths (Lederhendler 1994, 165–66). Moreover, in the possibility of a "great song of the future," Ginzburg adopts an optimistic tone that is more characteristically American than anything he had yet written.

Nevertheless, this brief Whitmanian coda is hardly a counterweight to the despairing, antiurban jeremiad that comprises the other 95 percent of the poem. Ginzburg's apocalyptic treatment of the American city reflects the strong antiurban and anti-American current in early twentieth-century Hebrew literary culture.[8] Indeed, his approach was even repeated by Bialik less than a decade after the first publication of "No-York." Bialik visited the United States for a five-month stay in 1926. His impressions, as recorded in a talk he gave after his return to Palestine, appear mixed but often quite positive, marked by his newly acquired appreciation for the

8. For a meditation on some of the European cultural contexts of this aversion to New York, see Buruma and Margalit (2004).

uniqueness and vitality of America and American Jews. He even referred to American Jewry as "one of the wonders of the Jewish millennial experience," a "miniature exodus from Egypt," and affirmed that "in our era of Jewish destruction, America has become the sole mainstay of world Judaism" (Bialik 1968, 170).

Yet in poetry, his visit took on quite a different cast. "Yenaser lo khilvavo" (Let it roar as it likes), written in New York and published in both *Hadoar* and *Hashiloah* in the summer of 1926, was one of the few poems Bialik published after settling in Palestine, and so attracted attention as a rare interruption of his late poetic silence. The poem centers on a sapling blooming in the springtime in New York, an image that represents the Jewish people in America who, despite the harshness of their surroundings, preserve their creative, spiritual potential. (The tree may also symbolize Bialik's renewed faith in his own dormant poetic powers.) Even in the heart of the hellish, polluted, city—"source of all human ills and the lap of all horrors" (Bialik 2004, 444)—the sapling buds just like "its fathers' fathers' fathers" did "tens of thousands of years ago, in primeval forests" (443). The presence of the tree grants the poet a momentary respite from the city's noise, a respite that he uses in order to prophecy the city's destruction. "Your end will be the end of Sodom and Nineveh," he tells New York, "and like all your brothers, fortresses of iron and stone, / Carthage, Tadmor, Ramses and Pithom" the American metropolis too "will be annihilated" (444). What will endure is the purity and virtue of the tree, whose persistence symbolizes new life (national renewal, individual-poetic renewal) and the higher order of God, which the city profanes. Bialik's poetic assessment thus remains the same as Ginzburg's: the American city is a contravention of God's will, requiring an apocalyptic deliverance and cleansing by Nature, and against which the Jewish spark of purity and goodness must contend. Whereas in his more prosaic talk, America is "the sole mainstay of world Judaism," in his poem, as in Ginzburg's and so many of the immigrant Hebraists', it is the "domain of Satan" (443).

2

The Poetry of an Upturned World

MODERNISM AND AMERICAN IDENTITY
IN AMERICAN HEBREW LITERATURE

WHEN GINZBURG WROTE "NO-YORK," the Hebrew language lacked, or had only just coined, the names for many elements of the urban scene. Footnotes in his poem explain such unfamiliar terms as *markevet tahtit* (lower chariot, a term for subway that has not survived in contemporary Hebrew usage) and *ma'alit* (elevator). Indeed, in the early twentieth century, literary Hebrew was hard-pressed to muster the idiomatic resources necessary to depict the modern city, particularly for writers with the traditional, small-town origins and sympathies of the Hebraists. As Robert Alter has observed, "the setting of Jewish immigrant life in America offered above all a densely concentrated, fiercely intense urban experience which was largely outside the imaginative ken and at first beyond the linguistic reach of Hebrew literature" (1994, 79).[1]

Yet, as Alter hints, the Hebraists' vexed relationship with the American cityscape ultimately turned less on the "linguistic reach of Hebrew literature"—which expanded rapidly in the early twentieth century—than on the aesthetic principles and practices of the Hebraists. The immigrant Hebraists include a range of writers whose styles and concerns differ from one to the next. Yet with rare exceptions these writers, and more specifically the poets, were generally known for their adherence to nineteenth-

---

1. Compare early twentieth-century Hebrew's lexical difficulties in a modern, urban landscape with the extraordinarily absorptive powers of Yiddish in this regard.

century aesthetic norms and values well into the twentieth century. In the first decades of the twentieth century, Hebrew poetry in Europe and Palestine began to reflect new, postsymbolist currents in international literature. Influenced by German expressionism and Russian futurism, poets such as Uri Zvi Greenberg, Avraham Shlonsky, and David Fogel pursued various lines of modernist experimentation in Hebrew verse. Meanwhile, the American Hebraists looked askance at such developments while they remained largely indifferent to Anglo-American modernism as well.

Menachem Ribalow expressed the prevailing opinion when, in the introduction to his 1938 anthology, he told the tale of modernism's international rise with evident dismay. As he described it:

> A storm swept through all literatures and rocked the foundations of poetry. And just as the kings of the nations were brought down from their thrones, so the kings of poetry were deposed from their poetic thrones. New and innovative movements arose declaring the death of the old. Radical modernism, called by various names, overthrew the "classical regime" and declared victory with joyful cries. (Ribalow 1938, viii)

"Only in America did everything remain on its foundation," he wrote, "Only America did not contribute to this madness." Elsewhere, Hebrew literature came to be dominated by "the poetry of *Sorrow* and the poetry of *Great Fear and Moon*," referring to influential expressionist volumes published in the 1920s by Shlonsky and Greenberg. Modernism was, in Ribalow's words, "the poetry of an upturned world," and it was attacked by the American Hebraists as blasphemous, ugly, chaotic, and irresponsible (viii).

Against the modernists overseas, Hebrew poets in the United States claimed to represent and defend the poetic virtues of clarity, purity, and restraint. Neither bohemians nor populists, they saw themselves as a Jewish elite, dedicated to preserving the sanctity of poetry in a profane world that scorned such institutions. They often expressed this cultural mission through the image of the biblical priest, a motif whose connotations—purity, continuity, loftiness, religiosity, elitism—resonated with these poets' collective self-conception. It is no accident that when the young Hebraist writer and critic Shimon Halkin attacked the modernism of the American Yiddish poets, he accused them of "sacrificing strange fire" (1969, 69), a

transgression of proprieties both poetic and religious. The modernists reciprocated, denigrating the elitism and traditionalism on which the Americans
prided themselves. The Hebrew poet Yitzhak Lamdan, then living in Palestine, responded to one of Ribalow's attacks on modernism by suggesting
that the American Hebraists "shake off the dust of pseudo-nobility" (1925,
92). "Bouncing in place to 'holy holy holy,'" Lamdan quipped (the reference
is to the traditional Jewish liturgical practice), was not the same thing as
taking a step forward (89). Even Bialik felt compelled to defend the work of
Greenberg to the American Hebraists. One of the talks he gave during his
1926 sojourn in the United States was a lecture in New York on the subject of "the New Hebrew Literature," in which he argued that Greenberg's
expressionistic style and sometimes shocking content were legitimate manifestations of his individual poetic voice and personal experience, rather
than being bad writing or sensationalism or signs of mental instability, as
many of the American Hebraists thought.[2]

The fact is that the basic cultural ethos of American Hebraism clashed
inevitably with the agendas and assumptions of early twentieth-century
modernism. Culturally, American Hebraism was to a great extent a continuation of the Jewish Enlightenment (Haskalah), transplanted to the New
World. In his history of the Histadrut, Moshe Pelli explains that his choice
of academic research was inspired by the Hebraists he encountered in the
United States, whom he calls "remnants of the maskilim [followers of Haskalah culture] of the old generation" (1998, 15). Pelli describes these men
as being

> like the elders of the Great Assembly, men in the likeness of the early Ger-
> man enlighteners: Euchel, Wesel and Satanow, Wolfsohn and Ben-Ze'ev.
> Who were these American Hebrew maskilim, eighty years after the end of
> the Haskalah period? Editors, enthusiasts, dreamers, fighters. Soldiers in
> literary battles great and small. Valiant warriors tilting at windmills. Pre-
> servers of the chain of Hebrew, sending letters flying into the air, ethereal
> nobility of the Haskalah. (15)

2. On Bialik's defense of Greenberg to the Americans, see Miron (1999, 94-100,
111–19).

Zvi Scharfstein similarly fits the Hebraist intellectuals in the United States into a taxonomy of maskilim. First, says Scharfstein, was the "old-style maskil" (1956, 189) who came to America in the 1880s and 1890s, enamored of Haskalah authors such as Mapu, Smolenskin, and Adam Hacohen, fanatically insistent on a "pure" Hebrew of biblical elevation and diction. Scharfstein describes one such maskil, a neighbor of his, who refused to read *Hadoar* because, as the man put it, "the writers of *Hadoar* slaughter and destroy our holy tongue" by allowing "Aramaic and Ashdodic words into the Hebrew" (193). By the end of the nineteenth century these first-wave maskilim were joined by maskilim influenced by the Hibat Tsion movement and its lachrymose poetry of yearning for the Land of Israel. This type was followed at the turn of the century by the "new maskil" (190), the Ahad Ha'amist whose Hibat Tsion sentimentality had been tempered by hard-bitten analysis. Finally, the "Zionist maskilim arrived," their thought inflected by nationalism and socialism.

Not that every Hebrew writer in America was a maskil in a strict historical sense. As Pelli notes, the Haskalah period was, properly speaking, already long gone. The characterization of the American Hebraists as maskilic has more a cultural significance than a historical one, indicating a set of cultural and ideological tendencies. To speak in broad terms, we may say that early twentieth-century Hebrew culture manifests two broad currents, which we might call maskilic and modern-national. In the former, Hebrew is a vehicle for Jews to move from the world of tradition into modernity. In the latter, it is a vehicle for Jews who are already post-traditional to move from modernity to Jewish national culture. These two currents were not at all mutually exclusive, and many a writer exemplified both at different points in his career or simultaneously. Nevertheless, they indicate different habits of mind and translate into different capacities for relating sympathetically to modernism in literature and culture. And the maskilic current was quite pronounced in American Hebrew culture.

Indeed, the Hebrew intellectual in early twentieth-century America was of necessity a maskil. In America there was no network of secular Hebrew educational institutions comparable in scope to the Tarbut schools of Europe, let alone the modern Hebrew vernacular environment that was developing in Palestine. The American Hebrew intellectual was therefore almost certainly an immigrant, who had emerged from the intellectual world of traditional Judaism and its educational institutions, and trod the path marked out by the Haskalah toward a more secular orientation while preserving an ardent allegiance to the Jewish people and the Hebrew language. In fact, some immigrants only embarked on this path after their arrival in the United States. (The poet, memoirist, and educator Ephraim Lisitzky, for instance, first became familiar with Haskalah literature while living in upstate New York.) In America, however, the maskil lacked a clear cultural function. If in nineteenth-century Europe the Haskalah was supposed to educate the Jewish people in how to participate in the modern world, in twentieth-century America the Jews were already avidly doing so, albeit without the education the Hebrew intellectuals felt was necessary. This lack of a popular function was one of the reasons Hebrew culture in America could at times become defensive and rarefied, resembling, in the critic Avraham Epstein's words, "a kind of exotic plant that had not yet adjusted to the climate and so required the atmosphere of a hothouse" (1952, 5). Modernization in America led perilously toward cultural assimilation, there being less scope for Hebrew cultural life in America, and so modern Hebrew culture occupied a more bookish sphere.

This maskilic cultural ethos was therefore at odds with modernism on a number of levels. The modernist eagerness to overturn established cultural institutions, literary canons, and artistic values was senseless to the maskil's faith in precisely such norms and achievements. The Haskalah was, after all, based on a profound esteem for Western education, literary standards, and shared values. Moreover, the Hebraists' tradition was under siege in America. They felt they possessed an ancient and noble culture that required defense against the forces threatening its disintegration. Their national and pedagogic concerns, made urgent by the degree of assimilation they encountered in America, informed a cultural project that was necessarily conservative—an endeavor to preserve tradition, not to celebrate discontinuity. In Palestine, radicalism, antitraditionalism, and the incorporation of popular culture and experience could be part of the Jewish national project. In America such trends were seen as dangerous to the survival of Jewish culture.

In addition, the literary-cultural conservatism of the American Hebraists may have been reinforced by demographic tendencies in the migration of Jewish writers. Although Jews did not often have a great deal of choice in where to reside or whether to move, it is clear that Palestine as a destination appealed to a more ideologically radical temperament, as well as to younger writers who might be more free of family obligations. The United States, on the other hand, offered economic and political security, within which Hebrew culture could be preserved, if not lived.[3]

One of the significant literary consequences of the American Hebraists' antimodernism was the difficulty they had in engaging urban experience. As has often been noted, modernism is intimately connected with the rise of modern city life, which both required new, post-Romantic techniques for its representation in literature and suggested new formal approaches to the writer: violent juxtaposition and shock, fragmentation and spontaneity, use of the mundane, the concrete, and the demotic.[4] Whereas modernist poets often used such techniques to explore and echo the city landscape, most of the Hebrew poets in America held instead to a Parnassian stance in which immediate reality, unless pastoral or lofty, was peripheral at best to the poet's concerns. In an early meditation on Yiddish modernism, Shimon Halkin expressed his surprise that this apparently vibrant poetry should appear "in America of all places, this mediocre country with its commonplace reality," and that it should be written "by the Yiddish poets of all poets—the denizens of the drab buildings of New York's Jewish quarter" (1969, 66). It was therefore not only that, as they often lamented, the Hebraists' surroundings were indifferent to their poetry, but also that their poetics made them indifferent to their surroundings.[5]

---

3. For discussions of the cultural and sociological differences between the American Hebraists and the writers active in interwar Palestine, see Govrin (1986) and U. Shavit (1992).

4. See, for instance, the engaging discussion of Wordsworth and the city in Donoghue (1991).

5. In making this point, I disagree with Eli Lederhendler, who emphasizes the social-literary isolation of the Hebraists—their lack of a readership—as the decisive factor in their alienation from America (Lederhendler 1994, 186–87). Lack of readership was certainly important (on this issue, see also Miron 1975). However, the Hebraists' own aesthetic beliefs and practices also helped to create their distance from and difficulty with America. Katz

An example of this dynamic is seen in Israel Efros's 1952 essay, "Epizodah amerikanit" (An American episode), in which he recalls the deep connection to the American milieu felt by his generation of Hebrew poets, who emigrated as young men to the United States in the first two decades of the twentieth century.[6] The essay's lyrical evocation of life in New York would seem to reflect the enthusiasm of these budding poets for their new surroundings. Efros describes the "various morning songs rising each day from the street," from the bell-like reveille of the milk wagon to the "songs . . . of the old clothes peddler, the knife and shears grinder, the umbrella repairman. . . . Each of them trilling his drawn-out tune like a cantor, so that they reached my ears on the fifth floor" (1971, 231–32). He mentions the crush of the subway commute to college lectures, Sunday getaways to the seashore, earnest discussions about poetry and God with a date in an East Broadway ice cream parlor. Yet, when Efros explains how this American scene manifest itself in his and his fellow Hebraists' poetry, he writes, "[m]ost important was the positive connection to and love for their new surroundings, and from this connection and the embrace of this vast, new variety, they began to pour forth in poems about nature, about mountains and seas, about the burning day sinking in the west. They wrote about love and, naturally, about death" (232). After rhapsodizing about the street hawkers and the subway, the university classroom and East Broadway, the evidence Efros offers for the Hebrew poets' "love for their new surroundings" is a list of generalities: "nature," "mountains," "death," etc. Not mentioned are the urban experiences these poets all knew, the difficulties of immigration and acculturation, the specificities of their lives in the United States. Efros not only finds the American influence on twentieth-century Hebrew poetry to be expressed primarily in such generalities, he is proud of this, as if convinced that the American scene had been successfully captured in the subject matter of mountains and sunsets.

(2009) devotes attention to the linguistic features of American Hebrew literature and their effect on readership.

6. Efros contrasted this generation with their poetic elders (e.g., Menahem Mendel Dolitzky) who came to the United States as mature men in the last decades of the nineteenth century and therefore found acculturation far more difficult.

This contradiction between the comparatively detailed depiction of New York in Efros's essay and his use of generalized nature motifs to indicate the Americanness of his and his fellow Hebraists' poetry is reflected throughout American Hebrew literature. The most involved depictions of urban experience, contemporary America, and the lives of Jewish immigrants are to be found in prose fiction, essays, and journalism, whereas such material is comparatively rare in the poetry. This shows that it was not only these writers' personal disaffection with and cultural isolation from their surroundings that determined their literary response to America, but their aesthetic beliefs as well. In their maskilic-Romantic conception of literature, poetry was the supreme literary medium, the purest genre of writing, and the central mode in which the new Jewish culture found expression. Indeed, most of the significant immigrant Hebrew writers were poets. And while one might write about less sublime topics such as New York City or the experiences of Jewish immigrants in an essay, a newspaper article, or a short story, poetry demanded loftier themes. It is therefore no accident that the American Hebraists incorporated modernist techniques into their fiction before their poetry—even when both were written by the same person. The case of Shimon Halkin is a perfect example. Reflecting on his literary output of the 1920s, he observes: "I wrote poetry as if in the time of Shelley, but in order to complete what was lacking I also wrote *Yehiel Hahegri,* which was one of the first modernist novels in Hebrew" (1971, 34). This literary schizophrenia (Halkin calls it "double bookkeeping") was not only stylistic and generic, enforcing a distinction between romanticism and poetry on the one hand and modernism and the novel on the other, but also thematic. The novel Halkin refers to, *Yehiel Hahegri,* deals with Jewish immigrants in New York, a subject he felt he could not broach in his Shelleyan poetry. Although poetry was given pride of place in American Hebrew literary culture, as practiced by most American Hebraists it was simultaneously the form least suited to penetrate into the realities of contemporary American life.

Let us return to Ginzburg's "No-York" which, for all its admirable verve and reach, shows at the same time the aesthetic constraints faced by the Hebrew poets in representing the city. Ginzburg lacked a sure poetic idiom with which to make the city visible. His New York is frequently obscured behind the poet's literary lenses, buried under the heavy neoclassicism and stock abstractions of Haskalah poetry on the one hand, and the tropes and gestures of Romantic and symbolist antiurban prophecy on the other. At the beginning of the poem, for instance, Ginzburg defends his use of free verse (although much of the poem is in hexameters), arguing that he is reflecting the "unpredictable, spontaneous" rhythm of the city. Yet in this justification he immediately turns to a nature lexicon: the rhythm of the city, he writes, "leaps like a waterfall" and "surges like a flood in springtime." Ginzburg also makes a wonderful analogy between the uneven margins of the free verse poem and the jagged New York skyline, yet in doing so he is unable to resist inserting a biblical formula, likening the long lines of the poem to Goliath—who at "six cubits and a span" is actually rather dwarfed by the city architecture (1931b, 263). The poem sometimes strains under the weight of forced allusions and unsuccessful metaphor, as when the Williamsburg Bridge is described as being "like the steed of Og, an iron giant that from shore to shore had leapt but was frozen in place by a sorcerer" (284), or when a rainstorm "comes to lay siege to the city" like "Agamemnon the king waging war on Troy with the elect of kings, the heroes of Greece" (276). Similarly, Ginzburg uses extensive personification to describe a snowstorm in New York as a war between the City Lord and the armies of "Old Man Winter." Ginzburg describes the battle's conclusion as follows:

> Drunk with triumph Old Man Winter himself then comes one
> 　　night through the gates of the city in a victory chariot,
> 　　and the army of winds goes before him, and the storm
> 　　announces his coming
> But the minions of the City Lord assault his chariot.
> They are marshalled against him in their thousands, with iron
> 　　shovels armed,
> And they nearly sweep Old Man Winter's chariot from the city,
> 　　as the determined clanging of shovels answers the storm of
> 　　his winds.
> And the battle is enjoined all the night,
> And when the Lord of the Sun arrives at daybreak he sees the
> 　　streets black and empty of snow as before, carts taking for
> 　　burial all evidence of winter, its lovely gems.
> 　　　　　　　(Ginzburg 1931b, 282–83)

Compare this epic register with Theodore Dreiser's recollection of the same reality—the practice in early twentieth-century New York of the city hiring poor and indigent workers to shovel snow. In his memoirs of New York in the 1910s, Dreiser writes:

> To see them following in droves through the bitter winter streets the great wagons which haul the snow away is fascinating, at times pitiful. I have seen old men with white beards and uncut snowy hair shoveling snow into a truck. I have seen lean, unfed strips of boys without overcoats and with long, lean, red hands protruding from undersized coat sleeves, doing the same thing. I have seen anaemic benchers and consumptives following along illy clad but shoveling weakly in the snow and cold. (Dreiser 1987, 234)

With a few line breaks, this passage could be taken for a poem by Dreiser's fellow Midwesterner Carl Sandburg, who had published his Chicago poems—one of the landmarks in the first wave of American poetic modernism—just a couple of years before Ginzburg's "No-York." Ginzburg's heavy and excessive classicizing (or aggadicizing, as the case may be) is a Haskalah legacy, pre-Bialikian in execution, and skirts the territory of the mock-epic—although I find that, strangely, this often adds to the poem's charm.

Even a Hebrew *poète maudite* like Avraham Zvi Halevy (1907–66) had difficulty finding an idiom for the seamy urban experience he knew well. The son of a family that combined traditional, Zionist, and Hasidic Jewish backgrounds, Halevy immigrated to Palestine in 1914 and then in 1924 to the United States where he remained, apart from several extended stays in the land of Israel.[7] He began publishing his first New York poems almost two decades after the appearance of Ginzburg's "No-York." Unlike many of the other American Hebrew writers, Halevy's poetry makes use of a symbolist register closer at times to the Yiddish poetry of Di Yunge than to Hebrew models. (This is not surprising, as Halevy translated extensively from Yiddish into Hebrew.) Something of a Jewish Baudelaire, he

---

7. For biographical material on Halevy, see Halevy (1968), especially the biographical essay by Yaakov Rimon.

wrote poems about the bars and cheap streets of New York, if not with sustained vividness or completely modernist fervor then certainly with a clearly authentic, experienced-based perspective and a willingness to depict scandalous subject matter. His poem "Ten Cents a Dance" for instance, describes one of the seedy New York establishments to which men would go and pay women for "dances"—that is, close contact for the purpose of sexual arousal. In a memorable image:

> One heavy-set man weakly clasps a lithe girl to the cascading
>   folds of his flesh;
> Like an old horse moving with difficulty, panting with exhaustion,
>   and whose face drips with sweat and twitches with pain.
>   (Halevy 1948, 68)

In the poem "Burlesque," which first appeared in 1938, Halevy even describes a man masturbating in a strip club, an image hardly imaginable in the work of any other Hebrew poet of his time. Yet he does so in ornate poetic diction: "the abundance of his overflowing love spills forth within his trembling, feverish fist" (64). Moreover, "abundance" (*shefa*) is a kabbalistic term for God's abounding presence, lending the line a further baroque pungency. This sort of irony is repeated elsewhere in the poem, as when Halevy describes men entering the hall seeking their "repair" (*tikun*)—again a mystical term given heavily ironic inversion, as a word for the ritual purging of sin is used to describe a sinful purging.

Halevy and Ginzburg (who was Halevy's teacher in the Tarbut teachers college in New York City in the 1920s) each depict the seamy side of the city. Yet for Halevy the city is not itself the source of the sin, nor does he posit nature as a pure alternative. Moreover, Halevy treats his subjects with an empathy—indeed, a complicity—lacking in Ginzburg's fear, outrage, and disgust. Halevy is an insider who describes the interiors of New York's dives, while Ginzburg stands gazing in from the outside. This different psychological-experiential stance is reflected in the formal and stylistic differences between these two poets. Halevy's poems favor a lyric-observational mode over an epic-declamatory mode, whereas Ginzburg, who wrote many lyric poems, nevertheless chose to engage the city mainly in his long "prophetic" poems. Ginzburg's city space is dreamlike and unreal, whereas Halevy creates a sense of real space, sometimes through the telling use of incidental detail. As the speaker makes his way to the dance hall in "Ten Cents a Dance," he hears the groan of a nearby train; this has nothing to do with the subject of the poem but makes for greater verisimilitude. He even uses particular addresses: the dance hall is on Fourteenth Street and Third Avenue.

Nevertheless, although his poetry displays a more modern and urban sensibility than most of the other American Hebraists, Halevy, like Ginzburg, finds it difficult to represent the city without recourse to predictable tropes, such as the heavy inevitability we find in his repeated ironic comparison of alcohol and cigarette smoke with the libations and incense of the biblical Temple. The combinations of myth and urban modernity seen in much of the Yiddish and English poetry of the time exhibit a greater range and complexity than we find in Halevy's New York poems, which attest to the often problematic character of the artistic encounters between the American Hebraists and the modern American urban environment.

In contrast to the Hebraists, the Yiddish poets of the United States responded with greater enthusiasm both to New York City and to literary modernism, developments that went hand in hand. A comparative glance at, for instance, Moyshe-Leyb Halpern's collection *In Nyu-York,* published at roughly the same time as Ginzburg's "No-York" is, if not entirely fair to the latter (Halpern was perhaps the finest Yiddish poet of his time), then certainly illustrative of the linguistic-poetic advantages enjoyed by the Yiddish poets in the writing of urban poetry. Halpern's New York poems surpass those of Ginzburg or any American Hebrew poet of the 1910s and 1920s, in terms of their representations of individual human specificity, imaginative involvement with both Jewish immigrants and non-Jews, register of poetic emotion, ability to depict the urban environment, psychological complexity and interiority, and capacity for humor.

Of course, the Yiddish writers also produced laments at their American exile and attacks on the city. Halpern's *In Nyu-York* is frequently marked by homesickness for Europe and acerbic complaints about the sordid reality of the "Golden Land." Sholem Asch's novel *Uncle Moses* describes New York as a "Babylon" and the Williamsburg Bridge as a foreboding "iron giant," in a manner similar to Ginzburg's New York poem (Roskies 2003).

Nevertheless, these same Yiddish writers were also far more likely to leaven such expressions with a sense of heady immersion in, celebration of, and identification with the American environment, which could become a positive imaginative space literarily, temperamentally, and ideologically in a way almost entirely absent from so much of the Hebrew work. "My city is New York," proclaimed the Yiddish poet Berysh Vaynshteyn in 1936 (Harshav and Harshav 1986, 671).

It is not surprising that Yiddish literature absorbed modernist trends more eagerly and quickly than did Hebrew because there was much less of a developed Yiddish literary tradition to displace, and a far greater spoken, vernacular presence than there was in Hebrew. As Benjamin Harshav has pointed out, there is also something of an inherent linguistic affinity between modernism, with its openness to the incorporation of "unpoetic" registers and new juxtapositions, and Yiddish, with its spoken, dialogic, associative, hyperconscious, and ironizing qualities. In addition, the social and ideological positions of the Yiddishists in the United States tended to be far more suited to the radical, the urban, and the new, than were those of the Hebrew writers. The former were more likely to have come from cities and large towns, rather than the smaller towns for which the Hebraists were so nostalgic. While most of the noted Hebrew writers in America were teachers and academics, their Yiddish contemporaries "were simple workers: Mani Leyb was a shoemaker; [Zishe] Landoy, a houspainter; [H.] Leyvik, a paperhanger; Halpern, a poverty-stricken jack-of-all-trades" (Harshav and Harshav 1986, 34). The Yiddishists were famously more secular, more politically radical, and less enamored of Jewish religious tradition or Zionist nationalism than were the Hebraists. And so, while it may not be possible to sort out cause from effect when considering the background, language choice, politics, and literary ideals of these writers, we can say that these traits tended to accompany and reinforce one another. Aaron Glants-Leyeles's father taught in a Hebrew school in Poland and wrote for the Hebrew periodical *Hamelits,* yet his son was devoted to Yiddish, to socialism, and to Territorialism, hardly an accidental trio. By the same token, it does not seem insignificant that Yiddish writers such as Judd Teller and Harry Sackler—both ardent Zionists and not particularly radical in politics—also wrote in Hebrew and in English.

Moreover, we find no equivalent counterpart among the Hebraists to the Yiddishists' frustration over their obscurity within American culture. In 1923, complaining of the superficial and misinformed treatment of Yiddish literature in an article in *The Nation,* Glants-Leyeles fumed, "[n]o other immigrant group has built an original, independent, and in more than one aspect American literature in the course of some thirty years than we Jews. Yet *The Nation* gets away with the silly cliché that every ex-reverend can supply" (Harshav and Harshav 1986, 797). Even more insulting was the response of the editors of *Poetry* to an issue of the avant-garde Yiddish literary journal *In Zikh.* As Glants-Leyeles reports, they wrote, "[u]nfortunately we cannot read your journal. We would like to know in what language it is printed. Is it Chinese?" At this, Glants-Leyeles wondered, "[h]ow long will Yiddish literature be unknown among the Gentiles? How long will they think of us—in literature—as Hottentots?" (Harshav and Harshav 1986, 798). Such statements are important precisely because they indicate the Yiddishists' desire to participate in an American cultural context. Harshav is surely correct in characterizing the literature of the Yiddish writers in the United States as "a truly American literature" (30), indeed, "an unjustly neglected branch of American literature" (5). Yet the Hebraists, who lacked this sense of American identity and sense of participation in an American culture, were not similarly troubled by their marginality in American culture. They did not especially regret their obscurity among Americans; they regretted only their obscurity among Jews.

To illuminate the way modernism, language choice, and American identity were intertwined in the different worlds of Hebrew and Yiddish culture in the United States, let us turn to the literary critic and editor, Shlomo Grodzensky (1904–72). Grodzensky's is such an instructive case because he had a foot in the world of American Hebraism, yet he was also a Yiddish writer and editor who was a devoted advocate of modernism. Born in Grodno, he came to America with his family in 1917. He soon had to give up formal schooling in order to work, but he remained a voracious and passionate reader all his life. He began to write for the *Yiddisher Kempfer,* a Yiddish-language Labor Zionist weekly that he was soon editing. In his late forties, after three decades in the United States, he moved to the State of Israel to be the editor of the Hebrew newspaper *Hador*. He was an articulate and humane public intellectual; his collection of essays, *Otobiografiah shel korei* (Autobiography of a reader), were it translated into English, would find easy fellowship with the literary criticism of the New York Intellectuals—despite his roots in Hebrew culture and Zionist politics, and his greater comfort with his Jewishness.

In the title essay of that collection, Grodzensky describes a series of literary primal scenes, moments or episodes that determined his sensibilities, biases, and loves as a critic and lifelong reader. In the first of these scenes, Grodzensky is introduced to modern Hebrew literature, reading Yaakov Fichman's Hebrew anthology *First Chapters* as a boy in a *heder metukan* (modern Jewish school) in Lithuania. Hebrew thus became, as he put it, "my first literature" (1975, 15). Despite his decades-long involvement in the Yiddish press and his affection for English literature, his first and deepest association with literature's magic—what he refers to, using a phrase from a poem by Yaakov Steinberg, as "the drug of lovely words"—is indelibly stamped as Hebrew. "It was curious to me," he writes, "and, it seems to me, to my friends as well, that my journalistic work was for so many years in Yiddish. For if there was passion in me, during my childhood and early youth, this passion was given first and foremost to Hebrew." Moreover, he says, "my passion for Hebrew was even more intense after I was brought to the United States at the age of twelve" (36). Although he soon quit his formal Hebrew schooling, he avidly followed developments in contemporary Hebrew literature and bought the latest Hebrew periodicals from a Canal Street bookstore.

Yet Yiddish, not Hebrew, was the language of Grodzensky's surroundings—his home, his neighborhood, the New York of his youth. This was the language of the political ferment all around him—a conjunction, he explains, of the "encounter with a democratic state" and its freedoms and the enthusiasm generated by the Russian Revolution, which broke out soon after his arrival in the United States: "[o]n the street corners of our noisy Jewish neighborhood, speakers' podiums were set up in the evening, upon which were delivered ardent and fiery exhortations and polemics. . . . the soapbox speeches, the proclamations of the Russian Revolution, the conversations of the adults at the table after work and on Sundays (the Jewish sabbath disappeared as if it had never existed) completely ignored the world of *First Chapters*" (16–17). Grodzensky faced the challenge of connecting the apparently exclusive worlds of Hebrew culture, on the one hand, and the revolutionism of the American Yiddish street, on the other: a disjunction he was able to bridge only when he discovered Poalei Tsion, a political movement that combined leftist radicalism with Zionism.

Interestingly, Grodzensky describes Yiddish as the language of his surroundings but not as a source of early literary passion. Instead, it functions as a medium for the second of his early literary primal scenes: his simultaneous discovery of English literature and modernism. "At a time when my spoken English was still halting and stammering," he recalls, "I began to read English literature with an enormous thirst" (17). The young Grodzensky came across a series of articles about modern American poetry in "a newspaper of the Ladies' Garment Workers Union, *Gerechtikeit* (Justice) was its name, that I used to borrow from one of the neighbors." The articles, penned by the Yiddish poet Aaron Glants-Leyeles, dealt with Edwin Arlington Robinson, Robert Frost, Amy Lowell, Ezra Pound, Wallace Stevens, and John Gould Fletcher. His curiosity sparked, Grodzensky "hurried to the public library and dove into the poetry section":

> In that library I discovered the world of English literature. My reading of the modern English poets, who were then quite young, determined for better or for worse my taste in poetry to this day. Only afterwards did I get to English poetry of earlier generations—and not in chronological order. Only after I read Robert Frost and Amy Lowell and Ezra Pound and T. S. Eliot did I go back (in this order) to the Romantics and the Victorians, to the poets of the seventeenth century (for whom I maintain a great love to this day) and the eighteenth century, and to Shakespeare. (Grodzensky 1975, 18)

The fifteen-year-old Grodzensky became "an avowed modernist," buying issues of *The Dial* and other "little magazines" as they came out. When he read the opening lines of T. S. Eliot's "Love Song of J. Alfred Prufrock," he experienced "a silent fanfare within" (20). In fact, this was a calling that would have significant literary-historical consequences more than thirty years later when Grodzensky helped introduce Anglo-American modernism into Israeli literary culture.

Grodzensky's love affair with modernism highlights a number of features that set him apart from the Hebraists. First of all, he was younger than nearly all the significant American Hebrew writers. (Gabriel Preil, born in 1911, is the notable exception, and Preil was one of the few American Hebrew modernists.) Grodzensky also immigrated to the United States earlier than most of the Hebraists—of the major Hebrew writers, only Preil and Avraham Regelson also immigrated prior to their teens—and he encountered Anglo-American modernism in his teens, not in his twenties or older as did most of the Hebraists. His loose relationship with formal education seems to have played a role as well. His neighborhood public library was, he writes, "my true, and perhaps only, school" (18). Having discontinued his formal public schooling, he had less exposure to the canonical English and American literature being taught in American high schools in the 1910s and 1920s. Similarly, he discontinued his formal Hebrew education, turning to Hebrew literary magazines rather than Hebraist colleges to provide his literary education in that language, freeing him to explore new literary currents that remained suspect among the Hebraist educators.

But it was of course Yiddish and, in particular, the radical, working-class, highly secularized Yiddish environment in which Grodzensky lived, so different from the traditional-maskilic milieu of the Hebraist intelligentsia in America, that set the stage for his seduction by modernism. This was a world in which "the Jewish sabbath disappeared as if it had never existed," in such stark contrast to the Sabbath-drenched imagination of a Shimon Ginzburg. It was not that Grodzensky simply chanced upon the "little magazines" of the time and so became smitten with modernism whereas, had he first read Tennyson, he would instead have embraced Victorian literature. As he tells us, he first encountered modernist poetry reading articles written by a modernist Yiddish poet in a union paper. If Grodzensky did not fall in love with literary modernism in Yiddish, Yiddish culture nevertheless enabled his love affair with Anglo-American modernism.

Moreover, it was not only that Yiddish and modernism were connected for Grodzensky, but that Hebrew and modernism were opposed. It is hardly coincidental that Grodzensky's embrace of modernism happened at the same time as his rejection of the Hebraist educational milieu and its literary and cultural values. Grodzensky's Hebrew teacher in New York was the poet and scholar Hillel Bavli, with whom he had a falling out just as he was discovering the joys of T. S. Eliot. Grodzensky saw his teacher, "lecturing on Bialik with his pince-nez and dreamy eyes" (23), as a "symbol of authority," and he felt compelled to throw off this authority, just as he was growing increasingly uneasy with what he then felt was the too openly rhetorical dimension of Bialik's poetry. Although Grodzensky does not remember the precise details of the argument he had with Bavli in 1919, he surmises that it involved his disparagement of Bialik. In response, Bavli grew angry and told Grodzensky that his place was still on the "students' bench" (*safsal hatalmidim,* 24). Grodzensky writes that he "decided at that moment, under the bridge of the El, that [he] would never again return to the students' bench," and he gave up formal Hebrew schooling ever afterward. Grodzensky tellingly notes that it was not only Bavli's condescending rebuke, but the flowery Hebrew phrasing in which he delivered it, that incensed him.

Thus, Grodzensky's break with Bavli resulted from a range of related issues that directly and indirectly concern his conversion to modernism. These issues include his critique of Hebrew romanticism (Bialik was "too explicit, there were too many overt positions"); the maskilic and European otherworldliness of the Hebraists (Bavli's pince-nez and dreamy eyes) and the nineteenth-century rhetoric and assumptions of their Hebrew (the *"safsal hatalmidim"*); as well as his Oedipal need to dethrone authority figures, and even his identification with the urban world of New York, symbolized by the train overpass that presides like a totem over his decision to leave school. And, given the presence of all these cultural elements, we will not be surprised at Grodzensky's much closer identification with America, in comparison to the Hebraists. "I never felt myself truly at home in the United States where I lived for decades," he admits. "Yet neither was I really afflicted with the sufferings of the alien. It seems to me that on some level of my being I am a sentimental American" (33).[8]

---

8. Grodzensky tells another anecdote from the early 1920s when Bialik had published a new poem for the first time in a long while, causing much happiness in Hebraist circles.

Ironically, Grodzensky's teacher was the one poet among the American Hebraists of that time to show a sustained interest in Anglo-American modernism. Born in Lithuania in 1893, Hillel Bavli came from a family that combined enlightenment and traditionalism in a way Lithuanian Jewry was known for. His father, a rabbi and maskil, had studied at the famous Volozhin yeshiva and from his school days there knew Abraham Isaac Kook (the future chief rabbi of Palestine and a major religious thinker) and Micha Yosef Berdichevsky (one of the foremost Hebrew writers of his generation). Bavli's father loved the poetry of the Haskalah and its nationalist turn of the 1880s, and he encouraged his son in both traditional study and modern literary pursuits. Bavli published his first poems in 1908 and was active in literary and Zionist circles in Vilna, where he moved the following year. Wanting to pursue higher education, something almost impossible for him as a Jew in tsarist Russia, he left for the United States in the summer of 1912. (His parents would follow after the First World War, and his father served as rabbi of a congregation on Staten Island, the site of a poem in which Bavli described the loneliness of a Jew trying to maintain his identity despite the meager Jewish community there.)

Bavli was one of the promising younger Hebrew writers, such as Shimon Ginzburg and Shimon Halkin, who arrived in the United States in the 1910s and who gathered around the figure of the elder Hebrew writer Benjamin Nahum Silkiner. He was a member of the Ahiever group, a precursor to the Histadrut, and helped with the launching of *Hatoren*. He took part in the creation of the Histadrut and was elected as one of the three initial secretaries of that organization at its founding congress in 1917. He was a critic and essayist for the Hebrew literary journal *Miklat;* and in 1923 he edited the anthology of American Hebrew writing *Nimim,* which included his essay on Negro poetry, the first such treatment in Hebrew. He studied at City College but finished his undergraduate degree in 1917 at Canisius

---

When a devoted Hebraist bookseller met Grodzensky in the street and asked him if he had read the poem, Grodzensky casually remarked that he preferred the modernist David Fogel to Bialik, knowing that his response would pique the Hebraist. The bookseller, when he recovered from his shock, spat in the street (a proper response to a heretic) and hurried away (Grodzensky 1975, 25).

College in Buffalo, where he was also a teacher at the local Hebrew school. Not long after his return from Buffalo to New York City, he was hired by Mordecai Kaplan to teach on the faculty of the Teachers Institute of the Jewish Theological Seminary, where he remained for the next four decades until his death in 1961.[9]

In the early 1920s, only a couple years after his blowup with Grodzensky, Bavli published a series of five articles on contemporary American poetry in the Warsaw-based Hebrew journal *Hatekufah*. In these articles, Bavli sought to provide his readers with a critical survey of new developments in American poetry. He provides considerations of the new American poetry as a whole, with individual studies of Robert Frost, Edgar Lee Masters, Carl Sandburg, and Amy Lowell. Limited as they are to those poets who had already come onto the scene in the mid-1910s, Bavli's selections may appear somewhat tame, at least compared to the reading habits of his ex-student Grodzensky, who was already on to E. E. Cummings and T. S. Eliot, after all. Nevertheless, his choices are not unusual for the time and serve to remind us that in the early 1920s, it was quite easy to take Amy Lowell and Carl Sandburg as major figures while ignoring, say, Wallace Stevens and William Carlos Williams (*Harmonium* and *Spring and All* both appeared in 1923, just as the last articles in Bavli's series were being published) and even, although with less justification, Ezra Pound and T. S. Eliot. With the exception of Amy Lowell, Bavli's focus is on the realist and regionalist strains in the poetry revival of the 1910s (Frost, Sandburg, Masters)—unsurprising, since he is writing for an international audience that would want to know about the social realities of the United States as well as its literature. Meanwhile, Bavli ignores other contemporary developments such as the expatriate modernism of Pound and Eliot, avant-garde poets such as Marianne Moore and Maxwell Bodenheim, and Jewish-American Whitmanians such as James Oppenheim.[10]

---

9. For biographical information on Bavli, see Malachi (1961/62). Malachi thinks Bavli may have been born in 1892 and not 1893 as most sources indicate.

10. By way of comparison, Louis Untermeyer, in his *The New Era in American Poetry* (1919), devotes separate chapters to all four of Bavli's choices as well as Ezra Pound, James Oppenheim, Vachel Lindsay, Edwin Arlington Robinson, Arturo Giovanniti, John Hall

The opening article describes the American poetry revival as part of the contemporary search for a distinctively American culture. Bavli traces its roots to Poe and Whitman who, he explains, stood in opposition to the prevailing materialism of American society and who sought to create a particularly American mode of expression. Whitman in particular "turned not to the dead past or the hidden world of the imagination" but to "the life of the people around him" (Bavli 1921/22, 437). Using "the living language of the masses," he "sought to destroy forever the artificial boundaries separating poetry from prose, and to abrogate traditional form." Whitman is the central model for the new writers of the twentieth century "who liberated themselves, or are seen to have liberated themselves, from the hypnotic influence of classic English literature" and who turned from "ancient mythology" and "the lofty and sublime heights" in favor of contemporary life and "prosaic everyday language" (439–40).

Bavli is anything but wholly enthusiastic about this modernist turn. His attitude throughout these essays is a mixture of fascinated interest and deep misgivings. This ambivalence is seen in the opening of his essay on Sandburg:

> When I first read the poems of this Swedish-American poet, I said to myself in shock and astonishment: is this poetry? And is one such as this a poet?—No! No!—cried thousands of voices from my youth within me. The hysterical bombast in these poems, the excessive, sometimes offensive realism that erupts from their lines, the crude vulgarity infusing their expression erected a barrier—to my mind, in any case—between them and the true legacy of poetry, which is noble and refined and favored with beauty and purity even as it treads this earth and crosses the muck of this life. The impression was almost repulsive. And yet it was impossible to forget this poetry. (Bavli 1921/22, 684)

It was precisely the "ruthlessness" and "crudeness" of Sandburg's poetry that Bavli found so memorable and affecting. Yet the strong, sometimes bewildering and offensive impressions made upon him by poems such as

---

Wheelock, and Charles Erskine Scott Wood. Untermeyer also deals with Eliot, Stevens, Williams, and H. D., but they do not receive chapters of their own.

Sandburg's clash with the conception, ingrained in him from his tradi-tional-maskilic youth, of the "true legacy of poetry, which is noble and refined." Given the "barrier" he finds dividing these two conceptions, Bavli responds by taking Sandburg's poetry out of the realm of purely aesthetic judgments, arguing that such literature should not be judged "by standards of beauty and art alone, since fundamentally it intends, as does the poetry of Whitman, not to sing but to call, to preach, to rouse." Sandburg's poetry is valuable because it "clears the air" and "prepares the ground." It is a salutary expression of a still-inchoate American culture coming into being, like an unfinished sculpture emerging from the rock.

In the case of Frost, Bavli offers an admiring but ultimately critical over-view of the poetry, discussing the collections *North of Boston* (1914) and *Mountain Interval* (1916), and translating in whole or in part poems such as "The Mountain," "The Death of the Hired Man," "Snow," "Mending Wall," and "Birches." According to Bavli, the "main value of Robert Frost" is as "a painter of the life of nature, and especially as a faithful interpreter of the souls of the modest and simple farmers of the New England land-scape" (1921/22, 453). Frost, writes Bavli, presents "life *as it is,* and not as it ought to be or as it might be pictured in the imagination of the poet" (450). Indeed, despite his admiration for Frost's psychological and dramatic acuity, Bavli views Frost's poems not as constructed texts that refract and create reality, but as documentary and imagistic portraits. Frost, he writes, is "a poet-painter" who deals primarily with "forms of reality themselves as they appear to him. . . . Life is greater to him than any beautiful theory, any lofty idea. . . . Therefore he presents to us natural scenes and states of soul naked and exposed . . . without any explanation or interpretation from the side" (442). By contrast, the poet-critic Louis Untermeyer, in his 1923 collection of essays *American Poetry Since 1900,* disputes the perception of Frost as simple documentarist: "Frost is never the photographic realist. His lines are lifted above mere representation by a clarity of phrase, a cleanness of epithet, a condensation that, without leaving the tones of conversation, continually tightens into epigram" (Untermeyer 1923, 17–18). Bavli, on the other hand, is struck by what he sees as a lack of rhetoric or overt argu-mentation in the poems, an absence of philosophy or polemic, and seeks to justify this to his audience with the refrain of "life itself" and "life as it is." Nevertheless, he finally rejects this mere realism:

> The imaginative faculty, that sixth sense given to poets, is hardly felt in the majority of [Frost's] poems. And in this is a flaw. While his landscapes are faithful and clear, his psychological descriptions superb in their accuracy and truthfulness, there blows a kind of chill from them all—like the cold that emanates from gravestones even when they are quite beautiful and artfully crafted—because the poet has not imparted to them the splendor of his living imagination or the luminescence of his waking soul. (Bavli 1921/22, 450)

Bavli implies a link between Frost's subjects, the "Puritan farmers" who are so often devoid of curiosity or imaginative warmth ("their lives pass without reflection or questioning or searching for answers" [445]), and the poet himself, who seems so content with reality that he refuses to transfigure or transcend it.

For Bavli, Frost's achievement amounts in the end to a localist verisimilitude stripped of the imagination. As for Masters's hugely popular *Spoon River Anthology,* Bavli admires the scope and intricacy of the book, yet he questions its unrelenting grimness and cynicism. "Is this America?" he asks (1922, 682). He muses that there may be some value in confronting "optimistic America" with such savage and bitter criticism, and he notes that the book's reception indicates that "the young generation in America" has "discovered something of itself, truly of itself" in its pages (673). Nevertheless, Masters's sallow, acid epitaphs excise the moments of happiness and inspiration in his poor characters' lives, indicating a failure of sympathy on his part. If Frost's works lack imagination, *Spoon River* lacks happiness.

Bavli's essay on Amy Lowell is subtitled "Imagist Poetry," and it mentions the first and second imagist anthologies, quoting generously from the preface to the latter. Yet of all the writers involved in these publications— including Pound, Williams, H. D., Joyce, Ford Madox Ford, Richard Aldington, D. H. Lawrence, and John Gould Fletcher—Bavli only names Lowell. His enthusiasm for her poetry, greater than that for the other three poets he deals with, derives primarily from the fin-de-siècle aestheticism and impressionism he finds in her work. Lowell, he writes, follows "the cult of beauty and art and thought alone" unlike "local, racial poets" such as Frost, Masters, and Sandburg who focus so exclusively on external reality (1923, 435–36). What Bavli admires, then, is what Ezra Pound derided as "Amygism" when he broke away from the movement he had helped to launch. Nevertheless, here too Bavli is critical, objecting to the imagist project as a whole in a manner that recalls his critique of Frost. Bavli critiques the imagist emphasis on visual surface, its cold superficiality. "For in its fundamental essence," he writes, "poetry is not a merely visual art, feeding on the play of light and shadow upon a screen, but is above all the art of the soul giving clear expression to the reflections of life's light and shadow in the dark cell of the heart" (440). The objectivity, realism, and rhetorical restraint of American poetry seem to Bavli a kind of paucity, not progress. Poetry, he argues, must "strip away the shell of incidentals from life in order to see the idea flashing within" (435).

Bavli's studies in modern American poetry show a curiosity and intelligent appreciation for some of the efforts of these new poets. Yet the premises and techniques of the new American literature are too foreign to his aesthetic beliefs for this curiosity and appreciation to translate into deeper sympathy or influence. Bavli attacks the antitraditionalism of modern poetry's dogmatic supporters, complaining, for example, that Masters is lauded only for his modernist work, though he has also written about "such 'ancient' things as light and love, about such 'conservative' subject matter as the legends of King Arthur . . . the fables of classical Greece, and even—hear this!—biblical ballads" (1922, 683). In this regard, what is most notable about these essays is what they do not say: Bavli never so much as hints that American modernism has any positive or constructive relevance to Hebrew poetry, whether that of the Hebrew writers in the United States or elsewhere. For Bavli, as for so many of the Hebraists of his generation, literary modernism was fundamentally in conflict with poetry's "true legacy."

How great the gap could be between these two things is indicated by the one poem I am aware of that Bavli published in English. "To Russia," a poem he submitted to the June 1917 issue of the *Canisius Monthly*, the college literary magazine, is a bad poem, though better than the other undergraduate doggerel in the magazine, and technically rather impressive in that Bavli's English had to have followed on at least four other languages: Yiddish, Hebrew, Russian, and German. (Bavli quickly learned English on his arrival in the United States, and he later translated *Anthony and Cleopatra* and *Oliver Twist,* among other works, into Hebrew.) The poem describes the ambivalent emotions—affection, resentment, hopefulness, and distance—felt by the young Jewish poet in the wake of the news of the February Revolution in Russia. Here is the first of its four stanzas:

> Russia, bleak Russia! empire of shadows,
>> Vale of deep sorrows and pain,
> Soaked with abhorrent blood and tear torrent,
>> Land of the martyred and slain!
> Russia, bleak Russia! my cradle of childhood,
>> And tomb of my youth's happy dreams,
> Land much beloved, black curses above it,
>> Mother—no mother meseems.
>> (Bavli 1917b, n.p.)

This is not an indication of Bavli's own Hebrew poetry, which while also frequently written in a Romantic, rhetorical vein, is decidedly more accomplished, far more fluid and less mannered. Yet the poem, in its clear wish to be a kind of Coleridgean ballad—poetry written, as Halkin put it, "as if in the time of Shelley"(S. Halkin 1971, 34)—does tell us a great deal about what Bavli expected from English poetry.

Bavli's distance from American modernism can also be seen in the many translations he included throughout his *Hatekufah* essays. These translations are generally well crafted and faithful and convey some flavor of each of the poets. They constitute some of the first translations of twentieth-century American poetry into Hebrew. What they do not achieve, however, is the sense of spokenness of the poetry, or the different colloquial shadings of the poets. This was perhaps inevitable, given the American Hebraists' remove from the Hebrew-speaking society of Palestine. Bavli's Hebrew biblicizes both Frost's New England cadences and Sandburg's Midwestern newspaper headlines. Yet part of what made modern American poetry so exciting to its readers was the sense that it was suffused with American speech, a vernacular quality also lacking in Bavli's own poems of the 1920s.

THE AMERICANNESS DEBATE

Ironically, it was precisely the Hebraists' opposition to modernism that became the core around which they first created a consciously American group identity. This process occurred in the course of what came to be called the "Americanness Debate," a series of polemics carried on in Hebrew journals in the 1920s. In these debates, a number of the most prominent and promising Hebrew writers in the United States collectively distinguished their literary values and practices from the Hebrew modernism developing in Europe and especially in Palestine. The mantle of "Americanness" now became a way of justifying their aesthetic and cultural traditionalism and of finding a raison d'être when Palestine was eclipsing all other literary and cultural Hebrew centers.

The first rumblings of the debate began in 1920 in several articles that appeared in the American-based Hebrew journal *Miklat*. In one essay, Shimon Ginzburg angrily complained that the arbiters of Hebrew literature based in Palestine were ignoring the contributions of Hebrew writers in the United States. This neglect, he charged, was not based on the quality of the latter's work, but rather was a result of those critics' and editors' ideological contempt for America and for Hebrew writers who chose to live there rather than in the Land of Israel. Upon seeing the words "New York" beneath a work of literature, Ginzburg claimed, the editors of overseas journals such as *Hashiloah* and *Hapo'el Hatsa'ir* declare that it has "the smell of America" and refuse to publish it. These editors assumed that Hebrew writers in America had forfeited their right to participate in the cultural institutions of the Land of Israel, since they clearly prized material comfort over the national struggle. Even writers who resided only briefly in the United States were held to be "tainted with sin" (Ginzburg 1920, 159).

Ginzburg's outraged response shows the beginnings of an ambivalent circling about American identity. The Americanness of the Hebrew writers in the United States is attributed to them by writers overseas and is considered an insult, a charge of materialism. Yet in sticking up for the "American"—as Ginzburg here designates Hebrew writers in the United States—he begins to accept this label, wanting to turn it from a badge of shame to a badge of honor. He asserts that the American Hebraist is even more admirable than the Palestinian because he turns "his thought to the Land of Israel" even while he is surrounded by "the seven layers of the American hell." Moreover, Ginzburg argues that "talent does not depend on country." In a sharp rebuke to Zionist considerations, he closes his essay as follows: "Concerning literature, what is America or the Land of Israel to me? If you have ability and something to say—go and say it. If you have nothing to say, even the merit of the Land of Israel will not help you" (160).

Another article published in *Miklat* the same year delved even further into the question of the Americanness of Hebrew literature in the United States. Yaakov Rabinowitz (1875–1948), an influential critic and writer, had lived in the Land of Israel since 1910, where he would cofound the important literary journal *Hedim*. Rabinowitz championed the young Hebrew modernists of Palestine, yet he maintained an enduring if often critical interest in the Hebrew literary center in America. In his 1920 article, "Amerika'iyut" (Americanness), he found both the promise and weakness of Hebrew literature in the United States embodied in the work of the poet Benjamin Nahum Silkiner. Referring to *Mul ohel Timurah* (1910), Silkiner's epic poem about Indian tribes in the New World, Rabinowitz praised the poem for its power and originality, regretting only that the difficulty of its language prevented it from winning a wider audience. (We will discuss Silkiner and the Indian motif in American Hebrew literature in the next chapter.) However, Rabinowitz went on to complain that Silkiner had since retreated to "the familiar and the banal" (Rabinowitz 1920, 463) in his poetry and that this decline was paradigmatic of the artistic timidity of Hebrew literature in the United States. Although it was understandable, Rabinowitz wrote, that the Hebrew writer in the United States should have difficulty in contending with new, American cultural realities ("If Odessa and even Warsaw" have not yet been assimilated into Jewish literary creation, "then how shall New York be?" [464]), he nevertheless insisted that it was necessary for these writers to persist in trying, daring to bring aspects of American reality into their writing, rather than turning back to the well-trod path of what has already been done.

Shimon Halkin, then twenty-two years of age, responded to Rabinowitz a few months later. In an article entitled "Americanness and Our Literature," Halkin argued that there was no such thing as Americanness, and therefore Rabinowitz's call for more of it was an impossibility. The argument may seem odd, yet it was drawn to a great extent from Halkin's observations of the American cultural scene at the time. American intellectuals of the day, noted Halkin, endlessly debated what Americanness was, while the young generation of American writers and artists looked ahead to the arrival of some "spiritual American type" to come (S. Halkin 1920b, 478). However, "actual Americanness, living and definite, has not yet been found." In the nineteenth century, "the outlines of a national literature" had emerged in the works of writers such as Irving, Cooper, Bryant, Thoreau, Longfellow, and Emerson, an American character reaching its apotheosis in "the mighty figure of Walt Whitman" (479). Today, however, there was no unified American character, and American literature was merely a collection of various regionalisms.

The reason for this lack of a national literature, Halkin claimed, was "the famous Melting Pot" (478), which had obscured the Anglo-Saxon, Protestant-American culture that came into being in the nineteenth century and which had not yet produced a new, distinct synthesis to take its place. Ever since "old Europe began sending masses and masses of foreigners to America," wrote Halkin, referring to the waves of immigration beginning in the last decades of the nineteenth century, these "different races and different cultures" have "enrich[ed] the country's spirit" while at the same time "blur[ring] its form and character." As a result, America now had a "culture in process" and had "not even created its own distinct literature" (479). Whitman may have been "the archetypal American poet," yet he was "only accepted by the freethinking reader" and "the younger poets," while so-called realists such as Twain and London had been unable to encompass the diversity and difficulty of American experience in their writing. With the exception of *Huckleberry Finn,* judged Halkin, Twain "did not dare to see American life as it is," and London had "ignored real life in his country" (479). American life was simply too various and unmasterable to be contained in the work of any one author.

Halkin's account of American culture is interesting for the use it makes of contemporary currents in American literary and cultural criticism. In the 1910s and 1920s, there was indeed an intense preoccupation among the American cultural vanguard with questions of American identity.

Halkin's arguments are traceable in particular to the analyses and polemics of the cultural nationalists who gathered around the journal *The Seven Arts*, critics such as Van Wyck Brooks and Waldo Frank. A generation earlier, William Dean Howells had already remarked on the decline of the national aspect of American literature in the period after the Civil War. "New England has ceased to be a nation unto itself," wrote Howells in *Literary Friends and Acquaintances* (1900), "and it will perhaps never again have anything like a national literature; and it will probably be centuries yet before the life of the whole country, the American life as distinguished from the New England life, shall have anything like a national literature" (quoted in Cox 1988, 764). Van Wyck Brooks, writing in 1917, considered it "a commonplace that immigration from without and migration within the Republic have prevented the formation of any structure in our society for literature to build a nest in" (Brooks 1968, 173). This echoed his earlier judgment, in *The Wine of the Puritans* (1908), that Americans were not yet a "race"—that is, not yet a coherent nationality that could give rise to a great spiritual and cultural tradition: "It seems to me that an artist can produce great and lasting work only out of the materials which exist in him by instinct and which constitute racial fibre, the accretion of countless generations of ancestors, trained to one deep, local indigenous attitude toward life. A man is more the product of his race than his art, for a man may supremely express his race without being an artist, while he cannot be a supreme artist without expressing his race" (Brooks 1968, 50). In his seminal work, *America's Coming-of-Age* (1915), Brooks uses the tale of Rip Van Winkle as an allegory for the passing of "that old innocent America which has fallen asleep," and which stirs somnolently to the thunderings of newly arriving "Jews, Lithuanians, Magyars, and German socialists" (Brooks 1915, 97). Halkin was evidently following this line of argument in his response to Rabinowitz.

Halkin's judgments about individual American authors also echo Brooks and his colleagues. His view—which, as we have seen, he shared with Hillel Bavli—of Whitman as "the archetypal American poet" and hero of the young generation of American writers finds obvious resonance with the writers associated with *The Seven Arts*. "Whitman," says Brooks in *America's Coming-of-Age*, "precipitated the American character" (118) and "laid the cornerstone of a national ideal" (121), an assertion echoed by fellow *Seven Arts* writers such as Waldo Frank and Louis Untermeyer. Halkin's assertion that Twain and London evaded reality was similarly influenced by these writers. Brooks made such arguments in his book *The Ordeal of Mark Twain*, published the same year as Halkin's essay, as did Frank in his galvanizing and influential diagnosis of American culture, *Our America,* published in 1919. In fact, Halkin reviewed *Our America* in *Miklat,* approvingly paraphrasing Frank's argument—common to many of the cultural critics of his generation—that America suffered from a soul-damaging materialism and moralism, traceable to its Puritan heritage. This argument may have struck a chord with the Hebraists, who were already critical of what they saw as American materialism and soullessness. Bavli, for instance, explained in his essays on the new American poetry that the "desiccating Puritanism" in American culture had, before the Whitmanian revival, "frozen any living, stirring feeling" in the American soul (Bavli 1921/22, 435).

Nevertheless, Halkin borrows quite selectively from these contemporary American cultural critics. He echoes their excoriations of American materialism and "Puritanism," but is far less interested in their excited charting of American cultural renewal. His argument to Rabinowitz that because there is no single, fixed, fully-developed, and all-encompassing national culture that can be called American, there can be no American influence on Hebrew culture, seems casuistic and detached from the literary and cultural ferment of the times. Moreover, Halkin implies that contemporary American culture not only cannot influence Hebrew literature (since it does not exist) but also that new (if fragmentary) manifestations of Americanness *should not* influence Hebrew literature. Although Halkin looks back admiringly to what he sees as the more innocent, agrarian, homogeneous culture of nineteenth-century America, what he now sees emerging is a collection of merely piquant regionalisms and doubtful modernist experiments. Hebrew literature, he argues, will be better served if its writers turn to the enduring treasures of world literature (including older American literature), rather than scrambling after contemporary American culture simply because they happen to reside in the United States.

Just as we find to be the case in Bavli's articles on American poetry, what is missing from Halkin's essays of 1920 is a sense of participation in the new American cultural currents. In his review of Frank, Halkin defends the United States, criticizing the skewed and stereotyped misapprehensions of America—based, he says, on "jealousy and short-sightedness" (S. Halkin 1920a, 307)—common in European and European Jewish treatments of the subject. However, he describes himself as "an honest observer" of the American scene, not as a participant in it. In terms of affect, throughout his review of *Our America* Halkin could as easily be writing of Japan. While an American Jewish cultural critic such as Frank could write of "our America," Hebraists such as Halkin and Bavli still thought of it as "their America."

These articles in *Miklat* were the first articulations of issues that would burst forth in a far more bold and developed manner a few years later in the Americanness debate proper. The debate (which again centered on the contributions of Rabinowitz and Halkin) was sparked by an essay (again entitled "Americanness") that Rabinowitz published in the August 8, 1924, issue of *Hadoar*. The essay's occasion was the appearance of *Nimim*, a showcase anthology for the American Hebraists, that was edited by Bavli and included recent work by Bavli, Halkin, Silkiner, Efros, Avraham Regelson, and Ephraim Lisitzky. Rabinowitz's review, printed in the most widely read American Hebrew publication of the time, offered a deeply critical assessment of Hebrew literature in the United States and provoked a series of fierce responses from the American Hebraists. It was in these responses that a new, specifically American identity was articulated by the American Hebraists.

As we have seen, Rabinowitz had already expressed doubts about the quality of Hebrew literature in the United States. Nor was he the first to do so. A decade earlier, the influential writer Yosef Haim Brenner had criticized this literature for its indifference to the realities of American and Jewish-American life—a charge repeated in each of Rabinowitz's essays. Yet neither Brenner's criticisms nor Rabinowitz's in his first "Americanness" essay elicited anything near the level of response that Rabinowitz's 1924 essay did.

The reason for this is not only what Rabinowitz said, but also when he said it. By the mid-1920s the American Hebrew writers, already doubtful about the future of Hebrew culture in America, sensed most acutely the gulf opening up between their dreams of a thriving Hebrew center in the United States and the developments that would give sole cultural preeminence to Israel. On the one hand, the possibilities for Hebrew literature in America had never seemed greater in comparison with Eastern Europe, where the Soviet Revolution was viciously extirpating Hebrew culture. Yet in 1921 and 1924, the United States Congress passed laws that drastically curtailed immigration from Eastern Europe. The American Hebraists, already anxious about the likelihood of raising a new generation of American-born Hebrew writers, found their most promising source for new Hebrew talent—immigrants—all but cut off. Meanwhile, the modern Jewish settlement in Palestine, or Yishuv, that had been so hard hit by the travails of the First World War now showed signs of rapid cultural ascendancy. A Hebrew-speaking society had emerged for the first time in two millennia, and a young generation of Hebrew modernists was gaining prominence in its literary life. Both linguistic and literary developments in the Land of Israel seemed to be speeding away from Hebrew culture as it was known in the United States. At the root of the Americanness debate, then, were two interconnected anxieties: about the future of the Hebrew literary center in America and about the nature of Hebrew literature in the Land of Israel. If Hebrew literature were passing from Europe, would it find its continuation in America or in the Yishuv? If the latter, then what was the purpose of Hebrew literature in America? And would Hebrew literature's character and legacy be assured in the hands of the modernists of Israel, who seemed so intent on overturning literary traditions?

According to Rabinowitz's 1924 essay, the problem with Hebrew literature in America was not lack of talent, but rather the continuing absence in America of what he called "an atmosphere sufficient for creative efforts in Hebrew" (9). What Rabinowitz meant by "atmosphere" was a level of cultural innervation and innovation, a literary environment in which writers were open to and nourished by their surroundings. Without it, these writers would continue to produce pallid, derivative work. As in his 1920 essay, Rabinowitz insisted that the lack of atmosphere could not be blamed on America itself, noting that the Yiddish writers proved success was possible. Indeed, he was actually quite sanguine about the prospects of Hebrew in America, arguing that, while a primarily spoken language such as Yiddish would be unable to compete with English and so eventually die out, Hebrew would thrive alongside its new vernacular partner, just as it had done for centuries alongside Yiddish. What needed to be remedied in American Hebrew literature, argued Rabinowitz, was its distance from reality, both in the sense of the Hebraists' reluctance to portray the environment in which they lived and, more fundamentally, their preference for aesthetic convention over the new artistic possibilities and influences around them.

This was not a simple call for local color—although many of the American Hebraists willfully misread his critique as such. Bavli accused Rabinowitz of seeking to strap poets onto the "Procustean bed of geography" (Bavli 1924, 5), and Ribalow claimed that Rabinowitz was an anticosmopolitan who wanted to "divide Hebrew literature by country" (Ribalow 1924, 6). Ginzburg asked if Rabinowitz would criticize a "Hebrew Keats" for not making his "Grecian urn" sufficiently American (Ginzburg 1925, 8). These attacks on Rabinowitz were unfair. (And it may be pointed out that, two years prior to Ginzburg's rejoinder, Wallace Stevens had in fact turned Keats's urn into a jar in Tennessee.) What Rabinowitz lamented was not a mere lack of Americana in the poetry of the American Hebraists—indeed, *Nimim* contained its share of "American"-themed material, including a poem by Silkiner about immigrants in New York and Bavli's essay on American Negro poetry—but rather what he saw as a moribund imperviousness to the world, the city, the local, the real. In its stead Rabinowitz recommended a literary dynamism, energetic and forward looking. "Less nostalgia for the former homeland, for Russia," he wrote, "and more reality—in the widest sense, of course, more adhesion to the ground under one's feet, to America" (1924, 11).

The American Hebraists' responses to Rabinowitz focused as much on concerns about modernism in the Land of Israel and about the future of Hebrew literary culture itself as they did on Hebrew literature in America, showing that an American Hebrew cultural identity was coming into being as an alternative to the direction of Hebrew literature overseas. One tack taken by the Hebraists was a sociohistorical critique of Hebrew modernism. According to this argument, Hebrew modernism was a symptom of the times—the upheavals of the First World War, the Soviet Revolution, and the pioneer conditions in the Yishuv—but would pass away as conditions settled down. Ginzburg, for instance, explained that because the Yishuv was a society still "in the making," it had produced a poetry "in the making"—incomplete and "still on the way toward the beautiful." Denouncing the "shrill stuttering" of poets such as Shlonsky and Greenberg, Ginzburg predicted that, as society in the Yishuv grew more "distinct," modernism would disappear like "morning mists dispelled by the rising sun" (1925, 7). By implication, American Hebrew poetry was a sober model of those literary values that would last beyond the ephemera of the times.

Ginzburg's arguments also reflected a second type of response, an idealist-aesthetic critique of modernist poetry, a Platonic outlook in which true poetry reflected lofty and timeless forms of beauty and truth, while modernism promoted *tishtush*—the blurred or indistinct. *Tishtush,* wrote Ginzburg, by definition "can never be beautiful," just as "the chaos of emotions is not true poetry" (1925, 7). This perspective was shared by many of the American Hebraists, from Bavli reacting in shock to Sandburg's Chicago poems to Ribalow fretting over what he called the "blurred" quality of modern Hebrew literature (Ribalow 1924, 6). Halkin, in his criticism, repeatedly attacked modern poetry for its twilight and murk. In an early essay, Halkin spoke at first with a reluctant, almost stunned admiration of the recent achievements of American Yiddish modernism. Read one of the recent collections of Yiddish poetry, he wrote, "and see if you don't stand there awed and amazed: good God! How much 'news' is here!" (S. Halkin 1969:1, 66). Yet Halkin went on to argue that, after one has gotten over the initial dazzle of their modernist pyrotechnics, one discerns that these poets deal only in superficial effects and lack those qualities that, for Halkin, define poetic greatness. Contemporary Yiddish verse "does not flow from a pure and deep source of poetry, but from a well of muddy waters that leaves in your mouth an insipid taste. You feel that this poetry does not enrich the stores of the spirit, does not exalt and uplift in the way of great poetry." It was, he claimed, a "poetry of shadows," a "wandering in the fog" (66).

A third type of response focused on literary-cultural concerns, and was seen in Bavli's rejoinder to Rabinowitz. Bavli emphasized that he was not opposed to innovation in literature. Nevertheless, he believed that the healthy development of a literary culture required a tension between revolutionary and traditional tendencies. The young modernists, however, were simply rejecting the poetry of their elders without understanding or integrating it. They demanded novelty for novelty's sake, he wrote, like "an infant who puts aside his playthings before he has yet sufficiently grasped their nature, and who is distracted from them as soon as a new toy meets his eye" (1924, 5). The danger of which Bavli warned was a too-rapid development, in which the still-fragile Hebrew literary culture would wither because, he wrote, the poetic ideas of the Hebrew Revival "have not yet had the influence they should and must have." Bavli's call for greater conservatism is therefore framed not as a resistance to the new or a stifling of literary vitality, but as a concern for the health of Hebrew litera-ture, which in the 1920s was still a not fully established entity and whose linguistic and spiritual resources the modernists seemed to be squander-ing. Ribalow similarly worried about the damage modernism might do to the bond between Hebrew literature and its audience, driving readers away by assaulting their sensibilities rather than cultivating their sympa-thy and trust—a particular concern in America, which had always lacked a sure Hebrew readership.

Bavli's outlook was a principled literary conservatism that sprang in part from a concern for the genuinely unpredictable and tenuous nature of contemporary Hebrew literary development. Moreover, his reservations were quite in line with the voices of resistance to some of the modernist firebrands in the Anglo-American world as well. Among the complaints editor Harriet Monroe received about the 1913 issue of *Poetry*, which included poems by Ezra Pound and William Butler Yeats, was one from the Nebraskan poet and *Poetry* contributor John G. Neihardt, who wrote as follows:

> Rebellion gets nowhere. Only slow growth ever counts. There is no new beauty. Literature is organic. We cannot banish our ancestors with a fiat. Important changes are not abrupt. Did the French Revolution bring democracy to France? Violence is the manifestation of hysteria. Real growth is imperceptible. You & Pound can't change natural laws. . . . My God! Have you forgotten that we are endowed with a great heritage? Will you & an impudent young man wipe out a tremendous past that has pro-duced us? (quoted in Parisi and Young 2002, 43)

Or, in Bavli's agricultural metaphor: "What our literature needs now is not innovation based on the extirpation of the old and the uprooting of the planted, but rather a renewal based on the turning of the ploughed soil" (Bavli 1924, 5).

The most elaborate and influential defense of American Hebrew poetry against its detractors overseas was Shimon Halkin's, first put forth in his 1924 essay "Hashirah ha'ivrit ba'Amerikah" (Hebrew poetry in America) and further elaborated in a later version of the essay, under the title "Paragonim ve'epigonim bashiratenu" (Paragons and epigones in our poetry).[11] Like other American writers, Halkin juxtaposed the characteristics of American Hebrew poetry—purity, temperance, clarity, sincerity—with the stylistic obfuscations and spiritual deficits of the new literary fashions. Like them, he complained of the obscurity and neglect to which Hebrew writers in the United States were consigned by critics abroad, when in fact they should be appreciated if only for the cultural obstacles they were forced to contend with in their country. "How many wars," he wrote, "must the creative artist wage in America in order to preserve his purity, to keep the aspect of the divine within him from being completely obscured by the unclean life sweeping him along with all its force" (1924, 10).

Yet the real novelty of Halkin's response was his claim that the character of American Hebrew poetry was a result of the influence of English poetry. Halkin's essay gave to American Hebrew poetry a literary-historical justification, arguing that its apparent conservatism was not an inability to embrace poetic innovation but was instead precisely the embrace of a

---

11. In my discussion, I cite both essays but rely mainly on the later one. Although it is longer and more developed than Halkin's original 1924 sally, Halkin's basic arguments—the influence of English poetry on American Hebrew poetry, the denigration of modernist poetry, the moral and aesthetic superiority of American Hebrew poetry, the loneliness of the Hebrew poet in America and the callousness of the critics overseas, the ethical-aesthetic bankruptcy of modern Russian poetry, the value of the eternal and unitary over the ephemeral and fragmentary—have all remained strikingly unchanged. This itself is significant, indicating the persistence of the Americans' aesthetic views over time, including Halkin's resistance to poetic modernism.

different (i.e., Anglo-American) literary tradition. As was only natural, these poets had absorbed the influences of their American surroundings and schooling and forged an identity distinct from Hebrew poetry elsewhere. Halkin claimed that, whereas Hebrew poets in Europe and Palestine had been influenced, often to an uncritically imitative extent, by Russian poetry and by forerunners of modernism such as Baudelaire and Whitman, the Americans reflected the aesthetic values of "Wordsworth, Shelley and Keats, Emerson, Tennyson, and Browning" (1969, 1:86). What critics attacked as the American Hebraists' traditionalism, their coldness of style and artistic timidity, was actually the rhetorical restraint, clarity of expression, philosophical lucidity, and unabashedly moral register these poets absorbed from English and American authors. Only a few years before, Halkin had claimed that there was no such thing as Americanness; he now argued that the antimodernist aesthetics of the American Hebrew poets was precisely a manifestation of their Americanness.

Halkin's understanding of English poetry reflected the spiritual and literary preoccupations of the American Hebraists, as well as something of his own Hasidic background. He emphasized in particular the metaphysical striving toward wholeness he found in nineteenth-century British poetry—in contrast to the stylistically and spiritually fragmentary character of modernist poetry. Modernism's concern with the flotsam and jetsam of experience, the grit of the local, registered for Halkin as unconscionable abdications of poetry's true calling. Missing from modern Hebrew poetry, he claimed, was "the central element in great lyric poetry: that graceful attempt by the poet to seize the isolated moments of his vision as they flow *from a single source* and to unify the isolated moments of life" (1969, 89; emphasis in original). English poetry, on the other hand, was "even in its lyric mode . . . not a poetry of ephemeral moments" but "an urgent, energetic, unceasing attempt to penetrate into the essence of all the world" (93). Halkin argued that "the influence of English poetry" reinforced the "spiritual seriousness" of the American Hebrew poets, a "seriousness almost approaching religiousness" and that had been "the foundation of Hebrew poetry in all its ages."

Halkin was also attracted to the moral and sentimental qualities he found in English poetry, particularly in the Victorians. In his novel *Ad mashber* (1945), we find a memorable embodiment of the moral mission of Victorian poetry in the figure of the college professor, Miss Watkins. A shriveled, corseted old maid, Professor Watkins lectures to a group of female students, zealously preaching the saving moral power of Victorian poetry, "which, as no other, and especially not the nightmare-besotted poetry of the generation, was destined to reform that whole generation of young, wayward women."

> —Yes, yes! . . . —the yellowish furrows of Professor Watkins's neck reddened above her erect, ridged fine cloth collar:—she knows that this course will not immediately influence the girls of the age, mothers of the future, birds who refused to recognize that their delicate wings were not given them to be singed in every flickering flame, but to take off flying . . . nevertheless she knows and understands that if there is yet any hope whatsoever for this profligate generation, only Victorian poetry whispers to the ear that perhaps there is still hope . . . the good in man would triumph in the end! The good and the pure, that is the only beauty, according to the deep, unshakable feeling of the immortal Victorian poets. (S. Halkin 1945, 56)

The professor's dried-up figure and didacticism might at first suggest that Halkin is mocking Victorian morality. Yet Halkin appears to admire Watkins's earnestness, and her antiquated appearance and decrepit physique correspond precisely to the baleful neglect of Victorian values by her students, the promiscuous, self-destructive "birds." Like Professor Watkins, the American Hebraists struggled against the times, advocating an anachronistic set of ideals to a wayward generation, refusing to countenance the notion that "the good and the pure" were outmoded values.

Halkin's claim that Hebrew poetry in the United States showed the influence of English poetry was soon adopted by many of his fellow Hebraists. Even Rabinowitz seems to have accepted Halkin's analysis, although he did not entirely approve of the results. And yet Halkin's thesis is highly doubtful. Prior to the case of Gabriel Preil, the only American Hebrew poets to evince the influence of Anglo-American poetry (Longfellow aside) were Halkin and Bavli, and it is debatable how significant such influence was. The American Hebrew poets were influenced for the most part by the norms and values of the Hebrew literary culture in which they developed, a culture shaped by the religious texts of traditional Jewish education and practice, by the enlightenment ethos of the Haskalah, by the rhetorical lexicon of the Hibat Tsion generation, and by the model of modernity offered by Bialik and his contemporaries. These were the lenses through which they read British and American literature, and that determined how they understood this literature and which aspects they found worthy of emulation. Indeed, it was only in the later version of Halkin's essay that he mentioned specific Anglo-American authors and literary movements as influences on American Hebrew poetry, suggesting that the influence of English poetry on the American Hebraists was less something Halkin revealed than something he gradually invented. It was not the case that British Romanticism and Victorianism, which Halkin first encountered in Russian, German, and Hebrew translations, exerted a determining influence on American Hebrew poetry. Rather, American Hebrew poets found affinities between their aesthetic ideals and certain facets of English poetry.[12]

Certainly, the encounters these poets did have with Anglo-American literature were based, as Halkin's essay shows, more on a reverence for canonical, nineteenth-century authors than on an appreciation for the complexities of these authors, interest in twentieth-century developments, or passion for specifically American poetry. It is significant that Halkin attributed the influence of Whitman to the modernists, not the Americans. Indeed, it was the modernist Uri Zvi Greenberg who first claimed Whitman for Hebrew poetry, three decades before Halkin published his translation of *Leaves of Grass*. In Greenberg's searing 1928 manifesto, *Kelapei tish'im veteshah* (Against the ninety-nine), he held up the example of Whitman, "that foreign beach-giant from America" (Greenberg 1928, 35) as a

12. For repetitions of Halkin's claims regarding the influence of English literature on the American Hebrew poets, see, for example, Efros (1971, 232–33); Epstein (1952, 1:10); Rabinowitz (1934, 72–73). Critics such as Shimon Sandbank and Arnold Band have questioned the extent of the influence of British Romantic poetry on Halkin (Laor 1978, 107, 200). For similarly skeptical assessments of the influence of Anglo-American literature on the Hebraists in general, see Spicehandler (1993) and Miron (1993).

counter to the poetic formalism and traditionalism he abhorred in many of the Hebrew poets of the time. Although we may question how acquainted Greenberg really was with his imaginary Whitman, "thundering in a baritone and not letting us sleep," his estimation for the American poet and his demand for the incorporation of this poetry into contemporary Hebrew trends is in striking contrast to the Hebrew writers of the United States, who translated very little twentieth-century American poetry into Hebrew, tending instead to focus their efforts on Shakespeare and other canonical English writers (U. Shavit 1992, 218). The choice of American poets translated by Shimon Ginzburg is representative: William Cullen Bryant, Henry Wadsworth Longfellow, Edgar Allan Poe, and Edwin Arlington Robinson. Bavli was the one poet to show some regard for contemporary American poetry, although, as we have seen, his was an ambivalent regard and, moreover, had limited impact on his own work. It is telling that, in the 1920s, when Bavli tried to persuade Halkin that T. S. Eliot was an important poet, Halkin remained unconvinced.

In fact, the first Hebrew writer to translate Eliot was the Lithuanian-born poet Noah Stern (1912–60), who resided for five years in the United States. Stern graduated summa cum laude from Harvard in 1934 and commenced a doctorate at Columbia before he left for Palestine. However, the literary career of this tragic figure (his life ended in mental illness and suicide), although bound up with American literature—he studied at Harvard with F. O. Matthiessen and later translated both Eliot's *The Waste Land* and Richard Wright's *Black Boy*—was not significantly involved with the institutions of American Hebraism. That is, while Stern was occasionally published in American Hebrew journals, his career mainly evolved (and was thwarted) through the journals and cultural institutions of the Land of Israel, which defined his status and context as a writer.[13]

Halkin provided a way for the American Hebrew writers to understand themselves as American. Yet their encounter with Anglo-American literature lacked the sense of historicity that accompanies a truly intimate

---

13. This is why, although he is a fascinating figure, Stern has not been treated in this study. For further references, see Stern (1974), Grodzensky (1975), and Miron (1991).

relationship with a language and its literature—as evidenced by the Hebraists' frequent though rather undiscriminating gestures of respect toward poets such as Keats, Longfellow, Shakespeare, and Tennyson. The Americanness debate was therefore fittingly concluded in the *Hadoar* anniversary volume of 1927, with Rabinowitz's response to what he felt were the misreadings of his critics, and in which he again urged the American Hebraists to pay more attention to recent developments in American poetry. "It is impossible to live always on Keats and Wordsworth," Rabinowitz counseled. "Leave Keats be. Let him rest in peace" (Rabinowitz 1927, 48).

And yet Halkin was not immune to the attractions of modernism. In 1925 and 1926, the young poet published three poems under a pseudonym. These attempts at writing the kind of expressionistic, licentious poems that he was attacking in his criticism provide intriguing insights into what modernism meant to Halkin. Interestingly, they depart from his other poetry of the time not only in their use of free verse and a more expressionistic register but also in their content, which dealt with sexual desire, the city, and race—themes that he would take up in his fiction but that never again made as explicit an appearance in his poetry.

In the first of the three poems, "Shkiah biNyu-York" (Sunset in New York), the poet meditates at sundown from the upper level of one of New York City's open-air double-decker buses, then popular with young lovers.[14] In defiance of the sunset and its intimations of mortality, he affirms humanity's irrepressible life force, manifest in the nocturnal couplings of New York's countless young men and women. Despite some compelling imagery, the poem is marked by a number of weaknesses, deriving in part from Halkin's ambivalence about his subjects: sex and the city. In the poem, New York is a triumphant "Man-God" (S. Halkin 1946a, 231), composed

14. First published, with slight differences, as "Shkiah me'al ha'bos'" (Sunset Over the Bus) in the November 6, 1925, issue of *Hadoar*. An apposite excerpt from a memoir of the time: "When money ran right, New York could still be an enchanting place for young love. There were long walks and picnics in the park, but my fondest memories are of those warm evenings spent riding the open-air, double-deckered buses, which sadly have gone the way of the Polo Grounds and Ezmerelda's Lemon Lime Soda Fizz" (Ryskind 1994, 25–26).

of its hordes of swooning young lovers. It is the embodiment of the mystical, dynamic persistence of eros. Yet Halkin has trouble associating this life principle with the city, as opposed to the traditional Romantic locus of nature, and he ultimately leaves the city to go out to "the fields, wrapped in mist." On the one hand Halkin attempts to celebrate New York, and on the other hand he presents the city as a "Babylon" (230)—corrupt, decadent, and indifferent. Moreover, we see that while Halkin counters the idea of death with a vision of New York's seething, libidinous energy, the desire he invokes is abstract and impersonal. Indeed, rather than some Whitmanian celebration of the body electric, the poem's tone suggests a more melancholy regard for the animal persistence of sexual desire.

Sexuality is foregrounded even more daringly in the second of Halkin's pseudonymous poems, "El hakushit" (To the Negress).[15] Here, the poet beckons a black woman to reveal her "true" self: a "daughter of the jungle" (234), rabidly sexual. The tragedy of past slavery and the woman's current position in society are not figured primarily as oppression, but as alienation from her true, primal, sexual desires:

> Arise, arise, daughter of the jungle, and throw aside your fine
> silk dress!
> Let your firm thigh shine, alive with muscles,
> so that its dark ebony blinds the watery blue eyes of the north
> longing for the joy of madness that flows vigorously in you,
> frightened by the joy of madness that flows vigorously in you.
> Arise and dance a whirling dance! Arise! Spill your joy of life
> in hot, steamy sweat, the fragrance of the negress excited by
> desire.
> (S. Halkin 1946a, 234)

The poem's racism is blatant, though hardly remarkable for its time. Indeed, it reminds one of "Heritage," a poem published a year before Halkin's by the Harlem Renaissance poet, Countee Cullen. Cullen represented his own blackness as a dangerously libidinal force—the primal, blood-based call of

---

15. First published, with slight differences, in the March 11, 1926, issue of *Hadoar*. Katz considers this poem as well (2009, 146–48).

Africa, an "unremittent beat" coursing through his veins, "treading out a jungle track," threatening to break through the veneer of civilization:

> Ever must I twist and squirm,
> Writhing like a baited worm,
> While its primal measures drip
> Through my body, crying, "Strip!
> Doff this new exuberance.
> Come and dance the Lover's Dance!"
>
> (D. Lewis 1994, 246)

In Cullen's case, one suspects that Africanness was also a figure for other forbidden lusts—i.e., his own homosexuality. The ineluctable blackness that so tortures the poet as it throbs in his own body was a perfect metaphor for a desire that had to be repressed, though it sprang from within his very being. Halkin's use of the motif of the Negress owes something to European modernist art (her "greenish-black skin" (S. Halkin 1946a, 234) and the "ruddy clay" of her eyes recall German expressionist images of black women) and probably to the European vogue for Josephine Baker as well. Yet it also has a history in Hebrew poetry, from the "black and comely" woman in the Song of Songs to Zalman Shneur's poem "In the Mountains," in which he compares the landscape to "an abandoned negress, / her eyes sparkling with desire, weakly sighing: embrace me! / Mist of desire rising from her lap, intoxicating, drowning every thought" (B. Harshav 2000, 2:133).

How little Halkin intended the poem as an insult is seen when we note his striking partnering of Jew and Negress, united in opposition to the depredations of life among "the watery blue eyes of the north." As the black woman is a creature of Africa out of place in the modern world, so the Jew is a son of the desert, who requires the Negress to reveal to him who he really is:

> Go out and dance, get drunk! And facing you I too will be
>   drunk,
> whose blood has also nearly forgotten the burning of the
>   desert,
> the distant heritage of the fathers,

> whose soul is imprisoned in a strange land of frost, among the
>   blue-eyed,
> its strong, blind joy grown weak.
>
> (S. Halkin 1946a, 235)

Negress and Jew are similarly encaged in a culture that has made them both forget the hot sun of their origins. Together, the poem asserts, they can topple the confining city-prison of their Wasp oppressors and "throw down the maze of stone walls / upon these hard, cold, blue-eyed people."

It is significant that Halkin later incorporated both "To a Negress" and "Sunset in New York" into a series of poems with the English (rather than Hebrew) title "Café Royal." (He left out a third, truly execrable poem, "To Be a New Yorker," which reprises some of the motifs of the other two poems—New York as sexual cosmos, the dancing Negress—with none of the intrigue.) Café Royal was the name of a Greenwich Village hangout at Second Avenue and Twelfth Street frequented by Yiddish poets. (Today it is a Japanese restaurant.) In using this title and its Roman alphabet, Halkin indicated a proximity to the bohemian, modernist milieu of the Yiddishists that would be little in evidence in the rest of his poetic oeuvre. This conscious association between his modernist experiments and Yiddish suggests that the antimodernism of the Hebraists was not unrelated to their perceptions of Yiddish and the Yiddishists. For the American Hebraists, Yiddish was the language of the Jewish masses who neglected Hebrew. It was the language of the radical politics that often denigrated Zionism and mocked attachment to religious tradition. And it was the language of a poetry whose confidence and success were envied by the Hebraists, even as they were made uncomfortable by its eager absorption of modernist trends. The antimodernism of the Hebraists was thus reinforced by their ambivalence toward Yiddish culture.

Halkin later claimed that these pseudonymous poems were not to be taken seriously and that he had written them on napkins in the Café Royal only to prove to the Yiddish poets and bohemians that anyone could write "those sorts" of poems (S. Halkin 1971, 33–34). Yet this explanation is unconvincing, for why would Halkin go to the trouble to publish and then reprint poems that were merely a minor literary joke? Rather, these poems, with their free verse and expressionistic style and their links to sexual desire, race, the city, and Yiddish, suggest some of the cultural and psychological dimensions of the American Hebraists' ambivalence toward the literary avant-garde.[16]

Moreover, for all their shortcomings, these poems did make an impression at the time, though not in America. In 1928, when Halkin first went to Palestine, Avraham Shlonsky, then the most influential leader of Hebrew modernism, was extremely eager to hear from him about the American Hebrew poet Lamed Dubsky—not realizing that Dubsky was the pseudonym used by Halkin for his three forays into "the poetry of an upturned world."

16. Shlomo Grodzensky was skeptical about Halkin's explanation of his pseudonymous poems (Grodzensky 1978, 48). A slightly different version of the episode concerning Halkin's writing of these poems is found in Boaz Shahevitch's biographical essay in the Halkin jubilee volume he coedited (Shahevitch and Peri 1975, 105–6).

3

Going Native

THE INDIAN IN THE AMERICAN
HEBREW IMAGINATION

It isn't worthwhile, in these practical times, for people to talk about
Indian poetry—there never was any in them—except in the Fenimore
Cooper Indians. But *they* are an extinct tribe that never existed.

— Mark Twain, *The Innocents Abroad*

THE ANTIMODERNISM AND ANTIURBANISM of the American
Hebrew poets contributed to these writers' evident attraction to Native
Americans. Of course, as Werner Sollors reminds us, "[i]mmigrant writers were generally fascinated by Indian themes—which European writers
sometimes regarded as the true America" (1986, 142). Native American
motifs were not absent from Yiddish American poetry; the poet Yehoash
translated Longfellow's *Hiawatha* into Yiddish, for example. Yet the figure of the Indian assumed a distinctively central place in the American
Hebraists' self-understanding. The Hebrew writers were nearly unanimous
in dating the beginnings of an estimable Hebrew literature in the United
States from the publication of Benjamin Nahum Silkiner's epic poem *Mul
ohel Timurah* (Before the tent of Timmura) in 1910. Moreover, as we have
seen, Silkiner's poem stood at the center of various arguments about the
Americanness of Hebrew poetry in the United States. The very possibility of a viable American Hebrew literature seemed to some of its prac-
titioners to hang on the promise suggested by Silkiner's importation of
"native" subject matter into the development of modern Hebrew letters.
Indeed, Silkiner's work was followed by two other book-length "Indian
epics" written by American Hebrew poets. In 1933, Israel Efros published

74

his *Vigvamim shotekim* (Silent wigwams), and four years later Ephraim Lisitzky's *Medurot doakhot* (Dying campfires) appeared.[1]

Given the Hebraists' alienation from America, turning to the Indian was a way for these writers to be American while simultaneously rejecting present-day, urban America. By setting their epics in a virgin, mythologized America, they could escape their harsh and disorienting surroundings while still claiming an American identity for their writing.[2] Moreover, they could soothe their gnawing sense of cultural purposelessness, exacerbated by the ascension of Hebrew literature in Palestine, by claiming for Hebrew poetry in America an important and unique mission, namely, that of expanding the horizons of Hebrew literature through the importation of distinctively American subject matter.

The Indian was therefore a perfect theme, expressing a critique of America even while typifying a more "authentic" Americanness. It could even be used as a counterimage to the greed, cruelty, and exploitation so often decried by Jewish immigrant writers in all languages. In Ginzburg's "No-York," for instance, he uses the image of an Indian chief as a noble counter to the horrific phantasmagoria of life in the big city. After recounting his anguished nocturnal wanderings through degenerate New York, the speaker makes his way to what is certainly Central Park, then as now a respite from the city's tumult. In "a hidden corner / to which the city profane does not reach," the narrator finds what was once "a Masada / of desperate Indian warriors," slaughtered by white settlers (Ginzburg 1931b, 273). This "dwarven palace"—probably inspired by Belvedere

---

1. For examples of the primacy accorded by the Hebraists to Silkiner's Indian epic, see Ribalow (1934), the introduction to Ribalow (1938), and Silberschlag (1973, 249, 276–79). For a discussion of the cultural significance of Yehoash's Yiddish translation of *Hiawatha*, see Trachtenberg (2004, 140–69).

2. See also the similar comments of Nurit Govrin (1988, 91). Katz (2009) offers an erudite discussion of the representation of the Indian in American Hebrew poetry, with separate chapters devoted to the Indian epics of Silkiner, Efros, and Lisitzky, as well as other works. We have independently arrived at similar conclusions in some cases, though our assessments of the "Americanness" of this literature and its relationship with modernism are quite divergent.

Castle, Central Park's oddly three-quarter scale fortress—is, in Ginzburg's imagination, still inhabited by the Indian "cacique" (*katsika* in Hebrew, a term footnoted by the poet along with "subway" and "elevator"), "an old man / clothed in white . . . prince of the dream-world, the ancient world that was destroyed." Just as in his earlier poem, "Bamigdal," wherein Ginzburg imagines a fantasy version of a Central Park locale in order to oppose it to the city, here he turns Belvedere Castle into an innocent pastoral island besieged by modernity. The Indian chief, the "only one who betrays the kingdom . . . of Moloch," lingers by an anthropomorphized pool—the debt to Bialik's famous poem "The Pool" is evident—that wistfully dreams of the "dense, virgin forests" and "joyful shouts of young redskins" that preceded the arrival of the whites. Menaced by the ugly reality of the city, cacique and pool retreat into their "dreams of the splendor and glory that have passed away" (273), while Ginzburg continues excoriating the factories and workhouses of New York. As the sole opponent of the industrial forces decried by Ginzburg, the Indian chief is linked with the displaced, disgusted poet.

The Hebrew poets' interest in Indians was not only a product of their personal and ideological alienation from America. It also stemmed from the aesthetic considerations we have already considered in relation to modernism. If modernist innovations seemed distasteful or discomfiting to the maskilic-Romantic sensibilities of many Hebraists, an effort such as Longfellow's *Hiawatha* made sense to them. The epic form suited their Haskalah-conditioned expectations of what poetry should be, and the subject matter, centering on the tragedy of the native people's encounter with the white settlers, seemed appropriately lofty and decorous. Through the first three decades of the twentieth century, much of Hebrew literary culture concurred. James Fenimore Cooper had already been translated into Hebrew in the nineteenth century, and a few years after the publication of Silkiner's Indian poem, *Hiawatha* was translated into Hebrew by the major poet Shaul Tchernikhovsky. The modern city, on the other hand, in Robert Alter's words, remained "largely outside the imaginative ken and at first beyond the linguistic reach of Hebrew literature" (1994, 79). Reviewing the anthology *Luah Ahiever,* in which Ginzburg's "No-York" first appeared, a writer for the journal *Hatekufah* judged Ginzburg's poem a failure, yet praised Ephraim Lisitzky's pastoral poem "Al hof Niagara" (On the shores of Niagara) as being "a truly American poem" in which "the American poetic influence of Longfellow" was readily discernible. Although it is questionable how much influence Longfellow had on each of the Hebrew Indian poems—Lisitzky was clearly captivated by Longfellow, whereas any such influence on Silkiner's Indian epic is more distant—his *Hiawatha* was clearly the main American literary-cultural model for both the production and reception of these works in Hebrew.

The esteem in which Longfellow was held by these writers and critics, however, only underscores the aesthetic and literary-historical disjuncture between the Hebraists and the American cultural environment. Longfellow was first translated into Hebrew around 1870 when Zvi Gershuni, a Vilna-born maskil who arrived in New York in 1869, translated the poem "Excelsior." Longfellow even wrote to Gershuni, thanking him (Kabakoff 1978, 270). In the period when the Hebraists were producing their Indian poems, Longfellow was still canonical grade-school reading, and yet—despite Longfellow's immense erudition and global literary appetite—most serious American readers and writers by then found works such as *Hiawatha* embarrassing in their seeming sentimentality, innocence, and aesthetic technique. "Longfellow is to poetry what the barrel-organ is to music," wrote the critic Van Wyck Brooks in 1915 (101), continuing in a manner resembling the critique of American Hebrew maskilic conservatism by the modernists of Palestine:

> To Longfellow the world was a German picture-book, never detaching itself from the softly colored pages. He was a man of one continuous mood: it was that of a flaxen haired German student on his *wanderjahr* along the Rhine, under the autumn sun—a sort of expurgated German student—ambling among ruined castles and reddening vines, and summoning up a thousand bright remnants of an always musical past. . . . But frankly what preparation is a life like this for the poet whose work it is to revify a people? (Brooks 1915, 101-2)

The more modernistically inclined among Jewish immigrant writers absorbed this aversion, or at least tried to. In his memoirs, Shlomo Grodzensky confessed that he still found a secret, guilty pleasure in Longfellow but, as a good modernist, kept it well hidden from his colleagues. Once, however, he accompanied a prominent Yiddish modernist poet on a visit to Marianne Moore. The poet asked Moore whom she thought were the most important American poets, laughingly adding: "Not Longfellow, of course!" The arch-modernist Moore surprised her Jewish visitors by responding: "How happy I would be if I were the author of a poem such as 'The Village Blacksmith'" (Grodzensky 1975, 23).

In spite of whatever lingering affection or respect they might have for Longfellow, most American writers and critics no longer saw his *Hiawatha* as an example of authentic Native American culture. Indeed, modernist circles in both English and Yiddish found in the more "direct" translations of Indian songs by ethnographers and anthropologists, from Henry Rowe Schoolcraft to Franz Boas, a shamanic directness that comported with their own experimentalism and love of the primitive.[3] In a different vein, Hart Crane took up Indian mythologies and mythological Indians in *The Bridge,* fusing such material with urban modernity to create a new and visionary American epic. The treatment of Native Americans in the works of the American Hebraists, on the other hand, often remains aesthetically and culturally in the ambit of the nineteenth-century American Romanticism of Longfellow and Cooper. By the aesthetic and cultural standards of American literature of the time, the Hebrew Indian epics can sometimes come across as quaint. As Robert Alter writes, with regard to the dubious notion that the Indian motif made this poetry more "American": "[s]uch dalliance with American exotica was of course a self-conscious act of willed acculturation, a symptom of the problem rather than a solution to it" (1994, 80). One suspects this has contributed to the marginality of American Hebrew literature: the Hebraists often place the Indian epics as the central literary achievements of American Hebrew culture, but they are among the most culturally uneasy and problematic works in these writers' output.

---

3. See Parisi and Young (2002) on the various issues of *Poetry* in the late 1910s that contained modernist translations of Indian poems. On the connection of such translations with modern Yiddish verse, see Trachtenberg (2004, 163–64). See Katz (2009) for a thorough examination of the American Hebraists' use of Native American sources.

What remains most compelling about the Hebrew Indian epics is not their supposed Americanness but their Jewishness, the extent to which these writers used their Indian narratives to dramatize aspects of modern Jewish experience. The Indian, a non-Jew yet entirely free from implication in the long history of anti-Semitism, was a safe figure with which to identify. These poets' interest in a "vanished race" reflects a range of Jewish national concerns, from cultural assimilation to the possibility of genocide. Their focus in all three epics on the displacement and demise of the Indians at the hands of the white settlers was a statement about anti-Semitism, European cruelty, and the plight of contemporary Jews, just as it inevitably foregrounded Zionist passions concerning land and sovereignty. In the figure of the tragic Indian, these poets could express the individual immigrant's sense of impotence, loneliness, and beleaguerment, as well as national outrage before the upheavals of modern history.

Ironically, it may be in this use of Indians as quasi-Jews that the Hebrew Indian epics also interact most directly with contemporary American culture. Walter Benn Michaels has argued that in the 1920s, the Indian became a widely used figure in American culture for white nativist purity, in contrast to the threatening hybridity of American identity brought on through immigration. Citing works of immigrant literature such as Anzia Yezierska's *The Bread Givers*, Michaels maintains that Jewish antiassimilationists made use of the same motif: "the nativist's vanishing Indian could function simultaneously as the [Jewish immigrant] alien's vanishing Jew: assimilation could be repudiated from both sides" (1995, 70), an argument that finds some correlation to the Hebraists' use of the Indian.[4]

The Jewish nature of the Indian is especially central in Silkiner's *Mul ohel Timurah*. For Silkiner, the Indian was a dark mirror in which the poet could contemplate the most extreme Jewish hopes and fears. His poem is remembered today, and was praised in its time, as the first significant

4. Michaels's book, while thought-provoking and sometimes illuminating in connection with the American Hebraists, is at the same time often exasperating because of its frequently abstract and arbitrary reading of American cultural history, as well as its rather ethereal conceptions of ethnic identity.

attempt to incorporate "American" thematic materials into Hebrew poetry. It was taken by his contemporaries as a kind of programmatic model for the Hebrew poets of the United States to follow. Nevertheless, this is something of a misreading. The supposedly American subject matter of the poem certainly was a novelty, yet to regard this as its defining feature misses the more fundamental aspects of the poem. *Timurah* is a highly personal, even idiosyncratic work, and its main referent outside of the soul of its author is not Native American or pre-Columbian culture, of which he seemed to know little, but rather the Jewish dilemmas of modernity. What Silkiner managed to do in this poem was to find a vehicle for national and personal concerns that was simultaneously perceived as American, and that, while unprecedented in its apparent subject matter, partook of the Romantic aesthetic of Hebrew contemporaries such as Bialik and Frischmann.

In what follows I will first analyze Silkiner's poem, then consider Efros's *Vigvamim shotekim* and Lisitzky's *Medurot doakhot*. As I will show, what is most striking about each of these "Indian epics" is the way in which their authors interjected their own experience into the figure of the Indian—ironically transforming into a strange yet potent truth the misbegotten notion, still maintained in the nineteenth century, that the Indians were Jewish lost tribes.

By all accounts Silkiner was something of a polymath, fluent in a range of languages. Lanky and painfully shy, he enjoyed nothing so much as spending his time reading through a personal library that included thousands of volumes. (Shimon Halkin even tells of a poem of his that was lost when Silkiner made the mistake of slipping the manuscript into one of his books, which was then swallowed up by his enormous library and never seen again.) Born near Kovno in 1882, he made his way at the turn of the century to Odessa, where he was briefly involved in the Ahad Ha'am circle. In 1904, he emigrated to the United States where he organized and contributed to a number of publishing projects, the most important of which was the launching of the journal *Hatoren* in 1913. Silkiner worked tirelessly to further the cause of Hebrew literature in America until his death in 1933. Mordecai Kaplan, who worked alongside Silkiner at the Teachers Institute of the Jewish Theological Seminary in New

York, wrote the following in his diary after Silkiner's death: "He was a rare type of man, gifted and modest, a genuine poet with a beautiful soul which found expression in all he did. Both he and Hoschander [another member of the JTS faculty] were unknown, uncelebrated men yet far more noble and heroic than most of those whose names are on everybody's lips" (2001, 1:515).[5]

Silkiner's first published work, *Mul ohel Timurah,* is a strange and poignant long poem of fourteen cantos and more than 1,500 lines. Silkiner's language is heavy with the stock phrasing typical of nineteenth-century Hebrew poetry, and the plot can at times be silly and quaint. Nevertheless, the poem remains fascinating. Its sentimentality and aesthetic limitations are easily offset by its startling refractions of modern Jewish experience, as well as the intriguing psychological dimension of the work. The poem's overt subject is the downfall of a native tribe at the time of the Spanish conquest of the Americas. Though vaguely reminiscent of nineteenth-century works such as Prescott's histories of the Spanish Conquest, the events of the poem do not appear to be based on specific historical models. Instead, they take place in Silkiner's Romantic and highly generalized imagination of New World geography and history, veering frequently into the supernatural. Yet this safely distant framework of a mythic, fantastical Indian past allows Silkiner to work over the traumas of recent Jewish history and of his own life. In the poem, the evildoings of the Spaniards, who were persecuting Jews in Europe at the same time as they were colonizing the Americas, not only allude to Jewish suffering in medieval times but also powerfully reflect the contemporary hardships of the Jews in Eastern Europe, from where Silkiner fled.

The poem entertains a number of other subjects as well. There is a protoecological, anti-industrial theme, as the tribe's downfall is linked with the exploitation of natural resources. The conflict between the tribe's chief and its spiritual leader reflects a long-standing tension in Jewish history between politics and religion, a tension that, since the Haskalah, was made

---

5. For information on Silkiner, see Ribalow (1934), Kabakoff (1988, 1990), and Katz (2009).

to reflect modern issues. Yet the poem's main concern, which although never trumpeted, saturates the work with anxiety and despair, is with the possibility of a people's disappearance. By projecting such a catastrophe onto an Indian tribe, Silkiner can meditate on the possibility of Jewish annihilation, whether by genocide or by assimilation.

In this regard it is significant that, although the poem centers on the chieftain, Mugiral—whose name recalls his people's bitter fate (*goral*)— Silkiner frames the poem as a story told by the aged Indian Timmura to his young daughter. Opening with a lovely invocation of sunset, the poem describes how Timmura's daughter, standing by her father in the dusk, is frightened at the sudden appearance of Mugiral, a man with a bent back, wild white hair, and blazing eyes. Timmura reassures his daughter: "I alone," he says, "know the events of his past and his present life; lean / Upon my arm and incline your ear to me and I will recount to you the Song of Mugiral" (Silkiner 1927, 83).[6] In this way, Silkiner places the events of the poem in an obscure, remembered past, converting the immediacy of Mugiral's epic into the pathos of a fading tribal memory preserved by a single old man. The poem begins precariously balanced between the possibility of cultural continuity (Timmura will recount to his daughter the history of the Silent Tribe) and the rapacity of time and loss (Timmura is the only one alive who knows this history).

The tale proper begins in the second canto with the story of Mugiral's cursed patrimony and doom-shadowed birth. When his father swears, in response to an ominous prophecy, to kill the unborn Mugiral "as he comes forth from his mother's womb" (94), Mugiral's mother flees into the mountains and delivers her son. Rather than face her husband's reprisals for her disobedience, she leaves the child in a crevice in a rock and throws herself into a ravine. This tragic story (and all the love relationships in the poem end

6. In almost all cases I cite the second, revised version of Silkiner's poem appearing in his 1927 collected poems. The first edition was published in Jerusalem in 1910. Silkiner revised the work with the help of Shimon Ginzburg and, to a lesser extent, Shimon Halkin and Hillel Bavli. Generally speaking, there are no significant alterations in the matter or style of the poem; the main impulse behind the revision was to clarify the syntax of Silkiner's long sentences, primarily through adjustments of word order and punctuation.

in death) is followed by the history of the Silent Tribe and their precursors. The Silent Tribe, we learn, was preceded by the savage Tribe of the Rocks, a proud and martial people who marked their victories over other tribes with wild celebrations in which they danced about ecstatically with the skulls of their enemies. Yet, when their chieftain is slain in battle, the Tribe of the Rocks fades into oblivion. Not for the last time, we see Silkiner's concern with the disappearance of peoples, as he writes how "this nation of heroes, whose memory is preserved in the howling wilderness, / And whose steps are etched in the flinty crags" eventually "vanished / From the Jacinth Valley . . . the force of their deeds had gone to waste" (101). The influence of Bialik's "Dead of the Desert," evident throughout the poem, is particularly noticeable in Silkiner's meditations on mythic, mysterious, vanished tribes.

The Tribe of the Rocks' place is taken by the Silent Tribe who, unlike their savage predecessors, live in near-perfect tranquility. The only event that interrupts the placid calm of their lives is their annual sacrifice. Every year, the chief randomly designates one member of the tribe to be slain and whose blood nourishes the "Red Rock." After the tribe witnesses the event, they assemble at their temple (*heikhal harahamim*) to view the statue of their deity, the Great Spirit or "Spirit-God" (*elnefesh*), an image described only in terms of its smiling countenance. When after a few days a flower blossoms at the base of the Red Rock, the tribe knows it will be a year of blessing. Silkiner's almost anthropological imagination is evidenced in this canto, as he seems to imply that the continual violence of the Tribe of the Rocks has been channeled by the Silent Tribe into a single yearly sacrifice.

The enemy arrives when "the white men of Spain descend / From the Mountains of Flint and stream into the Jacinth Valley" (105). Silkiner immediately reminds us of the Spaniards' historical cruelty, in a bitter reversal of the biblical image of saving pillars of cloud and fire:

> Rivers and rivers of blood and tears the men of Spain have
>   already spilt—
> By day clouds of smoke mounting skyward from the debris of
>   ruins,
> By night the light of pyres built for their god, who demands
> Sacrifices by the *thousands*.
>   (Silkiner 1927, 105; emphasis in original)

The Silent Tribe innocently welcomes the Spanish "Children of the Sun" and, though the chief of the Silent Tribe already has premonitions of danger, peace is declared between the two peoples. Not surprisingly, it is not long before disaster strikes.

Potera, the sinister Spanish lord, covets a horse belonging to a member of the Silent Tribe. In the manner of a Shakespearean villain (Silkiner was an enthusiastic reader of Shakespeare and translated *Macbeth*), Potera slanders the horse's owner to the chief, persuading the chief to pick him as the spring sacrifice—a violation of the random selection the ritual requires. The premeditated slaughter angers the Great Spirit, who punishes the tribe with a horrible drought. Gripped by famine, the tribesmen pray to the offended deity, but they receive no response. Potera then offers the starving tribe a deal: if they will mine gems from beneath the valley, the Spaniards will give them bread in exchange for the precious stones.

Desperate for food, and indifferent to the value of gems, they accept his offer. Yet this arrangement further corrupts the natural order of the valley. Personified throughout the poem in feminine and maternal terms, the valley is described here as being penetrated and violated by her children, the tribesmen mining for gems. Her loss of innocence then parallels that of the tribe, whose members begin to fight one another for the gems, the weak losing out to the strong, as "a chip of stone became more precious / In each man's eyes than his own soul, than the soul of his neighbor" (117). The Spaniards are not simply oppressors; they have introduced exchange-value into the valley—a taste of the tree of economic knowledge—and this creates competition, strife, and injustice. The exploitation of the earth and the exploitation of human beings are intertwined. (As we have already seen, however, this apparently anticapitalistic sentiment is less the expression of any deep commitment to revolutionary politics than it is a reflection of the American Hebrew poets' frequently antiurban, antimodernist ideals.)[7]

7. The episode discussed here also recalls biblical and midrashic treatments of the enslavement in Egypt and the building of the Tower of Babel.

The Silent Tribe now requires a savior. Hearing his people's suffering cries, Mugiral bursts forth from the Red Rock, in which he had been mysteriously ensconced since his birth. Now a handsome young man, he stands before the tribe and explains to them that the Great Spirit, angered by the corrupt sacrifice, has abandoned the valley. He tells them that they must descend into the earth and extract "black iron," and that with this metal they will make weapons: "Then a song of vengeance, sung / By the Tribe of the Rocks long ago, all of you shall learn, and you shall exact your vengeance / Upon the strangers who came and turned the heart of the Great Spirit from us" (121–22). It is indicative of the ambivalent role played by the poem's protagonist that Mugiral's first instruction to the tribe—to excavate metal from the earth—closely resembles the Spanish demand for gems. Moreover, the "song of vengeance" he teaches to the tribe resurrects the savagery of the extinct Tribe of the Rocks, an atavistic violence whose consequences Mugiral does not anticipate.

This violence is not described directly and literally. Never in the poem do we witness a Spaniard slaying an Indian or vice versa. Instead, we have an exaggeratedly nightmarish fantasy of blood, in which the night of the Indians' war of vengeance on the Spaniards is represented as a mythical tidal wave of carnage; "streams and rivers of boiling, reeking blood" inundate the valley, turning it into a "mighty sea . . . its red waves, capped and checkered with carmine brain" (123). One is reminded of Bialik's poem "On the Slaughter," written a few years before *Timurah* in response to the Kishinev pogrom of 1903. Indeed, it would not be going too far to propose that the violence in Silkiner's poem also draws on the nightmare experience of the pogroms, when streets really did stream with blood.[8] Silkiner delves into the emotional, pre-rational, even mythical dimension of the massacres, drawing on earlier Hebrew depictions of slaughter—from medieval martyrologies to rabbinic legends about the fall of Betar—in order to portray

---

8. Indeed, this was the surmise of Ginzburg, who also compared the poem to Bialik's "Megilat ha'esh" (Ribalow 1934, 29). Katz (2009) provides an excellent survey of the critical reception of Silkiner's poem.

a fantasy of revenge so intense that it resembles a volcano. Mugiral and the Silent Tribe show here what desires can be nursed in the hearts of the oppressed. Even when the last of the enemy have been slain, Mugiral and his tribe are found kneeling by the piles of Spanish corpses, "for vengeance and blood still yearning, craving" (124)—a parallel to the voice of unslakable Jewish rage we hear in Bialik.

The modern Jewish resonances of Silkiner's Indians are heard even more distinctly in the canto that follows. In the aftermath of the battle against the Spanish, the tribe must respond to a crisis of discontinuity as its temple and the statue of its deity have been destroyed. Silkiner depicts this crisis in terms that cannot but call to mind the cultural dilemmas faced by the Jewish writers and thinkers of his generation. Tomiya, the tribal priest, appears as a kind of Ahad Ha'amist, grappling with the fundamental questions of Jewish culture in modernity, with the uncertainty that follows the loss of tradition. Gathering together the builders and sculptors of the tribe, he commands them to rebuild the temple and its statue, lest the older generation die and "a new generation [be] born not knowing its fathers and their god" (127). This concern resonates throughout the poem, which as we have said is framed as the history recounted by Timmura to his daughter—an attempt to restore generational continuity through knowledge.

Tomiya goes on to note that the most difficult task falls to the sculptors, who must embody not merely the form but the essence of the Spirit-God. The subsequent inability of any of the sculptors to accomplish this task is nothing other than a reflection of the conundrums of modern Jewish culture:

> In vain did the sculptors, when they left the babbling brook,
>   disperse
> And go roving among the ruined heaps of the temple,
> To prod and dig beneath the piles of debris, and withdraw
> From the heaps of smashed fragments chips and splinters of the
>   statue,
> And order the pieces and arrange them and seek with tired eyes
> In these broken bits for the secret, hidden light of his spirit in
>   his smile;
> In vain did they leave the valley and go to the ends of the earth

And sit day and night in the temples of other tribes, keeping
   watch
Over statues of strange gods, and carving upon the tablets of
   their hearts,
Beating and pulsing with joy, innumerable lines and sketches.
                    (Silkiner 1927, 128)

What is a viable Jewish culture to look like in the wake of modernity's upheavals? Is it to be a repetition of the past, of tradition? Silkiner suggests this is not possible, as he depicts the failure of the sculptors who "prod and dig beneath the piles of debris" and "seek with tired eyes / In these broken bits" for a glimmer of true divinity. He similarly disparages the assimilatory impulse to copy from non-Jewish culture, as the creators who "sit day and night in the temples of other tribes" also fail in their task—a dramatization of the arguments of Ahad Ha'am's famous essay "Imitation and Assimilation." In both cases, Tomiya sadly rejects their efforts as inauthentic. Silkiner describes here the anguished period when the tradition has been destroyed, and a living continuation has not been found.

Perhaps unsurprisingly, Silkiner offers only the most obscure of resolutions to such perplexing challenges. In the ninth canto, "Secrets of the Sea," the fulfillment of Tomiya's task is conveyed through a somewhat opaque symbolism. The canto centers on Eitzima, an orphan who was taken in by the Silent Tribe after the mysterious death of his parents. When the Spaniards arrive and trouble besets the valley, the waves of the sea sing "an ancient song" (134) to him, describing the downfall of another tribe, the B'nei Rikvah, who are slaughtered by an enemy tribe on Mount Gahleh. Rather than be captured, the Rikvah chieftain defiantly leaps to his death, and on the spot where he dies a rock issues "springs of reddish-black blood." For centuries afterward, the Rikvah tribe drinks from this source and grows strong, dominating the tribes around them. Eventually, though, a "new generation of Gahleh"—the name recalls the Hebrew word for exile—"stopped fortifying their bodies / In the blood of the rock of wrath." They grow weak and passive, the "rock of wrath" crumbles apart, and the B'nei Rikvah soon fade into oblivion—the second tribe in the epic to disappear.

After hearing this tale, Eitzima goes to the place where the Rikvah chief died and takes fragments of the rock, from which he carves the image of the Spirit-God. When he takes it to the temple, Tomiya joyfully approves in the language of Psalms: "This is my god majestic in holiness! Before him on your knees bend down!" (136). Yet Eitzima is suddenly astonished to see that the statue's smile resembles his own. Strangely distraught, he sneaks away from the temple, and when messengers later tell Eitzima that Tomiya has died and that his last request was for Eitzima to take his place as priest, Eitzima remains silent, caught up in his own gloom.

His decision to accept the priesthood comes only after a further supernatural episode. When the messengers depart, he listens to the desert howl its forlorn entreaties to the sea. The desert claims that it will become a fertile, creative paradise, if only the sea will embrace it. A lovely girl rises from the waves and petitions the rocks that hem the sea to let the waters pass through to the desert. When she is ignored, her features become monstrous and she bites the "stone heart of the rocks" with "venomed teeth" (139). Still, the rocks refuse her entreaties, telling her that if the sea wants to meet the desert, it must find subterranean passages *"beneath the foundations of the earth"* (140; emphasis in original). When Eitzima hears this, he goes to the temple to take up the priesthood.

All of this is cryptic enough, yet a certain logic can be discerned in the canto. Eitzima is clearly a figure for the poet, for the creator who must interpret the mysteries of existence and nourish the spirit of his people. He is the one who successfully fashions the image of the deity, drawing on the elemental wisdom of nature (the song of the waves) and the inspiration of history (the rock of the Rikvah chief, a legacy of national strength and defiance through martyrdom). Yet like many of the American Hebrew poets, he is a lonely figure living on the margins of his society. Like a number of his literary contemporaries, from Bialik to Lisitzky, he experiences the pain of early orphanhood and abandonment. He is tormented by self-doubt and self-consciousness, as when he sees the resemblance between his statue and himself—a motif well known in Romantic poetry, in which the melancholy poet is often burdened by the inability to experience a divinity unmediated by his own mind. (Think of Wordsworth, Shelley, and Coleridge.) Yet despite this doubt and depression, Eitzima accepts the role of leader, and he does so in response to an allegorical conversation that centers on the image of the parched desert and its stifled creative forces. Silkiner here appears to be meditating on his own creative powers—and on America as a cultural desert?—that must be nourished through subterranean channels. This longing for creative inspiration also reflects the concerns of modern Jewish culture as a whole and its searches for spiritual renewal.

Also with its Jewish resonance is the poem's clash between political-military action (represented by Mugiral) and spiritual purity (represented by Eitzima, the priest). In the middle of the night, word arrives that the Spanish are returning to take revenge on the tribe; Mugiral is surprised to find the tribesmen with Eitzima in the temple, praying to the Spirit-God. The priest tells Mugiral that the midnight prayers are necessary since the valley has been tainted by the "night of Potera's vanities, and the night of Mugiral's wrath" (152). Mugiral is indignant at being blamed along with the Spanish for the tribe's predicament, and chief and priest begin to argue, pitting the demands of profane action against those of spiritual purity. Eitzima tells the chief that whatever his intentions, his violent lessons have made his people and their land impure. Mugiral defends himself: "You know that to save the valley, not to harm its spirit, I came. . . . You know that, had I not appeared, [the tribe] would have perished at the hand of the evil governor—" "As the Silent Tribe," Eitzima interrupts, "yet the earth would be full of their glory forever" (153). Eitzima prefers a spiritually elevated death to a spiritually corrupt resistance, but Mugiral does not accept this argument. Passive acceptance of fate, particularly when it would lead to his people's destruction, makes no moral sense to him. "The song of dying maggots in the dung has never filled the earth," he retorts, "[a]nd a mean death would only be the object of heaven's scorn."

For Mugiral, the only sensible response to the situation is physical action and military resistance—not prayer. He tells the tribesmen that they must uproot trees and carry rocks in order to build fortresses and fend off the Spaniards. (Note that every time Mugiral acts, he alters the natural state of the valley; first it was the excavation of iron, now it is the construction of battlements.) The tribe is swayed by his words, and the priest falls silent. The dark conclusion to this conflict occurs when Mugiral tells Eitzima to leave the temple, which his soldiers are going to turn into a fort.

The priest balks, telling Mugiral that he knows their doom is imminent and that he only wants to spend his final days in the temple. When the furious king kicks the statue, which falls and shatters, Eitzima falls too and breaks his neck, fatally enacting his ultimate connection with the statue.

The conflict here is familiar to us from the biblical tug-of-war between the realpolitik of kings and the suprahistorical faith of prophets. In particular, we hear in the exchanges between Mugiral and Eitzima the fateful clash between Zedekiah and Jeremiah. Moreover, these biblical themes had already been reframed and reworked by Haskalah writers such as Y. L. Gordon. As Silkiner's fellow American Hebrew poets Eisig Silberschlag and Hillel Bavli both pointed out, the Mugiral-Eitzima conflict clearly recalls Gordon's poem "Zedekiah in Prison." Writing from Zedekiah's point of view, Gordon was sympathetic to the king, who sought to protect his people through military and political action, in contrast to the pious resignation of Jeremiah—a passivity, Gordon implies, that has shackled Jewish existence up to the modern period. Mugiral's stance also resonates with the value Bialik places on Jewish self-defense in his poem "In the City of Slaughter." On the other hand, Eitzima's emphasis on the spiritual over the political might reflect a touch of Ahad Ha'amism. Shimon Ginzburg, meanwhile, saw in the Mugiral-Eitzima conflict echoes of the tensions between the young Jewish revolutionaries and their more traditionalist elders during the Russian revolution of 1905 (Ribalow 1934, 29).[9] It must be emphasized that in his dramatization of these Jewish concerns, Silkiner does not in fact allow the fate of the Silent Tribe to reflect a single, unambiguous ideological position. Sympathetic to both Mugiral and Eitzima, modern

9. Though it may be too crudely allegorical, one could extend Ginzburg's reading and view the Red Rock from which Mugiral bursts as a color-appropriate symbol for revolution, and even view the tribe's annual sacrifice that becomes corrupt as an echo of the earlier, nineteenth-century Russian Jewish experience of conscription into the tsarist army. On the other hand, Y. F. Lachower, in an essay more representative of the poem's lukewarm reception outside of the United States, maintained that while the subject matter was daring for its time, Silkiner's Indians were too remote and exotic to symbolize modern Jewish life effectively (Ribalow 1934, 38).

activism and traditional faith, he does not argue that either one alone could ultimately have saved the tribe.

Indeed, Silkiner makes the poem's denouement contingent on supernatural elements. On the eve of the tribe's destruction, Mugiral is visited by a mysterious and beautiful young woman who seems uncannily familiar to him. She tells the chieftain that they have long known each other, explaining that, as Mugiral descended into sorrow and depression: "I grew from the ground of your hut, like a child of darkness I grew, / You trembled with joy over me and spread your palms upon me, / And a vow of friendship and trust you swore to me, in the darkness of your soul" (175). This mysterious figure is an externalized embodiment of Mugiral's melancholy—his doubt and his despair, his nihilism and his solitude—as well as of his awful fate. She is a "child of darkness," of his darkness, and as his end draws near he cannot escape her. She asks Mugiral to come with her to the "Palace of Joy" and live there forever as her lover. When Mugiral refuses to abandon his people, she tells him that the Silent Tribe is already fated to be slaughtered by the Spanish. And when he says that he prefers in any case to die honorably with his people, she replies in a low whisper: "The twinkling stars know / Nothing of your death, and after you are gone the mighty sea will not mourn with its roaring" (176).

The central anxiety of the poem finds its starkest expression in these two lines. Silkiner meditates here on the possibility that a people's sufferings, and even its destruction, might take place unnoticed, undocumented, and unmourned by any higher power. Mugiral wants to redeem himself through a noble death in service of the tribe, and he unquestioningly assumes that his death will win him "awe and reverence." But from whom, the mysterious maiden asks: "The twinkling stars know / Nothing of your death." Although the stars remind Abraham of his eternal covenant with God, and the sea of the psalmist declares the divine glory, we have here a morally, humanly indifferent landscape. Silkiner's work contemplates this chilling possibility but ultimately tempers it, framing the destruction of the tribe in tragic but *chronicled* terms, letting Timmura tell the story to his daughter, who having been told will be moved to admiration and pity for Mugiral. Nevertheless, Silkiner's epic is a compelling reminder that before the Holocaust, Jewish writers contemplated the vanishing and the eradication of peoples. Silkiner is not focused solely on the event of genocide, but also on the long-term historical processes that have seen certain groups pass from the earth and others remain. Such concerns were certainly relevant for a group of Jewish literati who were ambivalent at best about their new home in America, and who often despaired of the possibility of a viable Jewish culture in the United States and in the modern world as a whole.

The woman silences Mugiral's protests with a passionate kiss, and he follows her on an ominous journey through the wasteland, to the "Palace of Joy." (To be lured away from one's people and their distress certainly would have had resonance for the émigré poet in America.) As they walk, Mugiral notices mysterious mounds rising from the arid land, and the woman tells him that her "treasures are hid therein" (177). Finally, they reach the desert's edge; beyond, all is wrapped in fog. Mugiral turns to the young woman and finds her transformed into an old crone. Rheumy-eyed and smiling with rotten teeth, she tells him to enter the mist, in which her palace lies. Understandably, Mugiral hesitates, saying he wants to see his people one last time. The "Silent Tribe is lost, not a single one remains," she says (178). She shows him an awful vision of what he has left behind: the tribe has been destroyed by the Spaniards, and snow covers the blood-streaked ruins of the valley. This vision culminates in a particularly bitter and poignant scene of the Spaniards celebrating their victory in a newly built church. "Peace descended with You to earth," sing the killers, accompanied by the sound of "an organ playing sweetly," while the last two surviving tribesmen slowly freeze to death in the winter storm outside (180).

Mugiral, pale and sickened, pleads to return, and he sets off through the desert accompanied by the old woman. This time he hears disturbing groans emanating from the mounds in the desert, and his companion tells him that he is hearing the weeping of her victims. When they arrive at the valley, she bids him farewell and asks for a final kiss. He recoils, though he sees that she has become young and beautiful once more. She tells him that she is going off to "another valley," and when Mugiral shouts that he will warn others about her, she responds with a smile: "And what is my name, which you would tell / Them?" (181). Outraged, he draws his sword, but as he strikes, she vanishes, disappearing into the morning air. The melodramatic, almost operatic ending of Mugiral's saga is marked by bitter rage against the murderousness and hypocritical piety of the Christians. The last pair of tribesmen become cruelly emblematic of suffering that is literally whitewashed as snow covers the bloody work of the killers. Moreover, the canto is permeated with Silkiner's anguished doubt in any ultimate sense of justice, a doubt felt in the ironic reversal of the biblical narrative that we see in the canto's final lines. Moses, the reluctant redeemer, asks God what he is to tell the people when they ask for His name, whereupon he receives the answer: "I am that I am." Here Mugiral, the failed redeemer, is gently mocked by a mysterious avatar of transience and death whose name he never learns.

In the last canto we return to Timmura and his daughter, who allow us a glimmer of hope at the end of the gruesome tale. Timmura finishes the history of Mugiral, explaining how he stole back into the valley to mourn over the ruins of his murdered people. Now he is only waiting to die, says Timmura. In his heart is a unique and mighty song, the "Song of the Sunset," but "it will never pass the lips guarding its secret" (186). It seems that Timmura's chronicle, the "Song of Mugiral"—and by extension Silkiner's epic—is a substitute for the never-to-be-revealed poem locked in Mugiral's broken heart.

Yet the final words of the poem are given to Timmura's nameless daughter. Having heard the tragic story of the white-haired stranger, she is moved to pity and utters the tender, lyrical prayer for Mugiral that concludes the work:

> Stars of evening, light his way,
> Stars of evening, light his way;
> Drops of brightness, drops of comfort,
> Flow upon him and anoint him.
> With grace and truth, against the wind,
> Grant a night of rest.
> And on the exhausted, weary one,
> Spread your dwelling of peace!
>> (Silkiner 1927, 186)

This small moment of brightness—and even, perhaps, of quiet hope—offered by father and daughter at the end of Mugiral's tortured life calls to mind an anecdote recorded by Bavli. Bavli recalls Silkiner's words after the death of the elder poet's daughter, who died before she reached the age of two:

> "I would like to know what happened to all the love and light we gave the little one," he asked, and then continued: "I can't believe that it's all lost forever. No!" He made similar remarks when, in moments of gloom, we would speak of the fate of Hebrew literature in America: "Is it possible that all we have done here in the field of our literature, with such boundless love and self-sacrifice, will really come to naught? No! I believe that every seed of beauty that we sow, no matter where, will not go to waste." (Bavli n.d., 117–18)

Certainly, *Mul ohel Timurah* was Silkiner's most personal poetic expression. It was not in his lyric verse but rather in this long narrative poem with its exotic subject, set in a distant, quasi-mythical past, that he was able to be most autobiographical and revealing. For Silkiner is Mugiral, is Timmura, Eitzima, and Tomiya. These are various aspects of his personality, giving expression to his sorrow, his rage, his uncertainty, and his tenuous hopes, as a young Jewish poet who had crossed half the world, trying to find a refuge for his people and their traditions. What so many of his contemporaries judged as an exploration of aboriginal America was a chronicle of his own soul.

The Indian epics of Israel Efros (1891–1971) and Ephraim Lisitzky (1885–1962) are both different from *Mul ohel Timurah,* as they are from each other. Neither Efros nor Lisitzky sought to use their poems as vehicles for the author's individual internal psychology to the extent we find in Silkiner's epic. These later Indian epics are instead comparatively more earnest in their attempts to use Native American motifs and subject matter in a naturalistic way. Nevertheless, in both Efros's *Vigvamim shotekim* (Silent wigwams) and Lisitzky's *Medurot doakhot* (Dying campfires), the image of the Indian remains a product of the author's personal concerns, colored by his cultural horizons and inflected by contemporary Jewish history.

Born about a decade after Silkiner and writing in the 1930s, Efros uses a far more modern Hebrew idiom than Silkiner. When we turn from

Silkiner's nineteenth-century register to Efros's poem, the linguistic effect is akin to bringing a fuzzy picture into focus. Moreover, this picture shows us a very different set of cultural models than those used by Silkiner. Whereas Silkiner turned to the civilizations of Central and South America—his Indians, when they were not expressions of his own anxieties and aspirations, distantly resemble the populations depicted in Spanish discovery narratives and early ethnography—Efros, writing a quarter-century later, draws more extensively from popular American and European stereotypes of the Indians, familiar from novels, plays, and films. We have the Pocahontas figure, a beautiful and passive Indian maiden with dark braids and deerskin dress; the taciturn chief; the shifty, warlike brave; the primitive, childlike (and sometimes animal-like) tribesmen; and, of course, the blonde-haired, blue-eyed, white hero. In many ways, reading Efros's book is like watching an old film from the silent or early sound era. It is extremely sentimental and anything but politically correct, yet not without a certain attraction.[10]

In all of this we see a more open relationship to American culture than was possible for Silkiner, whose epic was written only a few years after his arrival in the United States and long before the widespread presence of commercial films. Nevertheless, Efros's poem also reflects the poet's conflicted emotions about his American surroundings. The poem centers on Tom, a young English painter who has settled in Maryland in the seventeenth century. When he is expelled from the white settlement, he is taken in by a tribe of Nanticoke Indians, one of whom, the chief's daughter Lalari, falls in love with him. Whereas the white colonists are brutal and unfeeling—representing the America that pushes aside the sensitive soul—the Indians bring about in Tom a creative regeneration as he begins to paint their way of life and their myths—i.e., the Romantic-bucolic America that inspires the poet.

Efros follows many of the Romantic conventions of American literature and popular culture regarding the Native Americans, one of the most glaring being the taboo against miscegenation. Both Indian characters (Lalari

10. Also in the Western theme is *Zahav* (1942), Efros's long poem about the California Gold Rush. See Katz (2009) for a discussion of this work.

and her mother) who cross racial boundaries in the poem suffer and ultimately commit suicide. Similarly, in Lisitzky's Indian epic, the Indian protagonist chooses suicide over marriage to a white woman. In each case one might wonder whether this conformity to the prohibition against miscegenation simultaneously reflects a Jewish concern with mixed marriages—a subject that clearly comes up in Lisitzky's memoirs, as we will see in the next chapter.

The most overt contemporary Jewish element in the poem, however, is Efros's Zionist emphasis on territory and soil. Several times in the poem, Tom chastises the Indians for hunting rather than working the land, arguing that their way of life makes a strong connection to the land impossible and their dislocation by the white settlers inevitable:

> Thus you flit above the earth, not within her.
> And what is the wonder if, from beneath your feet,
> your rootless feet, the land withdraws
> and seeks to pass to those, to those
> who desire to make their feet into roots?
> (58–59).

In fact, Indians do engage in agricultural work—but only the women of the tribe; when Tom works in the field, the male hunters make fun of him for engaging in "women's work." Laying the blame for white usurpation of the land on the Indians themselves, Tom tells the Nanticokes that they must "Grasp the earth / with tooth and nail, hold on to the clods, / and then . . . no power in the world will be strong enough / to remove you from your place. That is salvation" (Efros 1933, 66). As Eisig Silberschlag noted (1973, 1:288), this diagnosis of the Indians' problems is resonant with the counsels of Zionist theoreticians such as A. D. Gordon.

At more than three hundred pages, Ephraim Lisitzky's *Dying Campfires* is the longest of the Hebrew Indian epics. It is also the least satisfying. While not devoid of interest—I will touch below on some of its surprises— the poem's ambition and scope are not matched by a commensurately developed talent, and the project as a whole lacks Silkiner's idiosyncratic broodings and Efros's gift for melodrama. Lisitzky founders on the contradiction between, on the one hand, his ambition to document something of the inner truth of the Indian, and on the other, the lack of historical specificity which results from his maskilic cultural referents. Lisitzky wrote his poem in the thumping meter of *Hiawatha*, used to fine effect in other contexts by contemporary Hebrew poets such as Tchernikhovsky, but something that English-language poets would have considered fairly retrograde by the turn of the century, let alone in 1937. Lisitzky's interest in Indian culture is primarily expressed through his introduction of various Native American myths into the narrative of the poem. Unfortunately, these insertions have an arbitrary quality—perhaps inevitably so because they are drawn indiscriminately from different native peoples, and thus their connection with any specific tribal culture is excised—and they often serve only to lengthen a poem that already feels bloated. In the prose foreword, Lisitzky admits that many of the names he uses are imaginary and that he has mixed rituals and legends from different tribes. He explains, "[m]y aim was not to provide a historical-folkloristic record, in which scientific accuracy is the main thing, but to rescue and gather within Hebrew poetry an echo of the songs of the vanishing Indians" (Lisitzky 1937, 3). Yet one wonders how Hebrew readers are supposed to catch an echo of Indian songs when Lisitzky has used Longfellow's English meter, which was borrowed in turn from Finnish poetry.[11]

As in the other two Indian epics, the depiction of the Indians in *Medurot doakhot* (Dying campfires) is often generic and sentimentalized. In the introduction, for example, they are portrayed in generalized terms

11. For more positive assessments of Lisitzky's poem and its engagement with American culture, see A. Mintz (2003) and Katz (2009). Stephen Katz's study is the most detailed treatment of the poem and of Lisitzky's use of Native American materials. Katz also makes the most emphatic case for the poem as an expression of the Hebraists' Americanness, in contrast to Robert Alter's reference to the Hebraists' Indian poems as a "dalliance with American exotica" (Alter 1994, 80) and my own reading of such poems as highly anxious and deeply ambivalent about their own Americanness. Katz goes so far as to conclude the following: "In presenting the lives and experiences of others, Lisitzky also added a new dimension to Hebrew literature, expanding it beyond its narrow, parochial confines. It is this process which, more than anything else, Americanized Hebrew belles lettres and those who contributed to it, giving rise to the Bellows, Malamuds, Ozicks, Potoks, and Roths of later years" (Katz 2009, 76).

as Edenic creatures, living "their lives in innocence and righteousness, hunting their game, catching their fish, fighting their wars and smoking their peace-pipes, singing their songs, dancing their dances, and raising up prayer to 'the Great Spirit'" (8). The poem's male heroes all speak, look, and act more or less like each other, and the female characters have even less individuality. This sentimentality and lack of individuation is, of course, hardly unique in the annals of non-Indian literature dealing with Indians. Nor is the stoic resignation to an unalterably tragic fate that Lisitzky ascribes to his tribesmen. In these ways, Lisitzky has successfully emulated his nineteenth-century American literary models.

What we might not expect to find in the poetry of Longfellow or the novels of Cooper, however, is an Indian echo of the Jewish-Arab conflict in Mandate Palestine. Early in the poem, the benevolent Vulture Tribe is forced to leave its usual hunting grounds, which have been desiccated by a terrible drought. But when the weak and hungry Indians turn to the forested lands nearby for food and refuge, they are cruelly repulsed by the Serpent Tribe. When the Vulture Tribe holds a meeting, the descriptions of the Serpent people's callousness and violence sound like Jewish complaints about Arab terror and intransigence. Here, the Vulture chief speaks of the Serpent Tribe's actions toward his unfortunate people:

> Deaf they were to our entreaties
> When we said our tribe is dying,
> We must find a place of refuge
> Ere our people will recover,
> Ere we heal from wounds of hunger.
> Yet you all know of the outrage
> Which they once inflicted on us:
> Chasing after youths of our tribe—
> Blameless were this group of young men
> Save that they had dared to take fish
> From the waterway at midnight—
> And they slew them with their arrows,
> Dipped in venom, dipped in evil.
>
> . . . .
>
> Can our self-restraint continue

When they act so insolently?
Shall we wait in days of famine
When our people die of hunger
While they withhold from our people
The abundance of the river,
While they swallow up the bounty
Of the forest which they rule o'er
Waiting till they next plot evil,
Till their arrogance increases,
And the wicked fall upon us,
Oust us from our home, the forest?
                    (Lisitzky 1937, 112–13)[12]

Reading this as a reflection of contemporary events in Palestine, we can hear the chief echoing the much-debated question of self-restraint versus retaliation in response to Arab attacks ("Shall our self-restraint continue / When they act so insolently?"). The moral argument that Arabs should share the land with needy Jewish refugees resounds in his rueful complaint: "Deaf they were to our entreaties / When we said our tribe is dying, / We must find a place of refuge / Ere our people will recover." And the mention of the mob attack likely refers to the Arab riots themselves.

The other notable departure from the conventions of American Romantic literature is the unambiguous opposition to the treatment of the Indians by the whites. Whereas the vanishing Native Americans were looked upon with a resigned pity in the literature and art of nineteenth-century America, the advancing whites were not portrayed with the extreme antipathy seen in Lisitzky's poem. In the introduction, Lisitzky describes the encounter between the whites and the Indians as follows: "From across the 'mighty waters' there came a white monster; before it, blood and fire and columns of smoke, and after it, utter destruction—and it poured out its wrath upon them, and persecuted them in anger and destroyed them from under the heavens of their homeland" (8). In the poem itself, the whites are

12. My translation of this passage departs somewhat from a literal rendering of the original in order to highlight its *Hiawatha*-like formal character.

manipulative and cruel, using their superior technology to cow and destroy the Indians, and intimidating the tribes into signing treaties, only to break them when they please. This portrayal of white expansion and its brutality links up with the Hebraists' negative attitudes toward urban modernity, as we see when, toward the end of Lisitzky's poem, one of the Indian women has a vision of the future—a future that is Lisitzky's present. She sees that the forest has been cut down, the marshes dried out, the fields destroyed, and the animals driven to extinction. The Indians survive only in tiny pockets, surrounded by whites and with almost no remaining traces of their culture. "Dwellings of stone," she prophecies, will reach to the sky, "Blotting out the golden sunlight, / Swallowing the lovely silence / With their noisy multitudes" (247). This vision recalls the despair and bewilderment of Ginzburg's "No-York," in which the Indian is the epitome of the city's victim, the outsider to the modern world of skyscrapers and factories. And the same sentiment surfaces in the opening of the first edition of *Mul ohel Timurah*, in which the shrill "rebelliousness and disobedience" (Silkiner 1910, 9) of the modern city is juxtaposed with the peace of Timmura's bucolic twilight.

Like the other Hebraists, Lisitzky here also portrays Christianity and its emissaries as arrogant, hypocritical, and cruel. Silkiner, as we have already seen, shows the Spanish conquerors in a church, singing hymns to peace while their victims freeze to death outside. Efros's poem, although less vehemently hostile to European designs, depicts a Christian missionary's blundering self-righteousness as he debates the Nanticokes about their religion. Lisitzky gives us Adam Anderson, an insolent priest with a gilded cross around his neck who harangues the Indians about the one true religion. The tyrannical nature of Anderson's mission becomes quickly evident as he makes it clear that Christianity is an offer the Indians cannot refuse. Any who persist in other forms of worship will be destroyed:

> more than
> One war have we waged while bringing
> The word of our lord, the Son of God,
> To the savage tribes and peoples,
> When they dared to rise against us,
> And we trampled them beneath us.
> (Lisitzky 1937, 225)

In such episodes we see Lisitzky's Jewish estrangement from the culture of the Christian West. He identifies with the Native Americans against the brutalities of the Europeans, a sentiment likely given additional force by contemporary events. In 1937, the ravaging white monster from across the seas must recall the Nazi beast.

This dimension of the poem expresses the American Hebrew poets' uncertainty about their place in America as well. This uncertainty was not one-sided: as we will see in the next chapter, the American Hebrew writers often saw aspects of the Christian dimension to the United States not as a threat but rather as a point of welcoming cultural affinity. The Hebraists' Jewish identification with the Indians in their poems is thus not a simple expression of hostile marginality in America, and it is telling that not one of these Indian epics portrays the whites as native-born Americans. Nevertheless, these tales of tragedy inevitably challenge any spotless picture of American history. It is significant in this regard that the figure of Adam Anderson can be seen not only as a general indictment of Christian violence, but also as a specific retort to Lisitzky's primary American model. When he depicted the cruelty of the priest in *Medurot doakhot*, Lisitzky doubtless had the ending of *Hiawatha* in mind, for Longfellow concluded his poem with a Christian missionary preaching to the Indians to rather different effect. This was a passage that Tchernikhovsky excised from his Hebrew translation of Longfellow's poem. Because it speaks so starkly to the tensions surrounding the figure of the Indian and its use by the American Hebrew poets, however, we should read the sermon in its entirety:

> Then the Black-Robe chief, the prophet,
> Told his message to the people,
> Told the purport of his mission,
> Told them of the Virgin Mary,
> And her blessed Son, the Saviour,
> How in distant lands and ages
> He had lived on earth as we do;
> How he fasted, prayed, and laboured;
> How the Jews, the tribe accursed,
> Mocked him, scourged him, crucified him;
> How he rose from where they laid him,

Walked again with his disciples,
And ascended into heaven.
    And the chiefs made answer, saying:
"We have listened to your message,
We have heard your words of wisdom,
We will think on what you tell us.
It is well for us, O brothers,
That you come so far to see us!"
                    (Longfellow 1993, 248)

4

I Am Not in New York

HEBREW ENCOUNTERS WITH RURAL,
SMALL-TOWN, AND CHRISTIAN AMERICA

"I am not in New York."
    —Gabriel Preil, *Sunset Possibilities and Other Poems*

AS WE HAVE SEEN, the Indian poems of Silkiner, Efros, Lisitzky, and others allowed these poets to find proximity to America while also maintaining a safe distance. These works express both a yearning for American identity and a deep unease about the Jewish future in America. Their wild settings allowed a trek into the American landscape, but a landscape that was bygone and romanticized, while their poetic encounters with exotic, non-Jewish figures—encounters with a certain erotic component—were safely imaginary, and the exotics themselves often rather Judaized.

Yet American Hebrew writers also depicted actual and present-day journeys into the America beyond New York City and the urban, immigrant milieu. Their alienation from the city and their Romantic appreciation for the natural world sent these writers, in reality and in their imaginations, away from the metropolis and out toward field and farm. Throughout the work of the American Hebraists we find an interest in rural and small-town America, thematically linked with an interest in natural spaces and with the place of the Bible in American Christian faith. It is perhaps ironic that these Jewish nationalists display such attentiveness to Christian America, and yet the Bible was necessarily the foundation of Hebraist literary culture, and the esteem in which "their" book was held by devout American Christians was a source of pride.

Other factors also contributed to the interest in rural and small-town locales. The Hebraists meditated often in their literature on the fate of Jewish farming and agrarian settlement projects such as the Am Olam movement. How such exercises in Diasporic nationalism fared in the United States would naturally implicate Hebraism and the role of these writers in America. In Harry Sackler's novel *Bein erets veshamayim* (Between heaven and earth, 1964), for instance, the Am Olam farmer Judah Novikov and his wife, Raizel, are presented as Jewish heroes, their New Jersey homestead worthy of glorification in epic literature: "[t]hey were the vanguard of a unique endeavor—to restore the descendants of herdsman and farmers who had become distant from their earth and thereby repair a strange historical dislocation" (Sackler 1964, 288). In a tragic mode, Reuven Wallenrod's story "Baleil prida" (On the eve of departure) centers in part on the disappointment of Aaron Zeitin, a Jewish immigrant who traded his New Jersey farm for a country store and finds himself caught between his unfulfilling existence as a storeowner in a small New Jersey town and his sense that a return to New York City is no longer possible:

> I should move now to cramped rooms on the sixth floor in the Bronx or Brooklyn? I should be a "border" in my old age? . . . Better for me to stay here in my store in Flatville, New Jersey, I'll sell stale Coca-Cola and ice cream, and stinking cigarettes, and I'll call myself Feivel Zeitin the farmer. Yes, farmer. My acquaintances in the city still call me that. (Wallenrod 1952, 113)

Zeitin's attempt at a farming life, so resonant with the ideals of the Zionist pioneers in Palestine, founders on the American generational conflict between immigrant and American-born children: his unruly son, resentful of and uninterested in his father's passion for farming and tree planting, has left home for Los Angeles, where he lives in shady circumstances. After he leaves, Zeitin's daughter Flora tries to cheer her father by helping him plant new saplings, but "it was a kind of game" (114), not an endeavor with a real future, and Zeitin trades away his farm. Wallenrod's typically atmospheric story transcends ideological allegory: the eve of Flora's departure from Flatville, during which the events and reminiscences of the story take place, is charged with the poignant melancholy inherent in all generational transitions and the passage of time. And yet, on one level, the failure of Zeitin's dreams of farming is certainly a metaphor for the inability of the Jewish national idea to succeed in Diaspora.

The portrayals of rural and small-town America in the literature of the Hebraists are quite varied in style and stance. They are sometimes auto-biographical in nature, reflecting the personal experiences of the author, though shaped and transformed according to aesthetic and ideological needs. Generally, prose fiction writers treat these episodes with more ironic detachment and provide more sociological detail, whereas poets tend to present these locales in a more idealized and symbolic mode. In this chapter we will look at several such episodes and locales in works by Lisitzky, Bavli, Efros, Halkin, Ginzburg, and others in order to show how these literary works illuminate the authors' relationship with America. We will pay par-ticular attention to the interest in agrarianism, to the ambiguous freedom from Jewishness presented by rural and small-town environments, and to the centrality of the Bible in these texts. Finally, we will look at Sackler's *Bein erets veshamayim* and its particularly intriguing depiction of a Jew-ish immigrant's attempt to reconcile the competing claims of Jewish and American identities in small-town America.

I had always been a lover of nature" writes Lisitzky (1959, 200) in his autobiographical-novelistic chronicle *Ele toldot adam* (translated into English as *In the Grip of Cross-Currents*). By "nature," he meant first and foremost the villages of Belorussian peasants surrounding his native Slutzk. As a child he looked at those thatched-roof houses as "charm-ing habitations" that inspired in him "a nostalgic desire to live there." Yet this was of course impossible for a Jew in tsarist Russia, and so, like many a heder boy, he satisfied these pastoral yearnings with schoolroom literature—namely, the agrarian worlds of the Bible and Talmud. In his imagination he created a bucolic landscape "just like the peasant villages I had seen," yet reconceived as Jewish through the biblical-Romantic liter-ary alchemy that found its classic expression in Abraham Mapu's wildly popular nineteenth-century Hebrew novel, *Ahavat Tsion*. Lisitzky's love of nature was therefore a split fantasy, torn between a Jewish world lifted from scripture and Haskalah romanticism, on the one hand, and the real but inaccessible world of the non-Jewish peasantry on the other. Only Zionism promised to unite these mutually exclusive worlds in the Land of Israel, where one could live as a peasant, a farmer, integrated into nature and connected to the land, yet still be a Jew.

America, on the other hand, was different. America presented to the turn-of-the-century Jewish immigrant from Russia the unfamiliar experience of natural and rural landscapes without the threat posed by a violently antagonistic peasantry. Unlike "Russia where my people are repressed and deprived of basic human rights," Lisitzky proclaims, "here I can walk down the street in a non-Jewish village and on the roads in its outskirts and meet someone who is not Jewish. We say hello to one another, even if we never met before—and I'm not afraid of him. There's no sign of dislike or contempt in his face—just good will and friendliness. That's another surprising thing to me" (1959, 241–42).

This comparative safety and acceptance could be very attractive. And yet it brought in its wake a different challenge: the temptation to abandon one's Jewishness. America famously allows a freedom, not only from fear, but from origins, from the immigrant's past. Despite their aversion to Americanization, their opposition to assimilation, the Hebraists were not insensible to this exhilarating liberty. Rural and natural landscapes become in their literature sites for rejuvenation, for encounters with the purity and wholesomeness effaced by the city. They also can become embodiments of this problematic temptation to cast off Jewish allegiance, responsibility, and identity and to become simply an American. This temptation is neutralized in the Indian poems because the settings are safely romanticized and historically remote, their erotic dimensions discernible but sublimated within the idealized framework of the poems, and because often the Indians are in some sense as much Jews as they are exotic others, and so convey the moral that one should stay within one's tribe. In the more contemporary American settings, however, the implied freedoms are living possibilities.

Such temptation is of course hardly unique to Jewish immigrants, let alone Hebraists, yet it does represent an exemplary moment of ambivalence in several works by the Hebraists. The ambivalence derives its force in part from the close association of American freedom with natural and rural landscapes. The Hebraists were culturally predisposed to the Romantic celebration of nature. They sought rural landscapes and admired the out-doors. When they could, they often left New York and roamed widely, and their literature is drawn again and again beyond the city. Yet such an embrace of America allowed and often required a slipping loose from the bonds of Jewish practice, community, distinctiveness. As a result, these American idylls could be dangerously, temptingly non-Jewish: assimilation into such surroundings was surprisingly imaginable, yet the loss of Jewish-ness was ideological anathema to these writers. So their cultural desires both propelled the Hebrew writers out into the American landscape and pulled them back into a nationalist isolation or imaginative inoculation from this landscape.

This is the case in the major turning point of Lisitzky's *In the Grip of Cross-Currents:* his decision whether or not to settle down as a farmer in rural Canada, with a non-Jewish woman as his wife. Around the age of nineteen, Lisitzky moved to the small town of Ahmic Harbor in north-ern Ontario to work as the Hebrew tutor and kosher slaughterer for the town's only Jewish family. Despite the friendships he makes and his sense of responsibility to the children he tutors, he repeatedly describes his stay in Ahmic Harbor as an escape from identity and allegiance. It was "an interval in my life, unconnected with either past or future" (1959, 208), exemplified by the heady anonymity he experiences during a midwinter sleigh ride: "[a]ll my aspirations to reform the world, and myself with it, disappeared. . . . I wanted to fly on, without thinking, with no goal, no purpose, no end in sight" (234–35).

When a mutual attraction arises with Becky, a local schoolteacher and the daughter of Scots immigrants, he considers leaving his Jewish past entirely behind him. Rowing at sunset on the lake with Becky, Lisitzky feels that "barriers of religion and culture, race and birth, heritage and tradition were leveled. All special considerations disappeared; consequences did not matter. Past and future merged in a present, newly created, a timeless real-ity" (257). In nature, figured here through the Romantic trope of the twi-light boat ride, identity becomes dispensable. When his friend Truex, the town freethinker and a veteran farmer, tells him that he can easily acquire a plot of land through Canadian homesteading laws, he decides to settle down in Ontario with Becky. As Truex tells him, "you're an enlightened man, and you know that distinctions of religion and nationality need not be a stumbling block in the way of people who love one another" (260).

It takes a deus (or Judaeus) ex machina to deter Lisitzky from his decision. An old farmer reveals to Lisitzky that he is a Jew who long ago married a Christian woman and found himself living apart from any Jewish community and now is consumed with regret over his long "marrano" existence. Lisitzky now decides that he must leave Ahmic Harbor forever to avoid "a similar ill-fated destiny" (276). Moreover, he links his encounter with the lost Jewish farmer to the new eruption of deadly pogroms in Russia (he left Canada around 1905), thus associating Kishinev with Ahmic Harbor: "[a]ll the people of Ahmic Harbor with whom I had been so close now seemed hostile strangers to me, as though they, too, had been responsible for the pogroms" (276). Yet he also expresses his uncertainty and ambivalence about his decision to give up Ahmic Harbor and admits, even during this "Jewish resurrection" (274), that America (and throughout his description of his Ontario sojourn he describes Canada as "America") may not be Russia:

> [D]espite my sudden alienation from the non-Jewish Ahmic Harbor inhabitants, I was seized with a feeling of nostalgic gloom which increased with every passing mile. I visualized these non-Jews among whom I lived and saw them again in their simplicity and uprightness and the generous hospitality they extended to me and was sorry to leave them. (Lisitzky 1959, 274)

What he is escaping when he leaves Ahmic Harbor is not, then, the possibility of a pogrom but the real possibility of losing himself in the Canadian landscape, of fulfilling his childhood fantasy of joining the peasants, at the price of his Jewish conscience. Instead, after a spiritual crisis in which he comes close to suicide, he decides to transfer his desire for national purpose to the realm of culture: teaching and writing Hebrew in the "wilderness" of America, an enterprise, he writes, that is "not unlike the bold vanguard pioneering carried on in Erets Yisrael [the Land of Israel]" (296). The Hebraist project, viewed here, is a continuation of the Am Olam Diasporic nationalist settlement work, but in literary-educational form. Jewish pioneering in America must be cultural, not agricultural, if it is to retain its

Jewish dimension. And indeed, Lisitzky went on to direct Hebrew schools in Buffalo, Milwaukee, and New Orleans, where he died in 1962.[1]

A moment similar to Lisitzky's rowboat romance with Becky occurs in Hillel Bavli's 1925 sequence of nature poems "Al brekhat Georg" (On Lake George). In the penultimate poem Bavli describes sailing on the lake with a non-Jewish woman: "You, daughter of bright Erin / and I—one of the sons of an exiled people" (1937/38, 1:126). As was the case with Lisitzky's boat ride, the romance is predicated on a silent, wordless experience beyond human language, in a natural environment figured in Romantic, idyllic terms:

> We have already forgotten even an echo
> Of vernacular or native tongue;
> A little longer and we will feel, will know
> The captivating language of the lake.
> (Bavli 1937/38, 1:126)

In order to leave their ethnic identities behind, Bavli and his companion must forgo ordinary human language, which would only underscore his Jewishness, either through his accent as an immigrant when he speaks the American "vernacular" or in his choice of national expression ("native tongue"), whether Yiddish or Hebrew. What "speaks" in this encounter is nature itself—the lake "weaves poetry, hews expression"(126)—the only medium in which the couple can be united.

Bavli had already given poetic testimony to the attraction of an Emersonian escape from the strictures of Jewish tradition. "Would that the thread of generations be snapped in me forever," he prayed in the poem "Mi yiten utso'ar nafshi" (Would that my soul be shaken [1919]): "And my heart and

---

1. Although some of Lisitzky's descriptions of his Ahmic Harbor sojourn appear to be embellished or idealized, there is a good amount of corroboration for the people he describes. The Brown family with whom he stayed were indeed real figures, as histories of the area indicate. Moreover, an amateur genealogist has posted to the Internet pictures of the headstones in the Ahmic Harbor cemetery, including that of a farmer named Truax (the spelling in the English translation of Lisitzky's memoirs would be an error) whose dates make him a likely candidate to have been Lisitzky's friend there; see http://freepages.genealogy.rootsweb .com/~murrayp/parrysnd/magnetaw/ahmic/truax1.jpg.

soul be like that of Primordial Adam, / Knowing neither law nor limit, nor the fetters of the past, nor the tradition of the fathers" (50).[2] Like Lisitzky, though, Bavli ultimately resisted such temptations. In the final poem of his Lake George series he abjures interfaith romance, addressing himself instead to Shimon Halkin, his fellow Hebrew poet and Jew. "Rise up, my brother, and let us go out to meet these wonders," he tells Halkin: "We will sing a last song to the glorious world / And our hearts will dissolve among the lakes and hills!" (127). This corrective to the previous poem allows for a union in and with nature, but one that does not require nature's wordless language. Instead, the male bonding of the poets lets them proclaim their "last song" in Hebrew and, for all the Romantic pantheism of the series, within safely Jewish bounds.

Bavli's most sustained poetic encounter with rural America, and the poem he is most associated with, is his long dramatic monologue, "Misis Voods" (Mrs. Woods). The poem, which first appeared in Palestine in 1924 in the journal *Hedim,* is spoken by a ninety-two-year-old widow living on her farm in the Catskills. Surrounded by a group of curious young visitors from the city, she holds forth, telling the story of her idyllic American childhood and her life in the mountains and expounding her philosophy of life. In the figure of Mrs. Woods, Bavli presents a picture of an "authentic" America, pristine and unspoiled.

One of the most striking things about "Mrs. Woods" is what is not in it: the Jewish presence in the Catskills is almost entirely absent from the poem. It is only alluded to obliquely in the audience of "city-folk" (Bavli 1937–38, 1:136) who come to hear Mrs. Woods dispense her wisdom, and who one assumes are Bavli's fellow Jews. This contrasts markedly with other Jewish writers of the time. The Catskills of Abraham Cahan's *The Rise of David Levinsky* (1917), for example, are of course the domain of Jewish vacationers; while at the same time that Bavli published "Mrs. Woods," the writer Maurice Samuel (who was himself significant for Hebrew literature in America as a translator of Bialik's poetry into English) published a poem

---

2. Spicehandler notes this as well (1993, 86).

in the *Menorah Journal*, the major English-language Jewish intellectual magazine of the time, with the English-Hebrew title "Al harei Catskill" (transliterated Hebrew for "Upon the Mountains of Catskill"). Samuel's poem meditated on the current state of American Jewry through a melancholy and satirical look at the Jewish Catskills, questioning the prospects of a group that has exchanged its sense of national mission, cultural traditions, and religious vitality for the shallow ephemera of American leisure fashions. An acid passage from Samuel's indictment of Jewish assimilation, ending with a pun on Wordsworth:

> And here in Catskill what do Jews believe?
> In *kosher*, certainly; in *Shabbos*, less
> (But somewhat, for they smoke in secret then),
> In *Rosh Hashonoh* and in *Yom Kippur*,
> In charity and in America.
> But most of all in Pinochle and Poker,
> In dancing and in jazz, in risqué stories,
> And everything that's smart and up-to-date.
> ("Milton, thou shouldst be living at this hour,"
> To hear the Catskills ringing with thy name.)
> (Samuel 1977, 372–73)

Hebrew writers did portray the Jewish Catskills, most hauntingly in Reuven Wallenrod's novel *Ki fanah yom* (1946; translated into English as *Dusk in the Catskills*, 1957), a poignant study of the immigrant generation's decline, set at a Catskills resort during the Second World War. Shimon Halkin, too, has one of the characters in his novel *Ad mashber* (1945) find temporary solace on a Jewish farm-turned-resort in the Catskills. The generic distinction discussed in chapter 2 holds once again: there was a time lag of at least a generation before Hebrew writers dealt at length with the Jewish sociology of the mountain resorts, and when they did so they did it in prose, not poetry.

Bavli's Jewishly denuded Catskills, on the other hand, is of a piece with a number of other works by the American Hebraists in which what was in reality a resort area is, in its literary representation, stripped of its commercial dimension and presented as wild or rural, pastoral or Edenic. Lisitzky's

Ahmic Harbor, for instance, was a vacation destination even at the beginning of the twentieth century; this was the reason his Jewish employers settled there and profited from their general store. Halkin's metaphysical meditations at Santa Barbara and the Michigan Sand Dunes are similarly located at what were vacation and resort locales, as is the case with Bavli's Lake George poems.

"Mrs. Woods," moreover, gives us the Catskills of pre-twentieth-century American Romanticism: the wild, pure, and rustic Catskills of the paintings of Asher Brown Durand and Thomas Cole; the untrammeled New York wilderness of James Fenimore Cooper; the gothic landscape of Washington Irving's Rip Van Winkle. Although not as remote or imaginary as the Indian worlds of Silkiner, Efros, and Lisitzky, this was nevertheless a Catskills that hardly existed anymore. A decade earlier, the critic Van Wyck Brooks had even used Rip Van Winkle as a parable for an America that had been irrevocably transformed by immigration:

> It is, in fact, the plain, fresh, homely, impertinent, essentially innocent old America that has passed; and in its passing the allegory of Rip Van Winkle has been filled with a new meaning. Henry Hudson and his men, we see, have begun another game of bowls, and the reverberations are heard in many a summer thunderstorm; but they have been miraculously changed into Jews, Lithuanians, Magyars, and German socialists. Rip is that old innocent America which has fallen asleep and which hears and sees in a dream the movement of peoples, the thunder of alien wants. (Brooks 1968, 97)

The "plain, fresh, homely, impertinent, essentially innocent old America" mentioned by Brooks still lives in Bavli's poem in the figure of Mrs. Woods. She describes a perfectly innocent rural American childhood, when she attended a one-room schoolhouse, sang "My Country 'Tis of Thee" and "The Star-Spangled Banner" with her friends for enjoyment, and every Sunday afternoon gathered with her family to hear her father read from the family Bible. Even the present-day setting of the poem, although intruded upon by the poet and other outsiders, remains rustic and quiet.

Indeed, Ezra Spicehandler has remarked that Mrs. Woods is "so innocent and charming that at times it demands our 'suspension of disbelief'"

(1993, 87). Certainly, she is a maddeningly static creature. In contrast to the troubled, lonely, and unsatisfied rural personae in the dramatic poems of Robert Frost, which Bavli had praised in his essay of a few years earlier, Mrs. Woods is perfectly happy and serene. "Ah, no, I am not lonely!" she avers. "There is no room for loneliness in the mountains / with all the beauty around you and all the work in the fields" (Bavli 1937–38, 1:139). She claims that even during the winter, when she is stuck at home with her dog as her only companion, she experiences "neither sadness nor loneliness, for life is dear and beautiful, / and even then its enchantments are many for any heart truly thirsty for beauty." The sense of unreality surrounding this woman with no sadness, regret, or tension in her life is increased by apparent missteps in Bavli's attempt to convey her folksy speech. Mrs. Woods occasionally punctuates her monologue with "*Moshe hakadosh*" (Holy Moses) or "*Peter hakadosh*" (Saint Peter), slightly unnatural exclamations that seem invented rather than heard. She is even introduced to us in the didactic pose of allegorical painting: she appears "in the doorway of her tiny cabin sitting tranquilly . . . bathed in the happy radiant beauty of a sabbath noon," with "one hand caressing her large white dog . . . and her other hand paging / the thick Bible laid open in her lap" (136).

The interest of "Mrs. Woods," then, clearly does not derive from the verisimilitude or depth of the character. Despite its first appearance in a Palestinian journal, whose audience presumably would have seen "Mrs. Woods" as interesting mainly for its glimpse of an exotic American type, and perhaps secondarily for the Zionist resonance of its glorification of a rooted, agrarian way of life, the poem is notable primarily as a set of fantasies and projections about America—an authentic and welcoming, yet also vanishing America—written at precisely the moment when popular nativist sentiment in the United States would culminate in the dramatic 1924 legislative restrictions on immigration, a policy that attempted to return America to a time before the transformative arrival of "Jews, Lithuanians, Magyars, and German socialists" with their "alien wants."

In this light, it is notable that Mrs. Woods is strikingly free of religious prejudice: "a Catholic church, a Baptist / or Presbyterian, or Hebrew, I don't discriminate between one sect and another, / between people I don't make distinctions" (144), she says. This authentic American specimen is entirely tolerant, welcoming all faiths and creeds, in her belief that the simple beauties of nature and truths of virtuous living transcend any one religious doctrine or group. Yet unlike Lisitzky's experience in Ahmic Harbor or Bavli's moment on Lake George, there is no temptation here. The ninety-two-year-old widow is a safely asexual figure, entirely unerotic, just as the landscape for which she is a synecdoche is entirely chaste and unseductive. What we have in the character of Mrs. Woods is a 1920s nativist fantasy made available to Jewish cultural nationalist needs and anxieties: an America that is free from anti-Semitism yet without assimilatory threat or power. Indeed, Mrs. Woods is a twilight figure, fossil-like, the last of an extinct breed. She resembles the Romantic "dying Indian" characters found in nineteenth-century American Romanticism, melancholy figures who merge with the landscape, symbolizing the passage of time and transience of empires, the inevitability of Indian demise and white ascendance. In this case, however, it is a matter of rural demise and modern, urban ascendance. And, as is the case in the Hebrew Indian epics, the poet here identifies not with the new wave (his fellow Jewish New Yorkers) but with the vanishing tribe (the rural Protestant).[3]

In fact, just as a number of the Hebrew Indians are like Jews, Mrs. Woods is much like the Romantic-maskilic Hebraist poets. Like them, she disdains the city. Bavli clearly sides with Mrs. Woods when she chastises her visitors:

> What do you know, you foolish city-folk,
> of the pleasure of country life? You disdain everything good
> and beautiful,
> and you darken the brightness of your life with dust and soot
> and noise

3. On the "dying Indian" figure, see Sollors (1986, especially 128–29). For a suggestive consideration of American nativism in the 1920s, see Michaels (1995). In 1941, Bavli wrote a "sequel" to the poem, "Demuyot beharim" (Mountain images), in which he revisits the home of the now-deceased Mrs. Woods and talks with her son, an indication that the tribe has not entirely vanished, although they still remain marginal and isolated from the rest of the world (Bavli 1955, 136–42). See Katz's different reading of the poem "Mrs. Woods," which does not view Mrs. Woods as an "Indian" figure (2009, 100–108).

> and competition and useless labor, and then when you end up
>   exhausted and broken
> you come asking: please, tell us, what is the secret of life?
>   (Bavli 1937–38, 1:137)

Also connected with the experience and outlook of the Hebraists are Mrs. Woods's reminiscences of her education in a one-room schoolhouse. Her description of well-behaved students ("quiet and polite and as serious as soldiers waiting for a command" [142]), eager to learn and reverent toward their beloved teacher, is the fantasy (and occasionally the hard-won achievement) of the immigrant Hebrew teacher, confronting conditions and attitudes in American Hebrew schools that were usually quite dissimilar to those portrayed in Mrs. Woods's reverie.

We also find in Mrs. Woods's monologue an echo of the frequent Hebraist critique of contemporary synagogal Judaism in America. Mrs. Woods laments that nowadays one does not find a sincere love of God in "the beautiful churches."

> They certainly don't go there for the sake of love of God,
> but rather for beauty and amusement's sake: some of them in
>   order to show off
> their fine, expensive clothes, to see and be seen,
> and many in order to look at the pretty young woman nearby
> so he might go out with her to a dance that evening in the very
>   same church.
>   (Bavli 1937–38, 1:144)

It is hard not to hear in this the many Hebraist complaints about organized American Judaism, its materialism and superficiality. Moreover, Mrs. Woods's preference for staying at home and reading the Bible instead of attending church has a certain resonance for the Hebraists' own emphasis on literary culture, rather than formal religious observance, as the basis for Jewish identity.

Mrs. Woods is one of the many rural and small-town non-Jewish characters in American Hebrew literature whose passion for the Bible is emphasized. Holding up her generations-old family Bible, she tells her visitors:

Every sabbath and holiday in the afternoon
all of us used to sit around the large stove,
dressed in our sabbath clothes, listening eagerly to father
read sweetly and eloquently from the Good Book.
There wasn't a church in the vicinity, so poor and small was
    our settlement,
But father—ever wise—would say to us:
"No matter! The good and merciful God has seen lovingly to all
and graced us with this book in which His Will is revealed to
    His creatures—
read it and see how the word of God and His Spirit fill you as
    well."
                (Bavli 1937–38, 1:143)

For the Hebraist, this enthusiasm for the Bible was a point of sympathetic connection with an authentic (i.e., nonurban, non-Jewish) America. In American Protestantism, in the faith of the American pioneers and settlers, the Hebraists were able to find an esteem and respect for their own culture. It is particularly telling that representations of the Christian Bible in Hebraist literature almost never include the New Testament, let alone the specifically anti-Jewish moments in the Pauline epistles and Gospel of John. Ironically, America at its most Christian became the most sympathetic for Hebraism.[4]

Of course, not all images of devout Christians are positive in the writings of the Hebraists. We have already noted the negative portrayals of the missionary priests in the Indian epics. It is usually the case that specifically American, Protestant and Bible-centered varieties of Christianity compare favorably to forms of Christianity that are identified with Europe, such as Catholicism. One thinks of the alienation manifest toward Catholic religious services in Bavli's poetic series "Behatserot el nekhar" (In the courts of a foreign god). In 1916, while teaching at a Hebrew school in Buffalo directed by Lisitzky, Bavli enrolled at the Jesuit-run Canisius College. This

---

4. For the colonial and nineteenth-century history of Christian Hebraism in the United States not historically connected with the Jewish immigrant Hebraists, yet resonant with it in certain ways, see Goldman (2004).

was perhaps a strange choice for a Jewish nationalist, though it was apparently the only school in Buffalo where he could finish his B.A. with a focus on literary studies. The literary reflections of his experience at Canisius indicate an intriguing mixture of attraction and aversion, interest and unease. We have seen in the previous chapter that in 1917 Bavli contributed a poem in English to the college literary magazine, under the perhaps less obtrusively Jewish name Aaron Ely Price, and under the same name he also contributed an English-language essay striking for its lack of any direct indication that he is a Jew.[5] In Hebrew, the main literary record of his time at Canisius is "Behatserot el nekhar," parts of which first appeared in *Hatoren* in 1917, and which was published in full in 1923. The eight poems grouped under this title each describe an experience, sometimes overpowering and bewildering, of the force and beauty of the Catholic rites—singing, organ music, church bells, statues, sermons, etc.—followed by a critique, self-censure, or ironization that undercuts the spiritual claims of the rival religion. In one of the poems, dedicated to Lisitzky, the speaker lurks at the back of a room in which Jesuits are praying and ironically muses that they are beseeching a resurrected Jew while a resurrected Jew—that is, Bavli, who has been resurrected in the national sense—is standing right behind them. Interestingly, the Bible is not part of Bavli's portrayal of Catholicism, and his time at Canisius is not presented as an immersion in America but as an apprehensive encounter with an intriguing but unfriendly rival.

When it comes to rural and small-town Protestants, however, the Bible is frequently a point of connection, an entry into the heart of America. We see this in Lisitzky's memoirs when he first accompanies his employer, Yudel Brown, on a visit to Becky's farm, and her father has his guests wait while the family finishes their Sunday Bible reading. Becky's father

5. Bavli presents himself in this essay simply as a Russian émigré, although there are some hints of his Jewishness, as when he refers to himself as one of "those foster-sons of Russia whom cruel persecution and life-long oppression have sent wandering and erring [the phrase is itself a Hebraism] across the seas" (1917a, 398). Concerning his name: Bavli was born with the family name of Rashigolsky and was at the time in the process of taking on the name Bavli. Price was the name of the uncle with whom he stayed when he first arrived in America.

apologizes, explaining that "it was his practice never to interrupt a reading of the Holy Scriptures" (Lisitzky 1959, 245). Lisitzky is not at all offended; on the contrary, he observes:

> There was no need for him to tell *us* how holy the Bible was, and with what devotion it must be treated. We were the children of the Old Covenant, who had given God's sacred book to the world. Bible reading was a tradition he had carried with him across the ocean from Scotland; it was particularly important to observe it in the New Country, as a bridge with Old Country tradition. (Lisitzky 1959, 245; emphasis in original)

The Sunday bible-study is a point of commonality, a Jewish entry into this rural Christian family, and the fidelity of these Scots immigrants to the holy scriptures connects them with the cultural seriousness of the Hebraists. Moreover, Lisitzky's relationship with Becky develops when he agrees to teach her biblical Hebrew, in exchange for which she instructs him in English poetry, which Lisitzky, like many Hebraists, saw as being saturated with biblical influence.

The Bible plays a similar role in Harry Sackler's *Bein erets veshamayim,* especially when the novel's protagonist, Avner, is introduced to Tom Wharton, the captain of a fishing boat in the small Long Island town of Eureka, in an episode set around 1910. When Avner expresses his envy of Wharton's extensive sea travels, Wharton cites Ecclesiastes in order to test the new Jewish arrival:

> "Better is the sight of the eyes than the wandering of desire," replied Tom Wharton, looking to see the impression his words made on his new acquaintance.
>
> "Ecclesiastes?" said Avner, not disguising his surprise.
>
> "Indeed," laughed Tom Wharton easily. And he immediately winked at Bruce and said: "Just as I thought, your friend would recognize that pithy saying, since it was his ancestors who wrote the book in which it was said. There's an advantage for him in knowing what the holy scriptures say." (Sackler 1964, 226)

Avner's friendship with Tom, which will be fateful for his stay in Eureka (we will discuss this at more length in the following), is initiated through the Bible, which the Christian Tom expects that Avner, as a Jew, will know, since it is in some sense his patrimony.

The Bible connected the Hebraists with the deepest wellsprings of American culture. However, this connection could be treated in ironic and humorous ways as well, as we see in works of fiction by Bernard Isaacs (1884–1975) and Shimon Halkin. Isaacs's "Amos mokher tapuzim" (Amos the orange-seller) tells the story of Izzy, a Jew who wants to be free of the immigrant past and his Jewish identity, and to immerse himself in America, "the true America" (1953, 10) as opposed to New York. Yet when Izzy moves to Florida and becomes a successful fruit seller and a revered figure among the non-Jews of Robertsville, this happens not in spite of but because of his Jewishness. Here, the biblical connection with America plays an ironic and somewhat ambivalent role.

The story is divided into three short sections, the first being Izzy's simultaneously blistering and humorous diatribe against his Hebraist roommates in New York City. This monologue is interesting in that, for all Izzy's anti-intellectualism (he attacks Bialik's poetry for having too many different interpretations), and his naïve and crudely uncritical embrace of anything "American," it still functions as a serious critique, written by a Hebraist, of the Hebraists' excessive bookishness and indifference to American reality. While his roommates stay inside working at their translations of the Bible into English and of Shakespeare into Hebrew, Izzy spends his free time pursuing America, its outdoors and its pleasures. He visits Niagara Falls, goes fishing at City Island, attends the Hudson River Festival and Regatta, all of which his roommates have not seen and, he argues, cannot see. "I want to be free," he proclaims, "free from all of your biblical verses and smart literary allusions, and to see America, all of America" (9). His roommates, on the other hand, cannot shed their rarefied, biblical-Romantic literary lenses. "Have you seen the Hudson River?" Izzy asks. "I know that you've sat down on the banks of the Hudson, but you were dreaming of the wonders of the Kishon River, and you couldn't even see the Hudson." Not only are these Hebraists uninterested in America, they are uninterested, Izzy contends, in its language as well. The only English they spend time with is that of Bible translations. "And do you think you'll learn your English from Amos shepherding with his gnarled crook, or from Ezekiel lying on his side?" mocks Izzy. "You won't learn from them how to speak fluent, melodious English with a young American woman. She's not interested in Amos's wrath and contumely, or in Ezekiel with his aching side" (5–6). Even if Isaiah were alive today, Izzy says, he would be out in the streets of New York "mixing with the holiday crowd and gathering and absorbing the impressions, colors, experiences, voices, and sounds, in order to disgorge them again in the form of a book" (7). Reminiscent of Rabinowitz's criticism in the Americanness debate, the Hebraists stand accused of failing to incorporate contemporary American reality into their literary output.

Izzy is a curious character, a kind of culturally apostate Hebraist. He is a lover of America and apparent maskil (he is fluent in Hebrew and familiar with, if contemptuous of, Bialik and Ahad Ha'am) who seeks to abandon the Jewish national ideal and embrace America totally. He is a highly articulate and persuasive speaker who detests bookishness, a rejecter of Jewish tradition who quotes the Bible instinctively and has a finely tuned spiritual sense. Part of the character's ambiguity inheres in the question of what language his eloquent monologue in part one is supposed to represent. Is it English, and therefore an enactment of the very embrace of the new world he advocates? Is it Hebrew, and so an undermining of that project? Or is he meant to be speaking in Yiddish, an invisible halfway house between his roommates' Hebrew pursuits and his own immersion in English? In any case, his highest allegiance turns out to be toward fruit: he is an aficionado of fruit, a veritable fruit worshipper, who works in a fruit store and views fruit as the very embodiment of America's goodness and blessedness. The high point of his attack on his roommates is a delightful paean to the banana, which he accuses them of failing to appreciate just as they fail to appreciate America.

Seeking to escape the Jewish past, Izzy moves to a town in Florida where, to his satisfaction, he does not see a single Jew. The second section of the story follows the structure, in miniature, of the classic immigrant narrative, recounting Izzy's arrival in the "new world" of southern Florida, his wonder at his new surroundings (now a southerner, he immediately develops a fondness for mint juleps), his travails and loneliness as he seeks employment, and his ultimate success by dint of hard work and a bit of luck. A couple points are worth noting within this conventional structure. First, the function of blacks in this section, while not central, points toward the ambivalent place of the Jew in black-white race relations in the south. Izzy cannot find work in the fruit stores of Florida: "[t]here are so many negroes who work for a few pennies," he realizes, "why would they hire a white worker for a higher wage?" (11). Weeks later, desperate for a job, he is finally hired by a Sicilian fruit seller when he rescues a crate of peaches dropped by a black employee. It is therefore in some sense because Izzy distinguishes himself from the black workers, who do their job idly and carelessly, that he is able to succeed. Another notable aspect is the way the story functions as a further instance of the failure of the Jew to attain his agrarian ideal, to truly return to the land. One Sunday, while exploring the outskirts of town, he happens on an orange grove at sunset and is enchanted by the spectacle of the "living fruit" (15) on the trees, trees that are filled with birdsong. His epiphany, however, is ultimately a melancholy one as he reflects that the fruit that he sells "in the store, in the crates, are dead, dead oranges" (15). The implicit realization is that, still working in a store just as he had done before arriving in Florida, he has not really transformed his existence. Though he has left New York City, he has in some sense come no closer to America.

The third section of the story is the ironic punch line. Izzy has eagerly tried to shed his Jewish past. Several years later, the owner of his own fruit store, he is a beloved figure in this overwhelmingly non-Jewish community. He befriends the priest of the local church (denomination left ambiguous, with both Catholic and Protestant traits), and when asked he contributes money gladly for the church's renovation. Yet he cannot escape being recognized as a Jew—not because of anti-Semitism, but because of his own penchant for biblical quotation, his ethical and moral probity, and the local priest's philo-Semitic reverence. This reaches its pinnacle when, in the final lines of the story, the priest overhears Izzy advise a female customer having difficulties with her husband and is filled with worshipful admiration for Izzy's counsel, his kindness (he doesn't charge the distraught customer), and his repeated use of biblical references:

The priest came toward them. He took off his hat:

"This is a holy place." And he turned to Mrs. Callahan: "Do you know who has sold you these fruits and vegetables? Amos, prophet of Israel, may God bless him."

"Amen," answered Mrs. Callahan with the sweet countenance of a religious pilgrim.

The priest donned his hat and hurriedly left the store. After a short while he returned with a huge Bible, covered in black satin, in his hand. "Take this holy book."

"The Bible? What do I have to do with the Bible? I'm a fruit-seller."

"And Amos, son of your people, was a shepherd, a herdsman, and you are his heir. Take it."

"But, but . . ."

Izzy wanted to return the strange, unwanted gift, but the priest had already left the store, and Izzy remained standing with the huge, satin-covered Bible in his hand. (Isaacs 1953, 16–17).

This ending is not only ironic but also intriguing in its possible implications. Izzy sought to leave his Jewishness behind and to "see America" without the Hebraists' biblical allusions in the way. Yet ultimately it is the Bible that marks and defines him and his reception in the non-Jewish community, as Izzy discovers that these "true" Americans see their world through biblical lenses too. Is the ending, then, a vindication of the Hebraists? In this reading, Izzy is surprised by the very source from which he sought to escape, and he goes to Florida only to find (or be found by) his inescapable Jewishness. On the other hand, the story's conclusion may describe a case of mistaken, or at least distorted, identity: the priest's Bible (Isaacs uses the Hebrew word "*bibliyah*," which indicates the Christian Bible) is no more the "*tanakh ivri*" (Hebrew Bible) of the first section than Izzy is the prophet Amos. In this less circular, less redemptive reading, we might take Izzy's vision of the living and dead fruit as a nationalist allegory, in which he has become a "dead fruit," detached from its living source on the tree. In any case, the story's conclusion is indeterminate: we simply do not know what Izzy will do with the unwanted book he is left holding. What we do find, however, is that the Christian identification of the modern Jew with his biblical past may be as confining as it is appealing.

Shimon Halkin describes a similar dynamic in his novel *Ad mashber*. However, the stylistic and narrative aspects of Halkin's novel, his stream-of-consciousness technique, and certainly his far greater brilliance as a fiction writer both intensify the irony of the encounter between Jewish immigrant and Bible-saturated, small-town Christian and hold this irony in a delicately balanced tension with the pathos of their curious interdependence. A former revolutionary who had been exiled to Siberia, Reuven-Irwin finds himself in a small town in Arkansas where he is warmly welcomed by Macleish, a prominent citizen, local judge, and Freemason. An avid Bible reader, we are told Macleish "had loved them, the children of Israel, all his life," though before Reuven-Irwin's arrival "he had not yet met one in the flesh" (S. Halkin 1945, 170). Their relationship is an intriguing mixture of reality and ruse. Macleish sees Reuven-Irwin, not as a poor immigrant and ex-revolutionary, but as a "symbol of the Eternal People, whom God Himself in His Glory called His servant" and who trails after him the "greatness of the Israelite past . . . like the ancient train on the robe of kings" (178). Inspired by his mythical-biblical apprehension of Reuven-Irwin, Macleish buys him a house, helps him to bring his fiancée over from Russia, supports him in opening a barbershop, and inducts him into the local order of Freemasons. Not the least irony of the episode is that, while the Jewish immigrant had changed his name from Reuven to Irwin in order to become more American, in small-town Arkansas Macleish insists on calling him Reuven-Irwin in order to preserve his biblical name.

And yet for all Reuven-Irwin's manipulative willingness to benefit from Macleish's mythologization of him, the relationship is not entirely one-sided. Reuven-Irwin is in fact an upstanding citizen who becomes genuinely enthusiastic about Freemasonry and prefers the small Arkansas town to "ten suffocating metropolises like New York" (164). The main problem Reuven-Irwin must contend with is the slow, quiet extinction of his Jewishness in this welcoming town, a dynamic he tries unsuccessfully and in bad faith to ignore. He frets that his infant daughter will one day have to be sent to New York if she is to avoid marrying a non-Jew. How to reconcile his preference for small-town life with his need to remain Jewish becomes an intractable problem, which "even Freemasonry cannot solve," and his ambivalence becomes increasingly palpable throughout his monologue, which swings from praising his new home to cursing it as "this sleepy town of stupid Gentiles" (177). Reuven-Irwin founders on the contradiction between his small-town existence and the demands of Jewishness, and for all his sympathy, Halkin seems to imply that Reuven-Irwin's problem is the problem of American Jewry as a whole: they can become American or they can remain Jewish, but they cannot do both for very long. As in the case of Isaacs's Izzy, the Christian embrace of Jews as a biblical people appears here as a distortion and a well-meaning but fatal trap.

Yet Halkin's ideological censure of Reuven-Irwin does not efface the humorous and human dynamics of his relationship with Macleish. The highlight of the episode is Reuven-Irwin's recollection of their first meeting, which in Halkin's shifting narrative technique (the entire episode is the recollection of another character, in fact) stylistically reflects Macleish's consciousness and point of view. Halkin sets the scene with great comic effect, as the immigrant, arrested for vagrancy, stands in the swelteringly hot provincial courtroom and attempts to respond to the judge's questions with the aid of a pocket dictionary, his accent rendering his grammatically mangled sentences completely unintelligible. The stylistic shift to Macleish's point of view occurs when the frustrated judge is suddenly seized with a surprising thought: "that this is an Israelite standing before him" (173). In a passage that combines *nusah* satire with an almost Joycean ebullience, Macleish, whose consciousness is clearly reflected in the indirect discourse, decides to confirm his intuition:

> With great confidence indeed he stood and sketched on a piece of paper the name י-ה-ו-ה [the Tetragrammaton], which he had trained his hand to write according to its form in slightly crooked Hebrew block letters since the day he entered into the covenant of the Freemasons, and he ordered the immigrant to read what he had written. And behold the wonder: the immigrant's face shone, and not only did he first read the name according to the letters and then according to their accepted reading passed down in the books of the Kabbalah, but then he stood and quickly added to that very piece of paper and in the same Hebrew script, though not broken and crooked like that of Mr. Macleish, the wondrous names: א-ל-ה-י-ם צבאות [Lord of Hosts], which were far beyond either the fingers or ken of the Right Honorable Judge Macleish, even though he had then already

attained the third of the first degrees of his lodge, namely: apprentice, fellow, master. Barely, just barely indeed did the Right Honorable Judge Macleish control the tumult of his spirit for a moment while he finished signaling for the lame officer who limped upon his thigh to leave the hall, and no one remained with him as he made himself known unto his fellow, as did Joseph in his day, and immediately he descended from his seat, the seat of judgement, and approached the immigrant and took his hand and pressed it silently and to the latter's mystification fled from the house, lest he be overcome with weeping. (S. Halkin 1945, 173–74)

Halkin pokes gentle fun at the judge's mystical-mythical apprehension of Jews—his confusion, for instance, at not being able to use his biblical and Masonic knowledge to decipher the significance of the immigrant's clothes and appearance: "[h]e had not imagined an Israelite in this way—could not determine the meaning of the strange symbols of his ancient costume either according to the Old Testament or the many books he had read in the wisdom of the great mason King Solomon" (173). Yet this episode is more than merely satirical. While the mock-serious biblical rhetoric, a well-known comic mode in modern Hebrew literature, effectively ironizes the episode, it does not efface a genuine poignancy. Stylistically, the passage is both satirical and an accurate representation of the biblical lenses through which the Arkansas judge views his encounter with the Jewish immigrant. The Joseph and Jacob references are comically incommensurate with the dusty courtroom scene, yet quite appropriate to Macleish's sense of life-changing momentousness and to Reuven-Irwin's equally life-changing arrival in small-town America.

A sense of shared cultural-nationalist estimation for the Bible and its narratives enabled sympathetic Hebraist consideration of even the most "exotic" groups of American Christians, such as southern blacks and Mormons. Lisitzky's collection of poems, Be'ohalei khush (In the tents of Cush [1953]), which is based on black folksongs, spirituals, and sermons and is the most extensive treatment of African-American themes in American Hebrew literature, goes beyond even the usual biblical connections between blacks and Jews based on shared histories of persecution filtered through the Exodus narrative. Lisitzky celebrates the biblical devotion of both groups through a series of poems presented as Hebrew versions of

Negro sermons. Lisitzky's imaginary black preachers retell biblical stories in contemporary guise—a kind of Midrash and a Hebraist imagining of a black imagining of an ancient Hebrew text. For instance, the story of Pinchas's zealotry against the Moabites in Numbers 25 is presented in the poem "Yisrael bashitim" (Israel at Shittim) as the story of a charismatic young black preacher's crusade against the gambling, drinking, and licentiousness within the black community. In "Vatedaber Miryam baMoshe" (And Miriam spoke to Moses), the conflict between Moses and his sister in Numbers 12 becomes an indictment of racism.[6]

The dynamics of race, identity, and literary influence in these poems are intriguing, as Lisitzky draws on a combination of firsthand experience with southern black Christians (he had lived for decades in New Orleans); stereotypes of black primitivity and violence (which actually seem to have had a galvanizing effect on his verse: this collection is far more interesting and vivid than his Indian epic); African-American folk literature; and Hebrew literary precedent—above all the novel *Ohel Tom,* the nineteenth-century Hebrew translation of Harriet Beecher Stowe's *Uncle Tom's Cabin,* which many of the Hebraists avidly read in their youth. In his review of James Weldon Johnson's anthology of Negro poetry, Bavli notes that, even after he met African-Americans firsthand, his childhood reading of the sentimental novel *Ohel Tom* shaped his perception of and emotional response to black Americans, both a closeness and a distance, effected through the biblical and modern Hebrew imagination (Bavli n.d., 280–91). As Lisitzky writes in the long narrative poem "Ezra hakohen" (Ezra the priest), the blacks he encountered when he first arrived in the American South

> appeared to him with the visages from that astounding world
> first revealed to him across the sea, when he was still a lad,
> in that foreign book entitled "*Ohel Tom,*" in whose pages
> the Hebrew garb lent Hebrew image to its content as well,
> for it placed them both close to his heart and far distant in time

6. See also Katz's extensive discussion of the representation of African Americans by Lisitzky and other American Hebraists (2009).

as he saw them like a tribe of Shem related to the tribes of his
    forefathers
fallen with them into slavery in Egypt.
               (Lisitzky 1953, 205)

Lisitzky both presents blacks as approaching their history through the
Bible and himself approaches blacks through the Bible. In "Ezra hakohen,"
Lisitzky tells of his quest to hear the story of black enslavement not through
books but through the dying generation of those who had lived through it.
He attends a black revival meeting where, far from feeling out of place, he
is welcomed as a Jew, "a shoot from the stock of the holy people" (207),
and told the location of an old-age home where he can meet an elderly black
preacher who had been a slave before the Civil War. The bulk of the poem
is the heartbreaking story of the elderly preacher Ezra, who begins his tale
with an extremely positive account of life as a slave under his kindly first
owner, a Jew from the West Indies named Cardozo, who taught him to
read and would preach to his slaves out of the Old Testament. The most
sustained voice of black history in the collection is therefore given his voice
by a Jew and through the Bible, reflecting the collection as a whole.

Bavli's long poem *Mormon mesaper* (A Mormon recounts), written in 1940, expresses admiration for and a sense of Jewish kinship with
the Church of Latter-Day Saints, based on the same cultural-ideological
dynamic that allowed the Hebraists their sense of proximity to other American "biblical" groups (allowing for the looser application of the term "biblical" in the case of the Church of Latter-Day Saints). With the exception of
the opening and final stanzas, the poem is presented as the monologue of a
Mormon tour guide at the temple in Salt Lake City; it recounts the history
of the Church of Latter-Day Saints from the revelation of the golden tablets
to Joseph Smith and through all the persecutions, wanderings, expulsions,
and massacres suffered by the sect, culminating in the arrival in Utah under
the leadership of Brigham Young, the miracle of the seagulls, and the determined creation by Young's followers of a society in which they can live out
their unique relationship with the divine. Implicit throughout are the poet's
fascination with and pride in this other chosen people, so evidently inspired
by the biblical-national epic of the Jews. Nor was this the only Hebraist

literary connection between Jewish nationalism and the Mormon Church, as we will see in the next chapter.[7] What makes Bavli's poem truly interesting, however, is that this mirror reflects in two directions: the Mormons are inspired by the ancient history of the Jews, yet nineteenth-century Mormon history demonstrates to Bavli in 1940 the possibility of present-day Zionist aspirations succeeding in the face of extreme persecution. After hearing the guide's tale, Bavli describes his own state of mind at the end of the poem:

> Reflections within reflections hovered in my imagination:
> camps of exiles, refugees from pogroms, future-looking
>   visionaries,
> a generation of pioneers, cultivators of the desert, builders of
>   cities,
> a sanctuary and a temple and a land redeemed.
>   (Bavli 1955, 134)

Precisely because of the Bible's importance as a link between these immigrant Jews and Christian America, this scriptural connection became fraught when seen against the dire background of the Holocaust. The catastrophe raised the question of whether American respect for the Bible would translate into concern for the suffering of Jews. Certainly, the long history of Jewish-Christian relations makes plain that Christian interest in the Bible has no necessary connection with sympathy for actual Jews.[8] This fact informs Gabriel Preil's grouping "Zer shirim katan la'Aviyah" (A little wreath of poems for Abijah). An author's footnote informs us that "[t]his cycle of poems was written in a house that was built in 1824 in Putnam Valley, New York by Abijah Lee, a devout Christian devoted to the Bible" (Preil 1954, 75). Preil's typical concern with chronological ambiguity, the competition between competing times and realities, is here sharpened into the sobering contrast between the pure and pious aspirations of this early nineteenth-century Christian, so passionate about the Bible,

---

7. Avraham Regelson also compared Mormons and Jews in his poetry (see Katz 2009, 89).

8. On the ambivalence of Christian Hebraists toward Jews, see Goldman (2004, 7–30).

and the destruction wreaked upon the Jews by his "kin," the Gentiles of Europe, in the twentieth century. "My fathers bequeathed to you eternal consolation," the poet tells Abijah. The Bible "caressed and adorned your youth, shaped the crystal paths of your deeds" (75). Yet this cultural-spiritual gift has not been requited:

> You were so close to my people's yearning sources,
> at their shore you leaned to quench your thirst.
> But in my day, your kin have shattered every last vessel,
> and stand with hearts of ice, in the wasteland they have sown.
> (Preil 1954, 75)

One of the Christian characters in Wallenrod's *Dusk in the Catskills* uses the Bible to castigate Jews, emphasizing the difference between the biblical figures he admires and the Catskills vacationers of today, for whom he holds a notably anti-Semitic disdain. He blames Jewish hotel owners for destroying the rural way of life and its biblically informed values. In response to these insinuations, the Jewish protagonist Leo Halper, who had himself wanted to remain a farmer and not a hotel owner, argues that Jews cannot be held responsible for modernity:

> "The new generation does not know the Bible, nor does it want to know what the Bible teaches. You know, Halper, it seems to me that it is partly the fault of those who built their hotels here. When we lived here on the land we did follow the Bible. . . ."
> "But there you are mistaken. It is no one's fault in particular. Neither mine nor yours. The times are different. It is the movie, it is the automobile, it is the airplane. Times have changed, Mister Stevens, and it is your fault as well as my fault, or, if you wish, it is neither my fault nor yours."
> (Wallenrod 1957, 112)

Similarly, Halper thinks back to when he first arrived in the Catskills as a farmer, and how Sam Douglas, "over fifty then, a tall strong friendly farmer" (38) welcomed him in the mode we have seen already in the examples above: "[h]e actually was happy that a Jew, a son of the Biblical people, had come to live amongst them." Yet Halper contrasts that period of closeness and sympathy to the current time, overshadowed by the Nazi terror, and the emotional gulf that now separates him from Douglas and his other non-Jewish neighbors.[9]

That the Hebraists might bridge this gulf is one of the desperate notions informing Shimon Ginzburg's powerful poem "La'ivrim ba'Amerikah miz-mor" (Ode to the Hebraists in America), written in 1939. Hearkening back to the redemptive image of lights at the conclusion of his earlier "No-York," this poem meditates poignantly on the Hebraists in America at the close of the 1930s:

> Like the few chains of lights, solitary yet connected,
> at an unfamiliar, snow-darkened train station,
> suddenly blinking into view among wintery fields
> forgotten somewhere between New York and Cleveland—
> I imagine you, Hebrews among the spaces of America.
> No one knows your seed here in this country, your holy seed,
> or the lost father and mother who have forgotten you,
> alone here on this night of winter, of stars and snow . . .
> (Ginzburg 1970, 119)

This ghostly company is solitary and sorrowful, but precious; beautiful but irreducibly alien to America: "the Potomac hears you, the Mississippi wonders at you: / for something flutters upon it, a shade of something lovely, incomparably lovely / and sad, and noble" (119). They are also the Jews who, in the dark night of the Nazi evil, are most aware of the suffering of their brethren in Europe. If most of America's Jews seemed to have only a vague sense of what was unfolding overseas, the Hebraists by contrast were like remote transmitters in America, wires broadcasting the anguish of the Jews of Europe: "day and night, as you work or rest, / like a viper from its

---

9. A similar dynamic exists in Avraham Regelson's poem "Arafel beKherem Marta" (Fog on Martha's Vineyard), in which the poet uses the Bible to initiate a conversation with a New England sailor. Speaking about the fog, Regelson tells the man: "This is what / my ancestors in Egypt called: oppressive darkness" (1945, 47). Yet the speaker is subsequently separated from the non-Jewish sailor by the consciousness of the Holocaust, which overshadows and undoes a Native American folktale told by the sailor.

den pursuing you, biting you with no cure / is the horrific curse of the exile and the scream of your brothers from the ends of the earth" (120). Midway through the poem Ginzburg describes an average American, John, a "decent and respectable Yankee," who

> sits on a sofa with smoke curling from his pipe,
> listening to the radio, confused at the barking
> of Hitler presiding over the slaughter,
> and weighs in his mind, hesitantly, whether to press one side of
>   the scale—
> when one of you appears and fades before him,
> with radiant eyes and modest step,
> and John turns suddenly, with bright face, and gazes upwards
> at the smoke of his pipe,
> as if he feels, tangibly, the passage before him of a figure from
>   the ancient source
> from which his forefathers drank . . .
>   (120)

A figure for America itself, John is not sure what to make of the situation in Europe or whether or how to be involved. Ginzburg's implication is that despite the marginality of the Hebraists, it is their ghostly, flickering presence in this dire and uncertain time that might possibly stir America to action—by being living reminders of that "ancient source," the Bible. Ginzburg's poem moves in the opposite direction from Jacob Glatshteyn's "Good Night, World," a Yiddish poem written at the same time, in which the poet leaves the non-Jewish world behind in disgust. In Ginzburg's poem, the Hebraists have an urgent mission to the Gentiles. Ginzburg does not describe intimacy or closeness: as in Wallenrod's novel, Ginzburg juxtaposes "John's tranquility" with the desperation of the Jews. Yet this tranquility can be disturbed by the Hebraists, embodiments of a biblical tradition, a spiritual-cultural debt owed them by Christian America.

Because the Hebraist writers were Jewish nationalists; because their cultural mission was profoundly bibliocentric—not simply in terms of types and narratives but in terms of rigorous literary-lingusitic devotion; and because they combined their modernity with a deep respect for traditional

Judaism, the American Hebraists were capable of a greater cultural proximity to devout Christians, whose devotion to the Bible (or, in the case of the Mormons, to a Jewishly inflected national epic project) was a form of cultural flattery, and whose piety and scriptural seriousness were sources of sympathy rather than alienation. These factors produced a different constellation of connections with other American and non-Jewish groups than we tend to find in Yiddish and Jewish-American literatures. There was no love of Christian anti-Semitism or conversionary zeal: the Indian epics and Bavli's poems on Catholic rites make the Hebraists' distaste for Christian persecution and exclusion plain enough. And, as we see in works by Isaacs and Halkin, the Hebraists could be aware of the constraints on and distortions of Jewish identity produced by a too-literal Christian embrace of Jews as a biblical people. Yet the Hebraists were often able to find in manifestations of American Protestant spirituality a sense of kinship rare in other Jewish literatures in the United States.

Small-town America was attractive to the Hebraists, but it could not resolve the conflict between Jewish and American identity, and in fact often exacerbated it. We will conclude this chapter by considering one of the most memorable accounts of how these identity dilemmas converge upon the Jew in small-town America: "Habrehah laYurika" (The flight to Eureka), book 3 of Harry Sackler's novel *Bein erets veshamayim* (1964). Sackler (1883–1974) is such an interesting case because, in contrast to so many of the Hebrew writers in America, he was relatively optimistic about the future of Jewish life and culture in the United States. Born in Galicia, Sackler was the great-grandchild of Rabbi Feivel Shreier, one of the most influential pro-Zionist rabbis in Galicia in his time. Sackler received a traditional heder education until the age of twelve, when he went to live and study with his great-grandfather, from whom he absorbed his love of Hebrew literature and passion for Zionism. After his great-grandfather's death, Sackler pursued secular studies in Radowicz, Czernowicz, and Vienna; in 1902 he immigrated to America, where he earned a degree in law, though he never practiced. Always included in histories of American Hebraism, Sackler was nevertheless one of its least typical members because of both his greater ideological comfort with the United States and because his creativity as a writer was not confined to Hebrew alone. We have already mentioned Sackler as the rare instance of a "triple threat," someone with literary accomplishments in Hebrew, Yiddish, and English, and we will consider aspects of his career as a Yiddish and Hebrew playwright in the next chapter. For much of his life, however, Sackler's literary aspirations had to compete with, and often took a back seat to, his community activism. He served as secretary general of the New York Kehillah (1917–18); he was on the staff of the Zionist Organization of America (1918–23), the Board of Jewish Education (1923–26), and the Brooklyn Jewish Community Council (1940–44); and he was an executive member of the Joint Distribution Committee (1945–55). As these dates indicate, his commitment to the writer's life was most active during the 1920s and 30s when he achieved his greatest fame as a Yiddish writer, and after 1955, when he focused most exclusively on Hebrew.[10]

Bein erets veshamayim reflects this linguistic comprehensiveness. It was begun in English, owes a good deal to the author's publications in Yiddish, and finally appeared in its entirety as a Hebrew novel (Kabakoff 1978, 187). It is generically hybrid as well, a fusion of the classic Jewish immigrant epic in the mode of Cahan's *Levinsky,* elements of sentimental melodrama, and autobiographical chronicle focusing on real historical events in the Jewish community as well as the author's search for Jewish meaning and personal equilibrium in America. These two dimensions, the social and the personal, are imperfectly synthesized. Although the first three of the book's five sections work on both levels, and would comprise a fine naturalistic novel in the mode of Cahan or Dreiser, in the final two books the autobiographical-anecdotal element disturbs the aesthetic balance. Description and characterization become spare and diaristic; the narrative slackens and turns idiosyncratic, relevant to Sackler's personal history but not to novelistic momentum. This part of *Bein erets veshamayim* is something of the equivalent to the years left out of Lisitzky's memoirs, between his departure from Ahmic Harbor and the near-attempt at suicide that ends the book.

10. For biographical information on Sackler, see Raisin (1927–29, 2:678–84); Zylbercwaig and Mestel (1934, 1519–24); and Silberschlag (1972).

Sackler seems to cast about for the ending, knowing that he wants to end with a positive sense both of the protagonist's life and of the role of Jews in the United States, but his personal narrative does not carry him to this conclusion in a novelistically satisfying way, and he tries to fill in the gap between autobiography and novel with melodrama.

The plot tells the story of Avner Stern, a Galician immigrant who, like Sackler, comes to New York at the age of eighteen and is also the great-grandson of an important rabbinical leader. We follow Avner's career from an initially promising start working for relatives, to employment in the sweatshops of the Lower East Side and involvement in radicalism, to a staid period as a teacher of immigrants, his acquisition of a law degree, his stay in the small town of Eureka, his career as a journalist in the Yiddish press, his army service during the First World War, and his final decision to become a writer and dedicate himself to the strengthening of Jewish identity in the United States. Throughout most of the novel Avner is haunted by a sense of aimlessness and lack of mission. His experiences are all shadowed by and reflective of a larger tension, between the freedom of self-invention in the United States and the loss of traditions and values from the Old World. At the center of the novel, this tension leads to what Avner calls his great "debacle" or "crisis" in the episode that comprises book 3, "The Flight to Eureka," in which he goes to live in a small fishing town on Long Island.

The plot of "The Flight to Eureka" runs as follows. Avner is now twenty-six years old. He has left sweatshop work after breaking the nose of an unscrupulous factory boss at the end of book 2. He has taken up teaching and acquired a law degree, during which time he befriended a fellow law student, Bruce Caldwell, a non-Jew who invites Avner to come to his hometown of Eureka. Avner takes up Bruce's offer and moves from New York City to Eureka. He works in Bruce's insurance firm and makes the acquaintance of various people in the town, including Tom and Carrie Wharton. Tom Wharton is the captain of a fishing boat, and his beautiful wife is something of a town scandal: a loose woman who, according to rumor, had an affair with Tom's brother, whom Tom drowned at sea in revenge. As the months pass, Avner feels increasingly alienated from Wasp Eureka. He is never persecuted but feels that he remains an outsider, at least to the town's "proper" families. This reaches a pitch during the winter holiday season, when the Caldwells leave him out of their Christmas and New Year's celebrations. When Avner realizes that his friend's family has invited many people from town to their New Year's party, he goes to the town pub and drinks alone, and is then discovered by Tom Wharton, who brings him back to his own New Year's Eve party, during which his wife secretly makes advances to him.

Avner grows increasingly resentful of the hollowness of his relations with the Caldwells and with the town as a whole. At a celebration of Bruce's passing of the bar exam, Avner quarrels and ends their friendship, such as it was, and is escorted home drunk by Tom Wharton and his shipmate Skip. Seeing him arriving drunk (and loudly declaiming Bialik poems), his scandalized landlady locks him out of the house in which he rents a room. Avner responds by angrily kicking in the glaziery on the door. To avoid further conflict, Tom and Skip bring Avner back to the Wharton house. The next morning Avner realizes that his time in Eureka has come to an embarrassing end, and he makes plans to leave town permanently in a few days. During this time, staying at the Whartons, he becomes consumed with the thought of Carrie's nearness and sexual availability.

The day he is supposed to leave, he misses his train and returns to the Wharton house, knowing Tom will be away leading a fishing charter. He confesses his love to Carrie in flowery terms that clash with his own clearly sexual interest and her shrill, crude manner. Carrie confesses her hatred for Tom but refuses to have sex with Avner unless Avner first kills her husband. They begin a rum-soaked vigil, waiting for Tom to return, Avner apparently ready to commit murder. When Tom does return, however, Avner is unable to lift a hand against him. He drops his weapon and is beaten up and thrown down the stairs. Arm dislocated and eye swollen shut, he is carried by Skip aboard Tom's boat, the boat from which Tom's brother Jack was drowned, and which now sets sail. To Avner's surprise, however, Tom does not kill him but transports him to New Jersey, to the farm of Judah Novikov, a kindly Jewish farmer. At the end of book 3, Avner is left at the farm, along with his shame at his total moral breakdown.

As can be seen, the plot is highly melodramatic, and yet the account is intensified by a confessional element that appears to run through the whole and by the ideological and psychological dimensions that intersect the plot at every point. Avner's "flight to Eureka" is an experiment in American-ness, the most extreme of Avner's failed attempts to come to terms with the United States. Indeed, he reflects that the journey to Eureka, while only a ninety-minute train ride from New York, feels as momentous to him as his transatlantic voyage to the New World eight years earlier. In New York, he still lived within an almost entirely Jewish world, but now he attempts to find his way into the "real" America, "entirely different from the one he had known in New York" (Sackler 1964, 202). The central predicament of the episode, then, is how to be Jewish and American—how to reconcile these identities, allegiances, and cultures—or, how to annihilate one's Jew-ishness in order to be at home in America.

Avner's struggle with this question is expressed throughout book 3 in multiple ways. When he first arrives in Eureka, for instance, he balks at working for Bruce's insurance company: he wants to take up manual labor of some sort, in order to show that Jews can do this kind of "real" work and so be "real" Americans. Bruce has to convince him that being a real American has nothing to do with manual labor, arguing that Americans have historically had no problem employing others (black slaves, immi-grants) to do the most physically demanding work. In another telling epi-sode several months into his stay, he goes drinking at the town pub one winter evening with Bruce and some of Bruce's friends. When they exit the pub, Avner is inspired to sing a Yiddish song from his childhood, at which point his friends disapprovingly say, "[w]hy don't you sing an American song, Avner?" (224), and they begin singing "Jingle Bells."

Perhaps the most poignant dramatization of the conflict between American and Jewish identity, and one with a clearly Hebraist dimension, is the bar mitzvah reception party for Avner's cousin Caspar, which Avner attends just before he leaves New York for Eureka. In the middle of the reception, Caspar is made to recite a Hebrew poem composed by Avner's uncle. The result highlights the generational conflict and crisis of continuity in American Jewish culture, and in Hebraist values in particular:

[Caspar] lifted up his head and began to mumble the foreign syllables as if his mouth were filled with gravel. At first Avner had great difficulty making out the strange sounds. And only after several minutes did his ear catch words about an ancient tree whose roots were nourished by the waters of the Jordan and whose boughs grew and spread to the ends of the earth. The birds nesting in the tree sang about the light of righteousness shining on the world and its fulness. And now that poem was flowing from the heart of the lad, still in the dew of youth, commanding him to . . . commanding him to . . . Anxiety clouded the boy's face; he began to stammer, and soon fell silent altogether. He had apparently forgotten the final verses. And when his father started to whisper in his ear, the boy turned his head away and said in a loud, contemptuous voice: "Ugh, father, I don't remember this foreign gibberish. Wouldn't it be better to say this in the language of America?" A wave of laughter and applause indicated that the people gathered there were of the same mind as Caspar. (Sackler 1964, 206; ellipses in original)

The very content of the poem reinforces the symbolism of the episode, as the boy recites a poem in the late nineteenth-century, Hibat Tsion mode (compare Tevkin in Cahan's *Levinsky*), emphasizing a sentimental-national Jewish tradition (the ancient tree with roots in the Holy Land), yet falters precisely when about to express what this tradition commands him to do. After the reception, Avner discusses the incident and its implication for Jewishness in America with his uncle and another maskilic landsman, Karenin. Karenin is hopeful that Hebrew will survive in America, and that "Americanness and Jewishness aren't mutually opposed" (207). He recalls the speech delivered at the reception by the Americanized rabbi, who insisted cheerfully on the complementarity of Judaism and Americanism. Avner, however, is coldly pessimistic here, and he responds that the rabbi "is satisfied with pleasant phrases about Judaism" (208), ignoring the possibility that Jewish tradition and American life may in fact be irreconcilable. "There are great advantages to American life," he says. "But it is possible that the tradition of our ancestors and the heritage of the past is the price we have to pay for it" (208).

Eureka is Avner's experiment in seeing whether "Americanness and Jewishness aren't mutually opposed," and it is interesting that Avner's career as a writer begins when this experiment begins to stall and sour. In the weeks following Avner's lonely and somewhat dissolute New Year's Eve experience, he begins to write down vignettes of life in Dubrovin, the town of his childhood. He notes that these exercises are in some sense a crucial distraction: from his desire to have an affair with Carrie; from his loneliness; and from what is becoming an increasingly significant force in his life, alcohol. But they also constitute a retreat from America and a return to the Old World, embodied especially in the figure of his great-grandfather, so prominent in these vignettes. Yet in the act of writing, Avner commences a process that, at the end of the novel, is meant to be a synthesizing bridge between the Jewish past and the American Jewish future. That is, literature is to become a vehicle for Jewish continuity, for the creative redeployment of Jewish tradition in new, modern forms. At this point in the novel, however, the Dubrovin of Avner's notebook is both a refuge from his failed attempt to embrace a "real" America and a painful reflection of that America as well, since Avner begins to question whether the clearly marked borders between Jewish and Christian worlds in his remembered Dubrovin are any less present, if less overtly visible, in Eureka. He ultimately sees his friendship with Bruce as a failure, not fundamentally different from the relations between Jews and Poles back in Galicia.

This conviction that he cannot be a part of this America, except possibly through a process of Jewish self-negation, becomes concretized in his sordid involvement with Carrie Wharton. The novel as a whole is to some extent organized around a series of sexual and romantic encounters with women: Malke Silberhaken from Dubrovin (who in America first becomes Molly Silver, and then the successful fashion designer Madeleine Chantelle); the Italian immigrant Celia Scarfo; Carrie Wharton; and Elka Alpert, whom Avner marries. In each case there is strife and conflict, which the authoritative narrative voices in the book present as expressions of the immigrant's confusion in modern America. Avner's erotic questing is seen as a manifestation of Jewish national uncertainty in a new, free environment, unyoked from traditional norms. Nevertheless, we should be wary of wholly embracing this purely sociological-ideological interpretation. Avner's life reflects the great migration from Eastern Europe to America, yet the novel also presents to us a protagonist whose erotic choices reflect his own individual psychology, and in particular his evident ambivalence about his mother, and his wife as a new mother-figure in his life.

The main voice in the novel to lay a national-ideological interpretation onto Avner's love affairs is his great-grandfather, the late Rabbi Uri

Bacharach, who appears to Avner in visions twice in the novel, in both cases helping Avner to understand how Jewish tradition can continue, in new forms, in modern America. The first visitation occurs when Avner is lying unconscious on Tom Wharton's boat, on his way, he presumes, to a watery grave in the Atlantic. In his delirium he sees his old heder teacher and his mother appear, reciting penitential prayers on his behalf in order to avert the death his sins surely merit. Then Avner sees his great-grandfather walking on the waves toward the ship. Rabbi Bacharach tells Avner that his sinfulness is not so great as he fears, as the ultimate Jewish sins are murder, which Avner refused to commit; idolatry, which Avner also refused when the Catholic Celia had asked him to convert for her; and sexual impropriety, which the rabbi explains has extenuating circumstances in Avner's case. Rabbi Bacharach explains that Avner's sexual transgressions are symptoms of modernity and immigrant dislocation. In a sympathetic, Rav Kookian manner, the rabbi delivers a striking midrashic reading of Genesis 33:1, in which Avner's sin would simply be a necessary facet of the Jewish need to survive in modernity. In their visionary exchange, the rabbi explains:

> "I spent my life in Dubrovin and I knew what to do and what not to do. Yet there are eras in which our nation is compelled to leave and migrate to new places. And such wanderings bring confusion, mistakes, and remorse."
>
> "Exactly. And the individual becomes swallowed up in the fog. Isn't there any escape from all this?"
>
> "Escape?" exclaimed the old man with a tinge of impatience. "And then who will go out in your place? When our father Jacob went to meet his brother Esau, he divided the people with him into two camps. Since then, the way of our nation in its struggle for existence is to be divided into two camps. One camp guards the old—as I do. And the other camp goes out to conquer the new—like you. Each one does what falls to it." (276–77)

In this extraordinary midrash, the continuity of the Jewish nation is ensured precisely by the differences between the guardians of tradition and the experimenters with the new. In this view, Avner's experience in Eureka is not a failure, but rather one individual outcome of the difficult collective mission to discover the way forward for the Jewish people in America.

As the rather forgiving Tom Wharton sees it, Avner's mistake was in trying to escape his Jewishness. He leaves a letter with Judah Novikov, entrusting Avner into his care and alluding obliquely to the events in Eureka as follows: "[t]he whole matter is strange and confusing. A young man who, by his nature, should be one of the Pharisees or a Levite officiating at the Temple, came to live among us and tried to be a drunken fool, a lecher and a brawler like one of us. But his transformation was a spectacular failure" (278). Wharton's essentialism makes Jews superior to non-Jews ("one of us") and maintains that by trying to live apart from a Jewish environment and shed his intrinsic and irreducible Jewishness, Avner only did violence to himself. Yet it is not clear that Avner sought to shed his Jewishness in Eureka, at least prior to the final day's events. His vague project seems to have been to see whether he could carry his Jewishness with him into small-town America, and there he found the limits to this project, albeit in a more violent and immoral manner than did Halkin's Reuven-Irwin, Isaacs's Izzy, or Lisitzky in Ahmic Harbor. It is telling, then, that book 3 ends with Avner at the Novikov farm—i.e., an agrarian, American locale that is simultaneously Jewish. In some sense this is the image of what he had sought, and did not find, in Eureka.

For the remainder of the novel, Avner continues to search for an American Jewish synthesis, at home in the United States but true to the sources and continuing national drama of the Jewish people.[11] He finds this in book 5 in the exhortations of a Wasp patrician he meets in the army. Captain Barlow holds forth enthusiastically on the idea that America should dispense with the melting pot ideal and adopt a cultural pluralist model of American identity in which each immigrant and national-ethnic group preserves its distinctive cultural traditions, contributing in this way to the richness of American cultural life. The melting pot, he argues, prevents America's minorities from truly enriching the nation and produces only a thin cultural pap. Thus, Sackler places the Kallenesque philosophy of

---

11. Book 4 of the novel is mainly interesting for the glimpse it provides into the world of Yiddish journalism and New York Jewish community politics in the years leading from the Bingham Affair up to the emergence of the New York Kehillah and the outbreak of the First World War.

cultural pluralism in which one would be authentically American precisely by emphasizing one's Jewish distinctiveness, in the mouth of a Mayflower Wasp. In a way distantly reminiscent of Bavli's Mrs. Woods, Barlow gives an American imprimatur to Avner's desire for a synthesis of Jewish cultural nationalism and American integrationism. The fact that Barlow is a professor in civilian life only adds to the American authority he bestows on these ideas. Moreover, Barlow is juxtaposed with the lieutenant Arthur Neumark, an American Jew of assimilated German-Jewish background who is hostile to Jewish affirmation and to Zionism. Neumark's assimilationist disdain for Jewish "tribalism" (426) is defeated by the force of Barlow's arguments, backed by his commanding officer's Mayflower pedigree and penchant for declaiming Whitman.

Nevertheless, Avner does not fully embrace Barlow's arguments on a concrete and personal level until the final pages of the novel, when he is visited a second time by the apparition of his great-grandfather. In a period of estrangement from his wife and intense depression and uncertainty about his life's purpose, Avner sits by the Hudson River, where Izzy's Hebraists could only see the biblical Kishon. Rabbi Bacharach now seconds Barlow's advice and tells Avner that he must put his energies into literature in order to show how Jewish tradition can survive and flourish in American modernity. If Barlow represents the imprimatur of American culture, Bacharach represents the sanction of Jewish tradition; he explains to Avner that Judaism has always undergone changes but that it possesses an unchanging core that must be given new expression in every age. This optimistic view typifies Sackler's conviction, so rare among the Hebrew writers in America, of the possible endurance of vital Jewish culture in the new world. For Sackler, speaking through Barlow and Bacharach, Jewish life in America entails new forms rather than negations of the "true core" of Judaism. This, pronounces Bacharach, is Avner's mission, to show this way forward through literature: "it is your task to express all this in their language; it is imperative that those wandering Jews, peripheral Jews, come to see something of the light in Judaism" (452).

This concluding epiphany is set in 1918, the year after Abraham Cahan published his own American Jewish immigrant epic. Yet Sackler's novel did not appear in book form for another half century after that, and it appeared in neither of the languages in which one would presume Avner found his cultural mission, i.e., neither in English nor in Yiddish. Instead, we have an impassioned statement as to how the immigrant generation can find its way in America, written in Hebrew and at a point well into the vanishing of this very generation. Indeed, *Bein erets veshamayim* (1964) was one of several novels of Eastern European Jewish immigration to America published by the Hebraists long after the period of this migration. These novels appeared, moreover, just as a very different constellation of Jewish-American novelists achieved their literary dominance, Reuven Wallenrod's *Be'ein dor* (1953) appearing the same year as Saul Bellow's *The Adventures of Augie March,* Samuel Blank's *Al admat Amerikah* (1958) being published around the same time as Philip Roth's "Goodbye, Columbus," and Sackler's novel published the same year as Bellow's *Herzog.* Writers like Bellow and Roth depicted contemporary Jewish life in America, the children and grandchildren of immigrants, not the earlier immigrant narratives. The Hebrew novels, on the other hand, filled an inescapably memorial function, belatedly chronicling a largely bygone immigrant milieu and mapping contemporary American Jewish life only in terms of its distance from the immigrant generation. They did so, moreover, not "in their language" and for the edification of American Jewry, as Rabbi Bacharach encouraged Avner to write, but rather for the benefit of a largely Israeli audience, all three having been published in Tel Aviv.

All this suggests that Avner's mission was ultimately unsuccessful. As he feared when he was in Eureka, the gulf between the Jewish national commitment of the Hebraists and their sense of belonging in America would remain ultimately unbridgeable. In their journeys into rural America, the Hebraists set out to discover the extent to which they might call the United States home. Yet they carried with them on these journeys an ideology that insisted upon seeing the United States not as a true national home, but as a temporary American refuge. How Sackler and other writers have imagined this notion of the American refuge, and its possibilities and burdens for Jewish national identity, is therefore the subject of the next chapter.

5

Messiah, American Style

MORDECAI MANUEL NOAH
AND THE AMERICAN REFUGE

"A hotel where people come and go is not a home."
—Reuven Wallenrod, *Dusk in the Catskills*

THE AMERICAN HEBRAISTS were not the only writers to take an interest in the figure of Mordecai Manuel Noah (1785–1851). Indeed, for more than a century, Noah's story has exercised historical and literary imaginations alike. How could it be otherwise? Diplomat, playwright, journalist, politician, and visionary, Mordecai Manuel Noah was an extraordinary individual. In the course of his life, he wrote and produced successful plays, fought a duel, established himself as a popular newspaper columnist, rescued enslaved American sailors during his tenure as US consul in Tunis, published an important book on his travels in Europe and North Africa, influenced presidential elections through his editorship of major newspapers, and served as judge and port surveyor of New York City. He was easily the most prominent and influential Jew in United States during the first half of the nineteenth century. Moreover, he has been described as the first public figure "to demand continuous recognition as both a devoted American and as a devoted Jew" (Sarna 1981, 159).

When Noah is recalled today, it is usually because of his plan to establish a Jewish colony on Grand Island, near Buffalo in western New York State. To this would-be "City of Refuge" (Noah 1999, 108) for the oppressed and persecuted Jews of the world, he gave the name "Ararat," a reference both to his own name and to the idea that the colony would be a temporary haven, a way station on the ultimate Jewish road to the Holy Land. Noah presented a cornerstone and inaugurated the plan in a highly theatrical ceremony held in Buffalo in 1825. Dressed in Shakespearean getup, he assumed the title of "Judge of Israel," and in the local Episcopal church, he delivered a consecration speech in which he claimed to "revive, renew and re-establish the Government of the Jewish Nation under the auspices and protection of the constitution and laws of the United States of America" (109), calling in addition for the ingathering of Native Americans as descendants of the Ten Lost Tribes.

Contemporaries such as Heinrich Heine found the scheme amusing, yet not a single Jew (or Indian) answered the internationally publicized call to settle in Ararat, and Noah admitted the following year that the project had come to nothing. Nevertheless, by the 1830s, his concern for the Jewish people had led him to espouse proto-Zionist arguments for the large-scale settlement of Jews in Palestine. "Every attempt to colonize the Jews in other countries has failed," he observed in an 1844 address. "Their eye has steadily rested on their own beloved Jerusalem" (138). Felled by successive strokes half a century before Theodor Herzl would launch the modern Zionist movement, Noah remains a figure who stands unabashedly at the crossroads of American and Jewish history. He was an American patriot who saw fit to crown himself Judge of the Jews, and he was a prescient forerunner of modern Zionism whose initiatives toward reestablishing Jewish sovereignty emerged from a quintessentially American audacity.

Small wonder, then, that in addition to a number of historical studies, the best being Jonathan Sarna's *Jacksonian Jew: The Two Worlds of Mordecai Manuel Noah* (1981), more than half a dozen works of literature have featured this colorful figure, including most recently the American graphic novelist Ben Katchor's *The Jew of New York* (1998) and Israeli novelist Nava Semel's *Iyisrael* (2005). Long after the death of the historical Noah, this important figure has continued to live on in the literary imagination. Writers in English, Yiddish, and Hebrew have all treated this character, their works inevitably turning upon the tensions inherent in Noah's simultaneous affirmation of both his Americanness and his Jewishness. These works function as bellwethers of attitudes toward both American and Jewish (or Israeli) national identities, expressing a range of ideological positions regarding ethnic, national, and linguistic belonging. The discussion that follows, then, examines how these writers have used the figure of Noah to try to reconcile Jewish national identity with the possibilities of American life, and it places American Hebraist treatments of Noah within the broader history and comparative context of these literary representations.

I first want to meditate on the general significance of Noah for the Hebraists and their cultural nationalist project, as compared with writers working in other linguistic and ideological veins. It is not that the Hebraists devoted obsessive attention to Noah, certainly not compared with their attention to the figure of the American Indian, an even more central motif for American Hebraist self-understanding (yet one that is also quite intertwined with Noah, as we shall see). The two Hebrew writers to treat Noah at length were Harry Sackler, one of the more anomalous Hebraists because of his equal devotion to Yiddish and English; and Yohanan Twersky, a writer of historical fiction who lived for two decades in the United States. Nevertheless, we may take these writers' divergent representations of Noah as exemplifying the poles between which American Hebraism oscillated, highlighting fundamental concerns of the Hebraist writers in and about America.

Noah's Ararat project presented a compelling model for the Hebraists' understanding of their place in the United States. The example of Noah could be used to write America into the drama of Zionism—was not Theodor Herzl, in his endeavor to restore Jewish political sovereignty, preceded three-quarters of a century by, of all things, an American?—thereby affirming the potential significance of the American Hebrew writers for the Jewish national project. Even more important, the concept of a temporary Jewish refuge in America had great emotional valence for the Hebraists, as it suited their ambivalence about seeing the United States as a permanent home. Noah himself had entertained the name "New Jerusalem" for his colony, but he decided on "Ararat," as it was not to become a long-term home for the Jews but rather a fortunate if impermanent haven. It was, he claimed, "an asylum" in which Jewish refugees might restore themselves physically and regenerate themselves intellectually in preparation for "that great and final restoration to their ancient heritage" (Noah 1999, 107).

Sackler's literary Noah is similarly emphatic that the colony not be considered a substitute for the Land of Israel. "To refresh oneself in Ararat—this is permitted," he says, "to remain there—forbidden" (Sackler 1943, 292). Or, as we find the thirteen-year-old Noah saying in a 1956 Hebrew children's book published by the Jewish Education Committee of New York, "[t]he ark of the Jewish people has found a place of rest [in America]. It has found its *Ararat*. But heaven forbid that we forget the holy city of Jerusalem" (Glenn 1961, 26). Thus, the tension between the Hebraists' Jewish nationalism and their commitment to America as "home" is mirrored in the concept of refuge, a term with interesting literary resonance in American Hebrew literature, extending beyond the works of Sackler and Twersky.

For example, *Miklat* (refuge) was the name of one of the most important Hebraist journals in the United States, edited during its short lifespan from 1919 to 1921 by Y. D. Berkowitz, the son-in-law and Hebrew translator of Sholom Aleichem and an important Hebrew author in his own right. Appropriately enough, Berkowitz left the United States for Palestine in 1924, never having shed either his conviction that America was only a temporary refuge on his path to the Land of Israel or his overall distaste for the state of Jewish life in America. As Avraham Holtz has remarked in regard to Berkowitz's fiction, "were one to judge solely from Berkowitz's accounts, one would have to conclude that America played havoc with Jewish culture and literature. Berkowitz viewed the American Jew as a coarse, luxury-seeking figure, unmoved by ideals and motivated solely by the dollar" (1973, 13). The title of the journal therefore presented American Hebraism as a cultural Ararat, vital but temporary, and no substitute for the one and only Promised Land.

Earlier, the nineteenth-century Hebrew satirist Gershon Rosenzweig had played on the notion of America as a "land of refuge" (*erets miklat*) in his irreverent *Yankee Talmud,* a send-up of life in America in Talmudic guise. "Our sages taught," runs this pseudoscripture, "that America was created for no other purpose than to be a land of refuge." Rosenzweig's punch line then links this "land of refuge" to the biblical "cities of refuge" to which murderers are allowed to flee—making fun of America as a kind of ne'er-do-wells' haven. He continues with another, oft-used Hebrew-Aramaic pun on the word "America": "Rav Safra said: Using astrology,

Columbus foresaw that in the future America was to be a land of refuge for all the wanton and empty-headed people of the world, and he implored that the land should not be named after him, and so they called it *ama reka* [an empty people]" (qtd. Scharfstein 1956, 34).

Another Hebrew word that may be translated as "refuge" is *miflat*, also the title of a story by Reuven Wallenrod in which he savagely exposes the psychic paralysis faced by Jewish nationalists who go on residing in the United States, never reconciling themselves to their American home. The story has a certain autobiographical kernel in that Wallenrod, like many of the Hebraists, spent a number of years seeing himself as only a temporary resident in the United States, planning to immigrate to Israel when it became financially and professionally feasible.[1] The story recounts the relationship between the appropriately named Gershon Dubin (an alien, as is Gershon in Exodus 2:23) and his lover of five years, Beatrice. Wallenrod ably characterizes the emotional and mental states of Dubin when his relationship with Beatrice collapses—his sexual hunger, jealousy, emptiness, and depression—but the story centers less on the specificities of their relationship than on the fundamental ideological contradictions in Dubin's life, the real reasons why he is unable to find happiness and why Beatrice leaves him. Dubin lives an existence in which his ideals and values find no correlation to the world around him. As did so many of the Hebraists in America, Dubin works as a teacher in a Hebrew school in which he is treated with the utmost lack of respect by both his students and the administration. At the same time, his Zionist pretensions are mocked by Jews who point out that he is unwilling and unequipped to go to Palestine. Out of inertia, fear, and an inability to find a positive outlet for his values in the American environment, he drifts along in his limbo-like existence toward the inevitable crisis.

The sneering contempt in which Dubin is held by both his students and Beatrice's radical friends is cruel, yet it mirrors his own self-contempt, the logical outcome of the contradictions of his place in American Jewish life.

---

1. Wallenrod lived in the Land of Israel during the early 1920s. In 1923 he came to the United States, where he taught at the Jewish Theological Seminary and at Brooklyn College. See Shaked (1988, 3:123–24).

His students know that the religious traditions and Hebrew he teaches are not valued by their own parents or community except through a kind of vague sentimentality—and for that matter, Dubin himself is not religious—and they resent studying things that bear no relevance to anything in their lives. This is the background to the outrageous disrespect they show their teacher, a disrespect that is paralleled by the school administration. When Dubin complains to the school's vice-president (and father of one of the most obnoxious students), telling him the truth—that the students behave for their English teacher because English is valued, whereas they run wild in their Torah class because Torah is not—he runs up against the worst sort of obtuse sentimentalism of the American Jewish community, a mind-set that will not acknowledge assimilation and so must retreat into comforting mystical-biologistic notions of a Jewish essence that will never perish. "Who can place a value on the Jewish soul?" the school vice-president asks Dubin. "Our enemies think it has vanished, when it suddenly rises up and stands in all its purity, all its holiness. The Jewish soul, the Jewish spark will not disappear: they are passed down from generation to generation . . . Consider, for instance, Doctor Theodor-Zeev Herzl, or the greatest writer in all the world, the ardent Zionist Max Nordau, or the greatest professor in the world, Professor Albert Einstein" (Wallenrod 1937, 90).

This feel-good blather is the diametric opposite of the Hebraist insistence on learned culture as bulwark against an all-too-real erosion of Jewish identity. Dubin's experience was common among the Hebraist schoolteachers: Berkowitz referred to the Hebrew school in which he taught as "this hell" (Holtz 1973, 22), and Lisitzky went so far as to compare Hebrew school teaching with black slavery! "I was delivered into slavery," he says of his work in the Talmud Torah of New Orleans: "Oh, the slavery of Israel, / in which the best of our poor Hebrew teachers have been placed / in the nation of America" (Lisitzky 1953, 208).

Beatrice's leftist friends, meanwhile, have an equivalent contempt for Dubin, whose national and religious allegiances seem to have nothing to do with the urgencies of the various workers' movements. They call him a "reactionary," accuse him of purveying the "opium" of religion. Though their Marxist enthusiasms are as puerile as the misbehavior of the children at Dubin's school (it is telling that Dubin recognizes the hate-filled looks of his students in the face of Beatrice's friend Karenin, who defends the Communist International's support for the Arab massacres of Jews in Palestine), these radicals, like the students, at least have the advantage over Dubin of finding expression for their ideals in their own lives' work. On the other hand, the bad faith of Dubin's life—and the lives of those like him—is repeatedly pointed out in the story, not least by Dubin himself, who is painfully aware of how disjointed and compartmentalized his life is. One object lesson is a young man named Perkins whom Dubin and Beatrice know at Columbia University, where they first meet. Perkins is an enthusiastic Zionist who speaks and lectures about life in the Land of Israel. But when Beatrice expresses her admiration for Perkins, Dubin exposes the truth to her:

> "Do you know him? Tell me about him," she asked.
>
> "A teacher in the talmud torah."
>
> "Why doesn't he go to the Land of Israel? He loves the land so much."
>
> "He'll go when he's sure that everything there is fine and dandy."
>
> "You're always dismissive."
>
> With a laugh he told her about Perkins. His acquaintances told him that Perkins had once gone to a training farm, but that he avoided all work, and at the first opportunity left for America. When his fellow townsmen would ask him about his trip, he would say: "My wish is to be useful to the Land of Israel . . . I want to perfect myself in America . . . To the Land of Israel, via America." His whole town accompanied him to the train station, dancing and singing: "We'll meet again in the Land of Israel . . ."
>
> "And here?"
>
> "Here he's a 'teacher' like me. He doesn't live in the Land of Israel, and he doesn't live in America." (Lisitzky 1953, 79; ellipses in original)

Clinging to the justification that America is a temporary refuge on the road to the Land of Israel, Perkins and Dubin have fallen into an existence as "teachers"—with scare quotes, as we see, since "teacher" becomes a term for Jewish nationalists who are avoiding the choices of life (though, it must be said, for often very palpable and pressing reasons) and so live neither in America nor in the Land of Israel but in a ghostly state between. One of Beatrice's friends, a former fellow of Dubin's in the Poalei Zion movement, enjoys battening sadistically on Dubin's psychic unhappiness and finally elicits an enraged punch in the face from Dubin when he pushes him too far by exposing his paralysis: "[l]et's be frank: so you've been a Zionist for decades, even a member of the workers' party, so to speak . . . Now then, first of all, you don't go there . . . and if you even went, would you work there? . . . Just between us . . . even here you don't want to work . . . even here you teach American children to recite the Shema . . . what could you do there?" (93; ellipses in original)

It is no surprise that Beatrice finally leaves Dubin. Dubin's very love for Beatrice forces him into the masochistic role of exposing his own inadequacies to her. She wants to live in the world, but Dubin seeks a refuge from it, and so she leaves him. The story ends with Dubin undergoing a total nervous breakdown, Wallenrod describing Dubin's madness as his final "refuge" (98).

The story depicts in extreme terms the psychic burden of the Hebraists in America. Although some Hebrew writers, such as Sackler, tried to synthesize their Jewish national allegiances with their sense of being part of the United States, others, such as Twersky, definitively rejected America in the end, immigrating to Israel. Sackler's and Twersky's treatments of Noah dramatize these themes and tensions as do, in very different ways, the treatments of Noah by the other writers we will examine. In reviewing the history of these literary representations of Noah, we begin, however, not with a Hebrew writer of the twentieth century but with a major American writer of the nineteenth century.

When William Dean Howells is mentioned in connection with Jewish literature, it is usually because of his championing of the work of Abraham Cahan. As is well known to historians of American ethnic literature, Howells, perhaps the most influential arbiter of literary taste in late nineteenth- and early twentieth-century America, hailed the author of *Yekl, A Tale of the New York Ghetto* (1896) as "a new star of realism," enabling Cahan's entry into the English-language literary world. Our interest in Howells, however, does not concern Cahan but stems instead from a novel Howells wrote a good quarter century before he lauded Cahan's tales of Lower East Side immigrant life.

Their Wedding Journey (1871) was Howells's first novel. Not often read today, it nevertheless stands as one of the more resonant meditations on American identity of its period, displaying in its ironic probings of the American scene and character easy fellowship with works by Howells's friend Mark Twain that appeared at the same time, such as *The Innocents Abroad* (1869) and *Roughing It* (1872). Admittedly, Howells hardly dilates upon Mordecai Manuel Noah in the novel; the reference to Noah is only made in passing. And yet a look at Howells's novel must commence our review of *Noahliteratur* because his meditations on American identity, the role of America's minorities, and the use of American Romantic tropes are, with the addition of considerations of Jewish nationalism, the basic materials of nearly all subsequent literary treatments of Noah. Following the American romances of Noah's own plays, writings, and life, our story begins with a well-placed reference in *Their Wedding Journey*.

As its title indicates, the novel follows a recently married couple on their honeymoon as they make their way to that already legendary post-nuptial destination, Niagara Falls. Based on an actual trip taken by Howells and his wife, the attraction of the novel derives from the parallel it sets up between its examination of America and the protagonists' reflections on their own relationship. Howells and his wife were in their thirties when they made their own trek to the falls, and the similarly aged protagonists of the novel are highly conscious of the fact that they are older than most newlyweds. To the clichés of their Niagara pilgrimage, and even those of their own romance, they bring an experienced, critical, and de-idealizingly self-aware eye. It is this cooler view that Howells and his characters also bring to their exploration of post–Civil War America, deflating Romantic icons and American myths.

Critics applauded this portrayal of, in the words of one reviewer, "our American life exactly as we see it" (quoted in Howells 1968, xxxi). Indeed, the novel, which followed on Howells's well-received Italian travel sketches, was intended as an affirmation of the worth and interest of American experience honestly portrayed. The character of the husband, Basil March, strikes this note in the opening pages, when the itinerary for this decidedly non-European voyage is provided:

> Basil had said that as this was their first journey together in America [the
> couple had met in Europe], he wished to give it at the beginning *as pungent*
> *a national character as possible,* and that as he could imagine *nothing*
> *more peculiarly American* than a voyage to New York by a Fall River boat,
> they ought to take that route thither. (Howells 1968, 5; emphases added)

Yet this gravitation toward the "peculiarly American" simultaneously risks
a disorienting and unsentimental questioning of what the national character is in a country that, like Basil and his wife, Isabel, is no longer quite in
the full flush of youth. Approaching its centennial at the time the novel was
written, the United States was going through myriad changes and seemed
to be in a position to test its own myths. As Howells wrote to a friend in
the same year the novel appeared, "I feel more and more persuaded that we
only have to study American life with the naked eye in order to find it infi-
nitely various and entertaining. The trouble has always been that we have
looked at it through somebody else's confounded literary telescope" (xiv).

Indeed, one of the most humorous moments in the novel comes when
the Marches arrive at Niagara and encounter Native Americans who fail to
conform to Romantic literary expectations, in particular that of the dying
tribe clinging tenaciously to its folk traditions while disappearing from the
face of the earth. At first, the Indians do seem to play to type: "like the
woods and the wild faces of the cliffs and precipices," their picturesque yet
unobtrusive presence helps "to keep the cataract remote, and to invest it
with the charm of primeval loneliness" (85). Yet when Isabel, purchasing a
souvenir trinket from an Indian woman, asks the name of her little girl, she
is disappointed to hear "Daisy Smith," and in "distressingly good English"
to boot. "But her Indian name?" Isabel persists. "'She has none,' answered
the woman, who told Basil that her village numbered five hundred people,
and that they were Protestants." Isabel complains afterward to her husband:
"[b]ut, how shocking that they should be Christians, and Protestants! It
would have been bad enough to have them Catholics. And that woman said
that they were increasing. They ought to be fading away" (86).[2]

---

2. See Sollors (1986, 102–30) for a relevant discussion of the cultural history of Indians,
Niagara Falls, and romantic love.

If the Indians, rather than fading away, seem to be becoming modern Americans, other putatively American groups who refuse or are unable to do so are likened to the image of the dying Indian. In this post–Civil War novel, a Southern gentleman at the Niagara resort is described in precisely these terms, with his combination of savagery and twilight nobility eliciting feelings of tragic pity. "He had an air at once fierce and sad," we are told, "and a half-barbaric, homicidal gentility of manner fascinating enough in its way" (95). Basil finds that he "can't help feeling towards him as towards a fallen prince" (96), in spite of the evils of slavery and war. "This gentleman, and others like him," he muses to his wife, "used to be the lords of our summer resorts. . . . Now they're moneyless and subjugated (as they call it)" (95).

Nobility, Indian or otherwise, is not the guarantor of inclusion in contemporary American life. The real key to this participation is money. Howells describes the Marches as being "of the American race, which finds nothing too good for it that its money can buy" (60). In the democratizing atmosphere of the market, class distinctions are famously irrelevant. On the steamboat from New York City up the Hudson River, the Marches observe a nouveau riche mixing unconcernedly with a "hereditary aristocrat," the latter representing "nothing . . . but a social set, an alien club-life" (43). On the other hand, a couple of Jewish immigrants on the boat, representatives of the mid-nineteenth-century wave of mass Jewish immigration, despite their foreign accents and stereotyped concern with commerce, seem to epitomize at the same time the giddy entrepreneurial spirit of the American scene. The Marches eavesdrop on these "two Hebrews," one of whom is holding forth on how to succeed at selling coats. "Isaac'll zell him the goat he wands him to puy," he says of an acquaintance, "and he'll make him believe it's the goat he was a-lookin' for . . . but the thing is to *make him puy the goat that you wand to zell when he don't wand no goat at all*" (42–43, emphasis in original). I do not want to ignore the anti-Semitic portrayal of Jews as obsessed with commerce, yet it must be pointed out that in the American environment, it is the "hereditary aristocrat" who belongs to "an alien club-life." The blue blood, like the Southerner, is the fossil, while the Jewish immigrants, observing that success in business is not merely to provide a needed commodity but to create an entirely new desire, exemplify the new American scene.

Niagara Falls is, appropriately, the central instance in the novel of the Romantic American myth, the primeval force and pristine beauty of nature, the golden mystery of the Indian past, which Howells seeks to test in the corrosive stress of reality, asking, as he implicitly does of the mature love of the Marches, what survives when romance is stripped away? And in fact, to skip for a moment to the resolution of the novel, something powerful does survive: romance, whether of a couple or a nation, is not solely a joke, a cliché, or an illusion. The splendor of the Falls overcomes the Marches, shattering the "patronizing spirit in which we approach everything nowadays" (103–4). This encounter with the sublime is not a simple sweet elation, but a breaking down. Confronting the sheer awesome force of the cataract, they find themselves "dispersed and subjected" (104), a pregnant phrase suggesting their own membership in some lost Jewish or Indian tribe.

Yet this affirmation of the enduring power of the Falls follows on a quite sustained attempt at de-idealization. As we have already seen, the Niagara's Indians are not the romantic solitary chief or maiden throwing themselves over the Falls. Howells notes the mundane, commercial aspects of Niagara, from the arrival of the Marches at the station when Isabel "was sure she should have heard" the sound of the Falls had it not been for "the vulgar little noises that attend the arrival of trains at Niagara as well as everywhere else," to the kiosks everywhere selling "feather fans, and miniature bark canoes, and jars and vases and bracelets and brooches carved out of the local rocks" (74). Howells's designation of these tourist knickknacks as "barbaric wares" seems to have as much to do with his meditation on the consumers as on the producers. The couple must contend with the jostling and noise of their fellow tourists, the importunings of commercial photographers. And the narrator, closely identified here with Basil, delivers a speech intended to entrap and neutralize the romance of Niagara in the web of historical consciousness.

"Niagara," the narrator begins, "is an awful homicide." It is drenched in a long history of bloodshed and barbarity, from the first inhabitants of the area, "abominable savages . . . leading a life of demoniacal misery and wickedness" to "the ferocious Iroquois bloodily driving out these squalid devil-worshippers," followed by the arrival of French settlers, who sowed "the seeds of war that fruited afterwards in murderous strifes," wars between the French and the English, Indian attacks on American settlements during the Revolutionary War, "the savage forays with tomahawk and scalping-knife, and the blazing villages on either shore in the war of 1812"—all these constitute "the memories of the place, the links in a chain of tragical interest scarcely broken before our time since the white man first beheld the mist-veiled face of Niagara" (89).

This meditation on the history of the Falls culminates in a reference that differs from what precedes it in that it does not involve violence or death. At the end of this history of bloodshed, and as the couple make their way across one of the islands near the Falls,

> they gave a sigh to that dream, half pathetic, half ludicrous, yet not ignoble, of Mordecai Noah, who thought to assemble all the Jews of the world, and all the Indians, as remnants of the lost tribes, upon Grand Island, there to rebuild Jerusalem, and who actually laid the cornerstone of the new temple there. (Howells 1968, 89–90)

We may quibble with a few details: Noah's cornerstone had nothing to do with a "new temple," and Grand Island is not quite as proximate to the Falls as Howells and many subsequent authors have imagined. Yet Howells's remembrance of Noah at the apex of his history of Niagara and its follies is quite perceptive. Noah's Jewish American fusions make him a necessary precursor to the novel's dizzy résumé of this new and changing, brash and hybrid America. Moreover, Noah is linked with Niagara as a symbol of an American vitality that, for all its folly, will never be completely ironized or dismissed. Noah is presented here as part of the true and ugly record of American failure and "yet not ignoble," just as all the de-idealizations of the novel eventually recede before a core of grandeur, a reaffirmation of Romantic aspirations, even if necessarily more hard-bitten and selective. Noah is therefore both part of the American past and a significant image for the American future, on whose threshold Howells stands, a totem for those "half pathetic, half ludicrous" dreams that nevertheless have a way of coming true.

How true, Howells could not have known. Yet Noah's significance as a precursor of modern Zionism would soon be mined. The first author to do this, thereby giving Noah a central place in a work of fiction, was

Israel Zangwill, the most prominent Anglo-Jewish intellectual to express the dilemmas of modern Jewish identity and to take a role in programs of Jewish national renewal. The author of such cultural touchstones as *The Melting Pot* and *Children of the Ghetto*, Zangwill chaired the 1895 meeting at which Theodor Herzl first presented his plan for a state of the Jews. As Zangwill's biographer Joseph Udelson notes, he "reacted to Herzl's program with a mixture of confusion, ambivalence, and skepticism" (1990, 156). Nevertheless, by 1901, Zangwill had become an impassioned Zionist and supporter of Herzl. More famously, he supported Herzl's Uganda initiative of 1903—the idea of setting up a Jewish colony in Africa, decisively rejected by the Zionist movement—and continued for some time after to champion geographic alternatives to the Zionist insistence on the Land of Israel as the location for a Jewish state. At least part of Zangwill's agitated ambivalence about Herzl's Zionism was his fear that the plan would not be realized and that, should this be the case, only "suicide, self-immolation remained as an acceptable alternative" (115) for the modern Jew.

All of these competing tendencies can be seen in Zangwill's story "Noah's Ark," which was first published in 1899. Zangwill imagines the fate of a German Jew who decides to take Noah up on his call to settle Ararat. Peloni (the name is the Hebrew equivalent of "so-and-so") is a maskil and Hebrew poet living in Frankfurt. (The character is not the only Hebrew poet in Zangwill's corpus: the "neo-Hebrew poet" Melchitsedek in *Children of the Ghetto* was famously modeled on Naphtali Hertz Imber. Zangwill seems to nod to the Hebrew poets who imagined the Jewish national revival in advance of much of the actual politics.) We first find Peloni loitering in the cemetery, an appropriate location for a Jew who feels there is no viable path in modernity. Disillusioned with the possibility of emancipation because of rising anti-Semitism—he has just been attacked in the street—Peloni soon finds Noah's proclamation posted on the synagogue door and, despite the derision of the other Jews, is captivated by the idea of Ararat. Disgusted by the passivity of his fellow Jews, he sets out for America, where he is entrusted by Noah with the task of planting a flag on Grand Island and waiting there to greet arriving Jews.

Given Zangwill's later career as a proponent of Territorialism (the advocacy of a Jewish state somewhere other than in the Land of Israel), it is certainly tempting to read this story as a foreshadowing of the Territorial-ist position. Indeed, when examining literary representations of Mordecai Noah and his Ararat plan, we must in each case determine to what extent the author is using Noah's project as a metaphor for Zionism, in which case Ararat is a figure for the Land of Israel, and to what extent the treatment is meant to be taken more narrowly as a commentary on the fate of Jew-ish nationalism outside of Palestine—keeping in mind that most authors indicate a combination of the two possibilities. In the case of Zangwill's story, although he would later be associated with Territorialism, we would do best not to insist on the more literal geography. Here, Zangwill's Ararat project is clearly a metaphor for Herzl's Zionism, and in fact, Zangwill's Noah is a figure for Herzl himself. This comparison was probably irre-sistible given the similarities between these two historical figures—both assimilated Jews, both journalists, both playwrights, both visionaries, both impresarios—and Zangwill (who shared some of the same traits) would not be the last to link them.

In this story, the comparison is not terribly flattering: Zangwill's Noah is self-regarding, vain, cocksure, and more interested in the theatrics of the plan than in the practicalities and work that might ensure its success. In short, Zangwill's Noah represents everything that both fascinated and worried Zangwill about Herzl. Yet although the Herzl/Noah portrait is somewhat critical, "Noah's Ark" does not reduce to a simple critique of Zionist politics. As Udelson notes, the story expresses Zangwill's attraction to Herzlian Zionism, along with his fear that if the plan should fail, there could be no viable Jewish future. It is a story of desperate hopefulness, or optimistic despair.

Zangwill presents Ararat not as an unworkable folly but as a plan that might very well have succeeded had numbers of Jews been willing to follow Peloni in heeding Noah's call. The backwater settlement of Buffalo, Zang-will reflects ruefully, will grow into a thriving town because of the initia-tive of its citizens; yet Grand Island remains unpopulated by any Jews save Peloni, who waits for months alone in the wilderness with his flag (which has seven stars, just like Herzl's initial proposal for the flag of the Jewish State). Niagara Falls, erroneously placed next to Noah's island just as How-ells had done, shifts in its symbolism from a promise of renewed Jewish vitality ("Force, Life, Strength, that was what Israel needed" [Zangwill 1938, 116]) to an indifferent fate that the Jews are powerless to resist: "[t]he very rainbows on the leaping mist were now only reminders of the biblical promise that the world would go on forever; forever the wheel would turn, and Israel would wander homeless" (118).

Zangwill's anguished consideration of the possible demise of the Jewish people links the Jews with the figure of the Indian, an oft-repeated comparison in American Hebrew literature, as we saw in chapter 3. At the end of Zangwill's story, the long-waiting Peloni finally receives a message from Noah that he has abandoned the Ararat plan. Noah now hopes for an even more unlikely Jewish restoration in Palestine, to be achieved through the outcome of imperial power struggles among Britain, Russia, and the Ottomans—in other words, contemporary political Zionism. Peloni, who has no hopes for Noah's new scheme, comes to the conclusion that the Jews have simply lost their will to live.

Peloni looks up to find the Iroquois chief Red Jacket standing before him. In fact, the Seneca chief of that name attended the real Noah's Ararat inauguration in Buffalo, but apparently he declined the invitation to join the Jewish city of refuge. In Zangwill's story, the Jewish immigrant and the Native American chieftain, "the puny, stooping scholar from the German Ghetto, and the stalwart, kingly savage" (121) converse, and Peloni realizes that Jews are like this other vanishing race. They "were indeed brothers: the Jew who stood for the world that could not be born again, and the Red Indian who stood for the world that must pass away. Yes, they were both doomed." Appropriately, then, Peloni dies in the Romantic fashion of the doomed Indian, throwing himself over the Falls. The cornerstone of Ararat, lying forgotten in the Buffalo Historical Society, is therefore not only the marker of Noah's failed project for Jewish political restoration but also "the gravestone of Peloni" (123).

Zangwill's story is an allegory for the hopes and fears connected with contemporary Zionism. Its interest in America is only inadvertent and metaphorical. By contrast, the other English-language endeavor of that time to feature Noah treats him in a purely American context, with only a passing reference to Jewish nationalism. The Noah of Alfred Henry Lewis's 1902 bestselling novel *Peggy O'Neal* is quite surprising. A Cleveland-born newspaperman and western ranch hand turned New York muckraker, Lewis was already the author of a successful series of Westerns when, responding to the turn-of-the-century demand for historical fiction, he produced this melodramatic page-turner.[3]

Basing his novel on the Eaton Affair, a scandal of the 1820s that had an impact on the presidency of Andrew Jackson, Lewis departs considerably from strict historical accuracy. Indeed, the very inclusion of Noah as a major character is striking, as Noah had nothing remotely significant to do with the Eaton Affair.[4] Nevertheless, in Lewis's novel, Noah is not only one of the central characters but also perhaps its most impressive. Whereas the Indians, Mexicans, and blacks of Lewis's Western novels are drawn with the racist condescension typical of the time, the Jewish Noah of *Peggy O'Neal* is exceptionally heroic, self-effacing, and capable. Though in reality, Noah was at that point in his life well on his way to becoming a portly family man, Lewis's Noah appears in the novel as a kind of early nineteenth-century James Bond: suave, quick-thinking, deadly with a sword. He exhibits the manly valor and willingness to shed blood when necessary that Lewis admired in Andrew Jackson and, one presumes, in Teddy Roosevelt in his own day. As the narrator observes (in the pseudo early-nineteenth-century diction used in the novel):

> Noah was of culture and quiet penetration; withal cunning and fertile to a degree. Also I found his courage to be the steadiest; he would fight with slight reason, and had in a duel some twenty years before, with the first fire, killed one Cantor, a flamboyant person—the world might well spare him—on the Charleston racetrack, respectably and at ten paces. (A. Lewis 1903, 72)

Elsewhere, Noah is referred to as "our cool gentleman of the red hair, the jet eyes, and the sharp Spanish swords" (341). As President Jackson says in the novel, "to me he is the man remarkable; fine, high, yet bold and quick, there will be no one to take his place when he is gone" (460).

---

3. For a biography of Lewis, see Ravitz (1978).

4. On the Eaton Affair, see Burstein (2003).

Lewis's Noah is not at all ashamed of his Jewishness. When an anti-Semite disparages him as a "Jackson Jew," he responds witheringly, "Jew, yes! My ancestors were poets, lawgivers—they read the stars, and collected the wisdom and learning of the world, when the slant-skulled fore-fathers of [some] I might indicate went clothed of sheepskin and club, ate their meat raw, and saved their fire to pray to" (109). And in the duel that follows, before which Noah learns that his opponent is one of the finest swordsmen in the state of Maryland, Noah professionally dissects his opponent's arm—"split it like a mackerel!" (131)—without breaking a sweat.

Yet nowhere in the novel is there the slightest mention of Ararat. Lewis's is a strikingly non-Zionist Noah. There is only one reference, speculative and in passing, to Jewish nationalism when the narrator muses that Noah, a descendant of David (both have red hair), "would be a present King of the Jews were it not that the latter owned neither country nor home" (72).

On the contrary, Noah is consistently used to emphasize the superlative American patriotism and loyalty of Jews. When the anti-Semite just mentioned says that he would like to expel every Jew from the United States, Noah returns, "[t]he Jew is as much the American as you. My father fought for this country; I have fought for it; the Jews found and gave one-third of that money which won the Revolution" (109). And it is not only Noah who makes the case for Jews as loyal and upright American citizens; the non-Jewish characters do so as well. "Your Jew makes a stout patriot," affirms the narrator, "I could want no better American than a Jew" (408). Writing in the midst of the greatest period of Jewish mass migration from Eastern Europe, Lewis affirms the Americanness and honor of Jews while leaving aside consideration of Jewish nationalism.

The first literary author to put Noah into Hebrew was Harry Sackler, who dramatized the Ararat plan in his play *Mashiah nosah Amerikah* (Messiah, American style) and whose novel *Bein erets veshamayim* we discussed in the preceding chapter. Sackler's Noah, like Zangwill's, has everything to do with the projects and pitfalls of Jewish nationalism. Yet the Jewish nationalism of Sackler's Noah is presented as profoundly American. Sackler's is an attempt to resolve the tensions between American and Jewish national identities, an approach in keeping with the author's personality and career. Although deeply devoted to Zionism and Jewish causes, Sackler's Zionism very much reflected the emerging American Zionism of philanthropic solicitude for the Jewish people rather than dedication to a specific political theory.

Nor was he a purist when it came to the linguistic debates and camps of his day. Indeed, as did very few other figures (Judd Teller comes to mind), Sackler moved with some success between the worlds of Hebrew, Yiddish, and English in the course of his long career as a writer and community leader. Though he was perhaps most committed to Hebrew, seeing to it that all his significant works were translated (usually by himself) into that language, his most public successes were in Yiddish, and he refused to foreswear or denigrate any of the three languages. Involved throughout his life in American Hebrew literature and culture, his status as a Hebraist in good standing was questioned by partisans of that language, just as he was never entirely accepted by Yiddishists as an ideologically loyal Yiddish writer. Speaking of the mutual suspicion between the Hebraist and Yiddishist camps, he explains: "I was innocently dragged along after both languages and both literatures at the same time. Ancient tradition and culture and new hope on the one hand; vitality and popular expression and utility for millions on the other" (Sackler 1966b, 26).

Sackler had been writing poems and stories in Hebrew since the age of fourteen, but he made his debut in print in Yiddish in a 1907 issue of the *Forward,* and in the 1910s he served as an editor for Yiddish publications such as *Dos Idishe Folk* and the *Morgen Zhornal.* By the 1920s, Sackler's Yiddish plays were being performed to acclaim throughout the Yiddish-speaking world, from New York and Chicago to Warsaw and Buenos Aires. He worked with such figures Morris Schwartz and Paul Muni, and his play *Yisker* was made into a silent film directed by Sidney Goldin and released in 1925 in both Europe and America.

At no point, however, did Sackler cease his literary production in Hebrew, though this never won him the popularity of his Yiddish work. He was active on the staff of *Hatoren,* and in 1920 he visited Palestine as a correspondent for both *Hatoren* and the Yiddish *Der Tog.* His Hebrew publications appeared in journals such as *Hadror, Shibolim, Luah Ahiever, Hatoren,* and *Hadoar,* and the Hebrew versions of his plays (several were written originally in Hebrew, some were self-translated from Yiddish or English) were also performed by amateur and small Hebrew troupes. In addition, he published works in English, including the novel *Festival at Meron.*

Typically, then, Sackler's play about Noah was first written and performed in Yiddish under the title *Mayor Noach* (Major Noah), and only later was it translated by the author into Hebrew, a Hebrew that often reads syntactically as a comfortably colloquial English or Yiddish. The Yiddish original appeared in print in 1928 in the author's collected Yiddish plays and had its stage premier in 1929 at Morris Schwartz's esteemed Yidishe Kunst-Teater. Schwartz played the title role. The production won positive reviews, with the notable exception of Abraham Cahan who, in a dyspeptic review in the *Forward,* argued that the play was mere historical research, lacking in dramatic tension (Cahan 1929).

By contrast, the critic Shmuel Niger and the poet Aaron Glants-Leyeles, both writing in *Der Tog,* found the historical dimension to be precisely part of the play's attraction. Niger in particular judged the play to be "an achievement in the world of Yiddish drama" (Niger 1929) and maintained that introducing his audience to the figure of Noah was not the least of Sackler's merits. Niger urged people to see the play in order to learn about this forgotten episode in American and Jewish history, an episode that showed that the modern Jewish national idea had surprising roots in the United States. By this, he meant not only that Herzl had been preceded by an American Jew but also that the very idea of a Jewish state had something particularly American about it in its audacity, bold pragmatism, and ecumenical faith. Noah is superlatively American in his boundless energy, determination, and optimism, and the United States—rather than nineteenth-century European nationalism—is the true model for the idea of the Jewish State. "Hadn't Noah all but seen with his own eyes how states had arisen from colonies," Niger writes, "how scattered settlements had begun to grow into a world power?" Sackler's play suggested to Niger that it was not simply oppression and persecution that drove Jews to messianic and redemptive projects. Freedom and relative integration, such as Noah had known in the United States, could equally inspire such efforts. In short, as Glants-Leyeles writes, Sackler had written "a truly Jewish-American play" (Glants-Leyeles 1929).

Sackler must have appreciated such responses: he took the title of Niger's review—"Messiah, American Style"—for the title of his Hebrew version of the play. Indeed, throughout the play, Sackler links Noah's proto-Zionism with an American combination of initiative, bluff, will, and dynamism. Of course, some of the chutzpah in Sackler's portrait of Noah is not confined to an American context, but plays instead on the same comparison with Herzl seen in Zangwill's story. That is, Sackler, a dramaturge-activist like Zangwill and Herzl and Noah, makes sure to emphasize the theatricality inherent in prestate Zionism, the way that the Jewish State was an act of imagination, an illusion becoming reality, a spectacle. "Tonight, my friend, you will see a wondrous production" (Sackler 1943, 298) says Noah to one of his companions—an old theater comrade, in fact—on the evening he announces the Ararat plan. "Your performance, Noah, goes well," admits another character on the day of Ararat's public dedication. "You are an expert at the creation of theatrical effects" (318). Indeed, Sackler later noted in his memoirs that some who had seen the play had been surprised to find such a de-idealized character—Noah is sympathetic, dynamic and good-natured, but not free of ego and self-promotion—used to symbolize Zionist leadership.

Even more notable is the ecumenical emphasis of the play. It is the Christian character Van Doren—who knows Hebrew and is knowledge-able about the Bible—who first supports the idea of a Jewish state, even when the Jewish characters still consider the idea to be a joke. "President of a Jewish republic," laughs one of Noah's Jewish companions when the idea is proposed that Noah might be leader of such a state. "Where? In Jerusalem?" "What is the meaning of this mockery, my Jewish friends?" responds Van Doren: "Why not?" (283).[5] Sackler similarly emphasizes the Christian faith of Samuel Leggett, Noah's real estate partner in the effort to acquire land for Ararat. The fullest expression of this ecumenical impulse

5. Van Doren is also the name of a character in Sackler's novel *Bein erets veshamayim* who is an impassioned Zionist and who joins the Jewish Brigade to fight in Palestine during the First World War. In the course of the novel, Van Doren and Avner have an admiring conversation about Mordecai Manuel Noah, whom they both recognize as an American precursor to the Zionist project (Sackler 1964, 390).

is seen in the striking tableau Noah (and Sackler) creates in the second act, when Noah consecrates himself to the Ararat plan by gathering together a Jew ("a symbol of the people Israel"), an Indian ("the symbol of freedom"), and a Christian ("symbol and model of what Christianity strives to be"), in what Noah calls a "holy covenant" (301)—and which takes place under a Jewish prayer shawl and with the help of the Reverend Addison Searle of the Episcopal Church of Buffalo:

> NOAH: Help me, Searle. (He and Searle spread the *talit* and wrap the three; in a ceremonial chanting) In the name of the God of the Universe, glorious God who created Man in His image, I proclaim the unity of all mankind in freedom, in noble striving, in mutual love and friendship!
>
> SEARLE: Forever and ever, amen!
>
> THE OTHERS: Amen! Amen! (Sackler 1943, 301)

Moreover, Noah's main antagonist in the play is a rabbi who is as opposed to the ecumenism of Noah's plan as he is to its proto-Zionism. Noah's opponents also include the elite of the Jewish community, who are reluctant to jeopardize their position in America by promoting Noah's scheme. However, it is Rabbi Peixotto who, until the final scene of the play, is Noah's chief opponent. Outraged by the pseudo-messianic heresy that is implicit in Noah's attempt to hasten redemption, Peixotto symbolizes the traditionalist opposition that would emerge against Zionism in Herzl's time. (Peixotto is not entirely unsympathetic, however; Sackler was not dismissive of traditional Judaism, and his play does consider critically the pretensions of the Zionist leadership in his own day.) Yet Peixotto also fills the role, well known in Yiddish and American ethnic melodrama, of the Old World traditionalist who tries to thwart the aspirations of the young American generation. In Sackler's play, Noah holds the inaugural ceremony for Ararat in the Episcopal Church of Buffalo not only because of the problems transporting all the participants and spectators to Grand Island (as it happened in real life) but also because this is a way of excluding Rabbi Peixotto, who had planned to disrupt the ceremony but cannot bring himself to enter a church. Act 3 ends with telling symbolism as a procession of soldiers, freemasons, notables, and Indians all march to the

church, accompanied by peals of cannon fire. When Noah's Christian partner Leggett cries, "[t]he great republic of the United States blesses Ararat!"
the rabbi holds his hands over his ears and laments, "[w]oe is me! Woe is
me! To a Christian church he leads them!" (318).

Sackler's play is an attempt to harmonize Jewish national aspirations
with American ecumenism and patriotism. Such harmonization is reflected
not only in the content but also in the genre. The play is not solely a historical drama but a comedy of errors. In Sackler's play, the Ararat plan
functions as a melodramatic device in Noah's relationship with his sweetheart, Esther Jackson, first dividing them, then uniting them when Esther
works to help Noah achieve his goals. In real life, Noah did not marry
until years after the Ararat episode, and Sackler has also changed Noah's
wife's name from Rebecca to Esther, presumably to pair an Esther with a
Mordecai and so lend a touch of *Purimspiel* to the play. As Sackler imagines it, moreover, the role of Esther is also clearly that of an emancipated,
free-spirited, American-born woman who can more than hold her own
with men. When holding a pistol, she brags that she has "never missed a
target at ten paces" (317).

The play ends, as comedies do, with their intention to marry, and the
final curtain falls on their kiss, a resolution intended to satisfy all parties.
Rabbi Peixotto, who comes across as not such a bad type after all, is assured
that with a wife by his side, Noah will be less inclined to pursue dangerous
schemes, while Noah vows that on the contrary, together with his new wife
he will continue working for the Jewish nation. Together, vows Noah, they
"will build a Jewish house" (or "a Hebrew house," in the Hebrew version),
and Esther agrees: "from our house Mordecai will begin anew his work of
building the house of the Jewish People" (330). This conclusion therefore
attempts to fuse the Zionist-historical and American-comedic plotlines,
celebrating the Noah/Jackson household as a renewed starting point for
Jewish nationalist projects. The happy American couple can fight together
for the Jewish future. Good Americans can be good Jewish nationalists.

Of course, the historical Noah had to contend with a significant
amount of anti-Semitism in his career. His political opponents were never
above trying to use his Jewishness against him. Sackler's play notes that
Noah's Jewishness was cited as a reason for removing him from his post as

US consul in Tunis.[6] Other tensions between Americanness and Jewishness show up occasionally in the play, as when Noah begins a speech to a group of Jews about the Ararat plan but is interrupted:

> HART: Excuse me, my dear Noah. When you speak of 'our people,' to
> whom are you referring? To the Jews? To the Americans?
> NOAH: *Our* people, mister Hart! The Jewish people. (Sackler 1943, 295)

Yet such are rare exceptions to the dominant mode of the play, in which Sackler articulates a particularly American kind of Jewish nationalism that is faithful to both American integration and Jewish national pride and is largely untroubled by the tensions between them—in short, the easygoing Zionism that would become the primary form among American Jews.

It was, tellingly, a review in the Hebrew *Hadoar* that questioned whether Sackler's apparent resolution of such tensions—comedic versus historical, integrationist versus nationalist—was not illusory. "At the end," writes the reviewer, "when the matter is settled through the marriage of Noah to Esther Jackson, everyone—both the actors and the audience—appeared to be fully satisfied with the outcome, with no regret on our part at the abandonment of the plan" (Wiener 1929, 292). This was, the reviewer continues, a "poor indication for the actors" who, it is implied, might have been able to convey a greater degree of ambivalence and contradiction. For the Hebrew critic, the happy ending, the synthesis of Americanism and Jewish nationalism, was too successful and therefore untrue.

This would certainly have been the opinion of Yohanan Twersky (1900–67, in the United States 1926–47). Sackler hoped that one could maintain one's Jewish and American national commitments with no irresoluble tensions. By contrast, Twersky, as the title of his 1954 historical novel *Eifo erets Ararat?* (Where is Ararat?) indicates, insisted that the Jew must decide where his genuine homeland is. It cannot be both Zion and America; one constitutes an abandonment of the other. Twersky's novel is therefore about

---

6. See Sarna (1981) for a judicious analysis of the role anti-Semitism did and did not play in this episode.

the unavoidable need to make that choice, on a personal and a national level. Despite his considerable attraction to American culture and American possibilities and the striking extent (greater even than Sackler) to which Twersky Americanizes the origins of Noah's Jewish nationalist project, the author answers the title's question definitively. The homeland of the Jews is not in the United States but in the Land of Israel, a perspective that Twersky himself embodied when, after living for two decades in Boston, he immigrated to Israel.[7]

As Gershon Shaked has noted, Twersky's historical fictions (he wrote a dozen such novels on subjects ranging from Rashi to Ahad Ha'am) are less attempts to recreate the past than ideological (Zionist) commentaries upon the present, structured around sentimental-melodramatic plotlines (Shaked 1988, 154). *Eifo erets Ararat?* is no exception. The novel is less concerned with creating an authentic historical atmosphere than it is with pondering the central ideological questions of the novel through any and all historical figures with which Noah might have come in contact—and even some with whom he most assuredly did not. As such, the novel includes internal monologues of Thomas Jefferson and Rahel Varnhagen, possible but extremely improbable encounters between Noah and such historical personages as Joseph Smith and Robert Owen, and anachronisms such as a subplot in which Noah must contend with a rival newspaperman named Greeley—presumably Horace Greeley, who would have been a boy at the time. Moreover, the novel frequently gestures overtly toward the contemporary world, as occurs in a post-Holocaust reflection on one early nineteenth-century German diplomat, about whom Noah thinks, "for all the culture he possesses a darkness rages in his voice—how much hate is in him for anything not his own!" (Twersky 1954, 137). The melodramatic dimension consists primarily of Twersky's addition of an entirely unhistorical romantic plotline in which Noah falls in love with and marries a British Jew named Miriam.

7. Twersky, who in America taught at the Hebrew College of Boston, became an editor at the Dvir publishing house in Israel. For a general overview of his other works of fiction, see Shaked (1988, 3:151–56).

The kaleidoscopic approach of the novel, in which anything and everything become pieces of the puzzle of Jewish destiny, is mirrored by the passivity of its central character, who mainly functions in the novel as psychological-ideological clay molded by the events, forces, and personalities around him. Twersky's Noah is a young idealist, a sensitive soul searching for meaning, for the solutions to his own identity and his people's predicament. Brave and always concerned with fulfilling his personal and communal responsibilities, he nevertheless lacks the vitality of Sackler's Noah and the egotistical drive of Zangwill's character, to say nothing of the martial determination of Lewis's. The historical Noah was a wheeler-dealer, a self-promoter, a man who made things happen and did not go through life—as Twersky's character often does—as the recipient of events. Twersky's Noah is never more insecure and uncomfortable than when he appears at the dedication of Ararat, robed as the Judge of Israel. In short, the real Noah was more of an early nineteenth-century American than Twersky makes him, the Hebrew novelist having instead created a figure who, one guesses, thinks and responds much as Twersky himself might have done in similar situations.

Although the character lacks presence, his ideological journey holds interest. The novel is constituted by the repeated posing of questions: what is the place of the Jew in America? Does America constitute a departure in the history of Diaspora? Is America a true home for the Jew? If not, then where? The novel concludes by demanding the choice of the Land of Israel. Yet this is presented as a difficult and painful choice, made reluctantly at the culmination of a long process. Indeed, with the exception of its final sections, Twersky's novel is saturated with tremendous enthusiasm for the United States. It seems no accident that Twersky translated Tocqueville's *Democracy in America* into Hebrew. America, Twersky seems to argue in the novel, is truly different—different, at least, from Europe. Although it is not devoid of anti-Semitism, America is a noble and often wildly successful experiment in tolerance and inclusiveness, instaurating ideals of liberty, creativity, and security that have so starkly eluded the Old World.

Thomas Jefferson becomes one of the many mouthpieces in the novel for these sentiments, describing how during a sojourn in Europe, he gained an appreciation for the United States:

How I began suddenly to miss this land, her soil, her climate, the equality here, the freedom, her laws, her people, her way of life. By God! How few citizens of my country realize how they have been blessed with blessings unlike those of any other nation or tongue. I must confess that it was only there in Europe that I myself began really to understand what I had understood before only in the abstract. (Twersky 1954, 233)

"Europe is too much immersed in her memories," Jefferson argues to Tonneville, an anti-American French diplomat, whereas in America, "the future is more precious than the past." "Is there no past in America?" Tonneville challenges. Jefferson responds:

"Certainly, monsieur, certainly! In 1776, I proposed that the seal of our nation would show on one side the Israelites in the wilderness—a column of smoke leading them by day and a column of fire by night—and on the other side our Saxon ancestors, from whom we inherited the principles of our government and its forms."

"Does my lord believe that the Americans are a chosen people?"

"Yes, monsieur Tonneville. I believe that this people is chosen by Providence just as the Children of Israel in their time, to give freedom and common sense to the world . . . To be a second land of Canaan for all the refugees from Egypt in our day!" (Twersky 1954, 233–34)

Here, Twersky emphasizes America's freedom from the past, which in the context of the novel implies a freedom from European anti-Semitism. He similarly emphasizes the extent to which America models its sense of national mission and uniqueness on the Jewish nation: a marriage of the Emersonian and the Puritan, in each case with favorable Jewish resonance. In another scene, Noah's future father-in-law is surprised that Noah, a Jew, could be the American ambassador to Tunis. Miriam responds, "[t]hat's the New World, father!" (128). Twersky's Noah visits a Spain in which the Inquisition is still active, but America is a place where he grows up with American naval hero Steven Decatur as a playmate, emphasizing the integration of Jews and non-Jews in the United States. Twersky shows the appreciation that Hebraists felt for America as against Europe, particularly in the aftermath of the Holocaust.

One of the most striking ways in which the novel indicates its Americanness is by tracing the origin of the Ararat plan to that quintessentially New World religion, the Church of Latter-Day Saints. Though some scholars have suggested that Joseph Smith may have been inspired to launch his quest for an American Zion by the example of Mordecai Noah, whose Ararat plan Smith would have heard about growing up in upstate New York, Twersky reverses the direction of this influence, having Noah derive his Ararat idea from Smith. Although the idea of a Jewish state or place of refuge is foreshadowed throughout the novel, Noah first articulates the Ararat plan following a chance encounter with fifteen-year-old Smith. Smith tells Noah that he converses with God, Jesus, and the prophet Mormon, and he prophecies his own discovery of the golden tablets of Mormon scripture. Noah, who in real life condemned the persecution of Mormons, here cautions the boy that people will attack him for his outlandish ideas, but Smith responds determinedly, "[p]erhaps they will. But America is large, and in time we will find a place to establish a new state . . . our Zion!" (241). "Why not establish a state-settlement for [the Jews] here in America?" (242) thinks Noah afterwards, deciding to undertake the plan. Twersky performs a neat trick in this historical genealogy, connecting Noah's Jewish national idea with an American source, yet a source that is, in turn, inspired by the example of Jewish national destiny—similar to Twersky's reference, noted earlier, to the proposed seal of the United States that showed the biblical Exodus, linking the American and Jewish nations.

And yet, although the Mormon project of creating a Zion in America may be successful, Twersky's novel is unambiguous in its conviction that the Ararat project is a failure, that the Jewish national idea can only be realized in the Land of Israel. Even during the height of his enthusiasm for the plan, Twersky's Noah is insistent that his American colony is only a temporary "refuge" (247), a necessary preparation for the long-term goal of returning to Zion. Given the enthusiasm and appreciation for America manifest in the novel, how does Twersky justify his rejection of it?

There are two main rationales for this rejection, both of which come to the fore in the final quarter of the novel and comprise some of the novel's most anachronistic registers, clear intrusions of twentieth-century perspectives into the early nineteenth century. The first such rationale is the concern that America will fail to live up to its ideals, the main manifestations of this failure being slavery and racism. This is ironic as the historical Noah, though often sympathetic to persecuted groups, became a staunch supporter of Southern slavery toward the end of his life. In Twersky's novel, however, he is presented as particularly concerned about the treatment of blacks.[8] And throughout the novel, Twersky questions America's ability to realize its ideals given its entanglement in race hatred. Almost immediately after Jefferson delivers the previously cited speech about American exceptionalism, he learns that his own nephew has murdered a black slave. The news horrifies him and causes him to question the entire American project: "[h]e believed so much in America, in the equality that existed here . . . and his own flesh and blood—a murderer of negroes!" (237). This concern over the poison of racism raises the possibility that, ultimately, America is not different from Europe and that anti-Semitism will flourish in the New World as it has in the old. In his sorrow, Jefferson remembers the correspondence he once had with Noah concerning the place of the Jews in America, and now he doubts his own earlier confidence in American enlightenment liberalism as a solution to the problems of the Jews. Is America really different, he wonders? The Inquisition, reflects Jefferson, "is also here, in the New World, the land of tomorrow. Here too glowers the thirst for revenge, awaiting a slogan and a leader. Especially in the south" (237). Jefferson's gloomy meditations clearly anticipate the Civil War, but they also indicate to what extent Twersky's novel reflects the author's mid-twentieth-century perspective on America. At the dawn of the US civil rights struggle, Twersky wonders what the outcome will be. And in the wake of the Holocaust, he wonders if "enlightenment alone is sufficient" (238) to withstand the poisonous hatreds that have dominated Europe and to make the United States an enduring exception to Jewish Diaspora experience.

8. In Alfred Henry Lewis's *Peggy O'Neal*, Noah is similarly emphatic that "slavery should be stricken down" (A. Lewis 1903, 457). Lewis and Twersky both seem to have associated Noah with the progressive and liberal currents, respectively, in their own day. For a treatment of Noah's later views on slavery and Southern states' rights, see Sarna (1981, esp. 108–14).

However, the threat of anti-Semitism in the United States is not the primary novelistic rationale for the rejection of America. Twersky is too convinced of America's crucial differences from Europe to base his rejection on such fears. "And will they slander us here too, and say that we poison wells?" asks Noah. "No," he affirms: "there is also a different America that, like Benjamin Franklin, seeks to pull lightning from the heavens and the rod from the tyrant's hand" (218). In the end, Twersky's most serious concern with America is not persecution but assimilation, not that enlightenment will fail in America but that it will succeed all too well. America is a melting pot, Twersky's Noah observes. It "swallows the uniqueness of peoples and turns them all into one new people" (296). And therefore, as he proclaims at the novel's conclusion, it must be rejected despite the indisputable physical security it offers:

> I am certain: in the shade of the American flag millions of our kinsmen will find safety, yet we must not look for our messiah here, but rather in the land that is ours, the land given us as our portion of the world, and which we cannot lose without our people also losing its hopes to live as a people among peoples! (Twersky 1954, 296)

Noah's Zionist argument is not that America will persecute its Jews but that a full Jewish national life cannot be lived in Diaspora: "[n]o, in America our people will not rise to its full humanity. Only in the land of our fathers can it dare to be what it truly is" (297).

Twersky reinforces these ideological conclusions with a series of abrupt and anachronistic introductions of twentieth-century American Jewish sociology into the novel, especially the figure of an integrationist Reform rabbi, who presides over a materialistic and desultory bar mitzvah celebration apparently intended to show the hollowness of American Judaism. Unlike Sackler's Rabbi Peixotto, Twersky's Rabbi Morgenstern (also the name of one of the most influential Reform rabbis during the period Twersky lived in the United States) does not oppose the Ararat plan on traditionalist grounds but on Americanist grounds. The plan, he argues, threatens all the benefits of American integration, offering Jews not "a state of our own, but a new ghetto" (264). In a speech that is clearly meant to take on dark irony in the wake of the Holocaust, Morgenstern argues that the

Jewish future will be secure only if based on an Enlightenment integration-ist outlook and that Noah's nationalism is a dangerous atavism, soon to be forgotten. And yet the bar mitzvah boy, Sidney, rebels against his bar mitzvah lessons and is dismissive of Judaism and his immigrant tutors. He is clearly a figure for the assimilation of the American-born generation, much like Caspar in Sackler's novel *Bein erets veshamayim*, discussed ear-lier. And the anachronisms in Twersky's novel multiply: Jewish immigrants from Eastern Europe, an Americanized and nouveau riche Jewish woman obsessed with her mink coats, the American-born child disdainful of the immigrant "greenhorn" (272).

As we see, Twersky's novel is not, ultimately, a meditation on Mordecai Noah and Jewish life in early nineteenth-century America but on Jewish life in mid-twentieth-century America. The novel answers the question of why Twersky himself would leave the United States in 1947, at the begin-ning of America's great postwar affluence, and move to the beleaguered Jewish protostate in Palestine. To answer this question, Twersky portrays an American Jewry that is more or less physically secure and financially prosperous but spiritually shallow and complacent, unwilling to consider the fragility of Enlightenment liberalism as a guarantor of Jewish security or its inadequacy as a guarantor of Jewish national vitality.

Sackler and Twersky come to opposite conclusions about the consequences of Jewish national commitment for American Jews. Yet for all their differ-ences, they speak the same language, both literally and ideologically. Both writers assume the need for a thriving national dimension to Jewish iden-tity that is distinct from American identity, even if it is (at best) complemen-tary or (at worst) contradictory to it. Both see the Jewish national revival in Palestine as, if not the culmination of Jewish history (as in the case of Twersky), then at the very least a central concern (as in the case of Sackler).

In the case of the two most recent imaginative explorations of Noah and his Ararat plan, the authors are worlds apart, not only in terms of lan-guage—one writes in English, the other in Hebrew—but in their basic stance toward Jewish identity and the significance of Noah for it. Both authors explore the archeology, fault lines, and nature of Jewish identity, but they are little in agreement as to what this identity is or whether it even exists.

Ben Katchor's graphic novel *The Jew of New York* (1998; first serialized in the English-language newspaper *Forward* in the early 1990s) is a meditation on American Jewish identity, set in 1830 following the Ararat episode. Noah is not one of the novel's main protagonists; instead, he makes appearances throughout as a background figure, yet he is central in that his presence helps to tie together the story's loosely, often accidentally related strands. Like Zangwill and Twersky before him, Katchor imagines Jews who come to settle in Ararat, only to be disappointed when the plan is not realized. Unlike these Zionist writers, however, Katchor is enchanted with marginal Jewishness, with Jewishness as marginality, obscurity, the faint traces of immigrant Jewishness discernible at the margins of mainstream culture or blended almost indistinguishably into its center. He displays this affection for a kind of esoteric archeology of vanishing ethnic Jewishness in his "Julius Knipl" comic strips, which have appeared in the *Forward* and other newspapers and are devoted to a subterranean history of the denizens of New York's Garment District and other aging Willy Loman-like figures, mining the blandest of urban landscapes for mystic significance in a manner that recalls the essays of Walter Benjamin. These strips have been justly praised for capturing a certain poignant lugubriousness that seems (at least to many of us who do not work in manufacturing or sales) to attach to obscure and mundane physical objects such as newspaper weights, paper placemats, flagpole ornaments, ball bearings—and their salesmen—moldering quietly throughout the aging eastern cities of the United States. Katchor himself is a red diaper baby—his father was a Jewish communist from Warsaw—and he has made out very well indeed for a comic book artist. He has been lionized by the the *New York Times* and the *New Yorker,* is the recipient of Guggenheim and MacArthur "Genius" Grants, and has even been the subject of a documentary film.[9]

The vision of American Jewish identity that is discernible in the "Julius Knipl" strips is thrown into sharper focus in Katchor's Noah book, which shows and even seems to celebrate the centrifugal forces pulling Jews away from organized community and traditional observance into the wilder,

---

9. For a profile of Katchor, see Wechsler (1993).

more hybrid domain of American society, whether in the city or on the frontier. The main thrust of Katchor's book is to cast doubt on all "authentic" or "original" forms of Jewish identity and, by extension, to render suspect forms of Jewish community or belonging that depend on rigid boundaries and definitions of what is and is not Jewish. This happens in myriad ways throughout the novel: discussions of the importance of Jewish continuity take place over oysters, and kabbalistic diagrams inspire French fabric patterns of haute couture. Interconnected with this unraveling of origin and authenticity are the running themes of mistaken identity, deceit, and masking—the multiple gaps between representation and reality. *The Jew of New York* commences, therefore, with the preproduction of a play titled "The Jew of New York," which is a grotesque and anti-Semitic satire of Mordecai Manuel Noah, presented in the play as a decrepit Shylock with a "ghetto stoop" (4)—all of which announces these themes of theatricality, representation, stereotypes, and authenticity, in connection with Jewish identity. Similarly, in the opening pages, another Jewish character, Nathan Kishon, is found sprawled out under a bedsheet in a town square and mistaken for "a naked Indian" (3) by the trader Isaac Azarael, reminding Azarael, in turn, of a lecture he once heard claiming that American Indians are members of the Lost Tribes. Again, mistaken identity and dubious origins are the touchstone. Kishon, meanwhile, continues the themes of the authentic versus the bogus: we discover that he is a Jewish ritual slaughterer, found guilty of passing off nonkosher meat as ritually proper.

In one of the most representative episodes, which occurs midway into the book, the authenticity of both Holy Land and American origins are exploded. The arrival in New York of Enoch Letushim, a messenger selling soil from the Holy Land, produces a seven-panel sequence of scenes from "the crooked streets of Jerusalem and its environs . . . where unscrupulous guides" (47) point out to "credulous pilgrims" where the various events of the biblical narratives occurred. "All these places are described as the true and genuine places where the events actually took place in the times referred to," says the narrator, quoting Chateaubriand's early nineteenth-century travel guide to the Holy Land, "though it is well known that even Jerusalem itself does not stand on the same spot of ground which it occupied in the time of Christ." There is, in this view, no way of ever really arriving at the "true" City of David, let alone other sites, and those who think they do are simply allowing themselves to be gulled. Yet Letushim is curious to know whether, by contrast, an authoritative history of American places can be determined, and so he turns to a Native American whom he sees in a hotel lobby to ask what stood on the site of the hotel before the arrival of the whites. "I've only been here a few days," apologizes the Indian, "I come from Buffalo" (49). No voice of native truth is to be found here. In fact, Letushim discovers that this Indian is in cahoots with an itinerant Jewish Hebrew teacher, and he recites Hebrew prayers, biblical passages, and sabbath hymns to the amazement of paying audiences, who are told that he is "a rare, living member of one of the 10 lost tribes of Israel . . . rescued from the wilds of upper New York state." Not only is the Holy Land a fake and a scam, then; aboriginal America is, too.

There is apparently not much sympathy here for fixed or supposedly authentic forms of identity. It is not only that we encounter no authentic or stable identity that is not revealed to be a mask or misunderstanding. We also hear the most forthright plea for clearly defined categories of authentic Jewishness from the most anti-Jewish character: Dr. Solidus, the author of the play "The Jew of New York," introduced as "a pamphleteer of anti-Semitic sentiments" (64).[10] Solidus complains, "[h]ere in America, through assimilation and intermarriage, I fear that someday all of these [Jewish] traits will become diffused within the general population—and in that, the real danger lies! There will be no Jews left, as I know them, to write about" (68). It is the anti-Semite, then, who is most upset about the fluidity of Jewish identity, particularly in the United States. Noah, on the other hand, criticizes Solidus's play because of its stock characters, warning the playwright that an American audience will not find these predictable stereotypes believable. The point is elaborated further when Vervel Kunzo, a rather improbable New York fieldworker for the Verein für Kultur und Wissenschaft der Juden, observes that "[t]he Jew is not a museum specimen

---

10. The use of the term "anti-Semite," not coined until the 1870s, is one of the many anachronisms in the book. Katchor does not pretend to be engaged in historiography, describing his work as "the dreams of an amateur historian" (Wechsler 1993, 66).

to be admired on Sunday afternoons. Like all social beings he is subject to constant change and development—a creature of his surroundings" (85).

And indeed, the fate of the one Jew who literally becomes "a museum specimen" seems to be an allegory for the danger of attempting to fix authentic forms of identity rather than acknowledging its inherent randomness and malleability. When Kishon, who wanted to join the Ararat colony, discovers that Noah has made no provision for any settlement, he is taken in by a fur trader named Moishe Ketzelbourd, "a baptised Jew who had lived for so many years in the wild that he no longer maintained any religious affiliation" (11). In many ways, Ketzelbourd is the book's central character in that he epitomizes the Jew beyond identity, the Jew in the American wilderness who becomes increasingly inscrutable and indefinable. As Kishon spends more and more time traveling through the American wilderness with Ketzelbourd, his own traditional Jewish observances erode. Yet at the end of the book, the mentally unstable Ketzelbourd is shot, and because no one knows quite what to make of this bestial woodsman, his body is stuffed and mounted under glass for exhibition. "It is a creature unlike any I have seen before—defies classification!" claims an amateur zoologist (84). Kishon, meanwhile, is "recivilized" by the members of the organized Jewish community, who provide him with proper clothing and an eligible bachelorette for marriage in order to avoid scandal and to reaffirm the boundaries of identity and decorum.

Given such object lessons in the heavy, even murderous hand of identity categories and community boundaries, it is perhaps unsurprising that Katchor's treatment of Noah's Ararat plan is somewhat acid and dismissive and that Zionist and Jewish national themes are either absent or similarly disregarded. Of course, Katchor's vision of early nineteenth-century America as a whole comes across as a rather joyless landscape populated by lonely, obsessive eccentrics—intentions to the contrary are not helped by his relentlessly unlovely, gray-washed panels. Many of the plotlines are faintly whimsical at best and sometimes seem driven primarily by low and leaden humor, as in the case of the kabbalist whose mysticism is based on the transcription of the sounds of eating into English letters and who thereby ascends to the mystical state of *greps* (Yiddish for belch), or the entrepreneur who wants people to invest in his plan to carbonate Lake Erie.

Noah's Ararat is enfolded into these kinds of pointless follies and suspected of being "nothing more than a land speculation scheme" (12). Katchor further imagines the insulted response of the Indians, who reject Noah's invitation to Ararat and who "cannot be subsumed by Major Noah's tribe of Jews" and "understandably expect trickery and deceit" (15). If there is a Jewish national resonance to Katchor's treatment of Noah, it is not a particularly positive one. But, as we have seen, *The Jew of New York* casts doubt on the very existence of a stable or collective Jewish identity, let alone one that might attain a destiny of any grandeur or brightness.

The obscurity into which Noah and his Ararat plan have fallen is a recurring theme in the literary representations of Noah. Katchor, of course, seems to thrive on the experience of oblivion, his comic strips conjuring a secular tradition of urban esoterica to which he assimilates Noah. The narrator of Lewis's *Peggy O'Neal* blames the eclipse of Noah's fame partly on anti-Semitism, concluding that Noah's "modesty, coupled with that vulgar dislike of Jews by ones who might otherwise have named him in the annals of that day, has operated to obscure his name" (A. Lewis 1903, 72). Sackler lays the blame for the failure to preserve Noah's memory on his coreligionists. The third act of Sackler's play opens with the soliloquy of the engraver Seth Chapin as he works to prepare the foundation stone for Ararat:

> They say that the Jews' power of memory is great, and that they remember their friends no less than their enemies. If this is true, then my name will be eternally remembered. Certainly the Jews will not forget the first person to make something concrete for their republic . . . Congratulations, Seth! You've already found your place in the history books! . . . All my life I've carved sweet, little lies to honor the deceased. (Pauses) Can it be that the foundation stone of Ararat is also a sweet, little lie? I wonder! What will history make of the matter? (Sackler 1943, 306)

The irony is clear here, as Noah (let alone the engraver of the Ararat stone) was relegated to the dimmest part of American Jewish memory and the foundation stone itself was forgotten for generations. As Sackler wrote later, when the play was in its Yiddish stage production in New York, "one of the leaders of the Zionist movement in America" approached him during the intermission and "asked me wonderingly if the comedy's protagonist was a historical figure or if I had invented the entire Ararat episode from whole cloth" (1966b, 22). And in Nava Semel's novel *Iyisrael*, one of the characters also reflects on an almost entirely forgotten "half-mad playwright . . . who dreamed up the dizzy idea of establishing a state for the Jews" yet "whose name no one knows today" (265).

In Semel's novel, however, the reference is not to Noah but to Theodor Herzl. In the alternate universe of *Iyisrael*, Herzl has died in obscurity. Noah, on the other hand, successfully established his city of refuge, which in the year 2001 of this alternative timestream has existed successfully both as a Jewish state and a member of the American republic for 176 years. Other authors—Zangwill, Twersky, and Katchor—have imagined what might have happened had one or two Jews actually responded to Noah's call. But no one, not even Katchor, has endeavored novelistically to imagine what Jewish history and Jewish identity might be like today had the persecuted Jews of the world come to live on Grand Island in the state of New York. This is the novelty of Semel's cleverly inventive, thought-provoking, and deeply touching book—her anti-*Altneuland*, as it were.

Semel's novel, the fifth by this prolific writer (also a children's author, journalist, critic, and member of the board of governors of Yad Vashem), is a meditation on Jewish and Israeli identity as they connect with homeland, refuge, and physical and spiritual survival. Like Katchor, Semel also wants to know whether there is such a thing as Jewish identity and what it consists of. Yet the contrast between these two latter-day Noah books could not be greater. Unlike Katchor, Semel is convinced that there is such a thing as Jewish identity and that it is deeply and complexly intertwined with what it means to be Israeli. As one of the non-Jewish characters in the novel asks himself, "[w]hat kind of Jews are these Israelis?" (36). Or, as we might elaborate the question, which Semel does novelistically, would a different history—one without the State of Israel and with a Diasporic yet physically secure, territorial Jewish existence—create a different Jewish people? Is Israeliness therefore an accident, something not intrinsically connected with Jewishness? Would Diaspora itself mean something different under such circumstances? What is the Jewishness that inheres in Israeliness and that can maintain its commonality even in such an alternate history? To begin to answer these questions, Semel conducts an experiment: using her parallel universe as an imaginative control group, as it were, for the Jewish people, she dismantles Israel and Israeli Jewishness in order to see what remains, to discover the common Jewish substrates. Semel's purpose is not didactic, but observational: one does not conclude the novel with a final, articulated definition of Jewishness. Yet neither does her exercise in historical deconstruction seem to me an anti-Zionist exercise in wiping clean the Jewish slate (State). By imagining the absence of Israel—this is the wordplay of the novel's title, which can mean both "Isra-Island" (the name given to Noah's state in the alternative universe) and "not Israel"—Semel approaches more profoundly what her country is and means.

This exercise is the last of a three-part novel. In the first part, which takes place in September 2001 of our own universe, Semel imagines an Israeli descendent of Noah discovering his forebear's title deed to Grand Island and running off to see what is now a bedroom community of Buffalo, New York. The episode allows the non-Jewish police detective, asked by the Israeli consulate to locate their missing citizen, to pose questions about Jews, about Israel, and about Jewish and Israeli identity as he attempts to track down the Israeli. The second part takes place in September 1825, the week before the inauguration ceremony for Ararat. Here, Semel imagines Noah visiting Grand Island in the company of a Native American girl, the last native inhabitant of the island. This middle section is understood to be the pivot of the novel: the decisions of the two characters, Noah and Little Dove, determine whether history arrives at the events of part 1, in our own universe, or part 3, which takes place in September 2001 of this alternate timestream. Similar characters, themes, and situations crop up in all three sections, their variations creating sometimes uncanny effects. Most striking, perhaps, is the focus on Native Americans as Jewish parallels, a motif that returns us to Zangwill's story and to the American Hebraists' implicit comparisons of Jews and Indians. The detective of part 1 is of Native American descent, but he is in flight from his ethnic roots and keeps up a running mental dialogue with his deceased Native American grandmother, who becomes increasingly intertwined in his head with the deceased Jewish father of Noah's Israeli descendent. The second part rests on the encounter between Noah and Little Dove during the course of what is to be her last night on her people's island. And the Jewish state of part 3 is, we discover, a fusion of Jewish and Native American culture, exemplified by the state flag (a Star of David above elm leaves) and bar mitzvah ceremonies modeled on Native American vision quests.

Historically—if that is the word one uses when referring to the alternative history of part 3—the consequences of Noah's success in establishing his Jewish state are enormous. As noted, the State of Israel never came into existence. The Middle East is described by one character as a sleepy and boring region, never in the news. Moreover, according to the logic of the novel, the presence of Noah's Jewish state not only means the nonexistence of Israel, it also means the nonoccurrence of the other major event of modern Jewish history, the Holocaust. Although in this alternate history the Nazis were able to vent their hatred on gypsies, homosexuals, political dissidents, and the disabled, the Jews of Europe were able to leave and come to the United States because they were admitted into the Jewish refuge of Iyisrael. Indeed, Noah's impulse for creating his Jewish refuge is, as Semel indicates in the first two sections of the novel, his quasi-prophetic fear of the Holocaust, about which he has nightmares in part 2, and to which he alludes in the title deed that resurfaces in part 1. Far more than Twersky's or Katchor's books, Semel's novel presents us with a post-Holocaust Noah, his name alluding to the most horrific deluge in Jewish history. The nonoccurrence of the Holocaust in part 3 is at least as central to the logic and effect of the novel—its ability to ponder the nature of modern Jewish identity—as the nonexistence of the State of Israel.

Given these vast historical differences, one is struck by the continuities and similarities that remain. Normalcy continues to elude Jewish existence, which even in its Iyisraeli form is marked by unease, exile, and difference. Noah's utopianism has had considerable success in providing a refuge for Jews, but only on the small space of Grand Island. Anti-Semitism still exists. Violent hatred yet stalks the earth—both the first and third parts of the novel are punctuated by the mass murder of 9/11—and Jews are still seen as outsiders in the world beyond Iyisrael. There is no Arab-Israeli conflict in this alternate universe, yet the Jewish possession of Grand Island, which was formerly Native American territory, is not uncontested either, suggesting that when people refuse to grant refuge to those in need, only hatred can result. Throughout all of this, the question of how the State of Israel is and is not reflected in Iyisrael is constant. Liam Emmanuel, the descendent of Noah in part 1, insists that the differences are fundamental: "in contrast to Grand Island, Liam Emmanuel explained . . . Israel was from the beginning the place of [the Jews'] heart's desire, from which they had been forcibly uprooted" (113). Yet the novel incessantly works over the motif and implications of the refuge—often using the Yiddish term *boydem* (attic), a tiny hiding place—posing the question of whether the State of Israel is also a kind of *boydem* for the Jews. What, Semel asks, is the difference between homeland and refuge, state and *boydem?*

The method of the novel is the intricate working and reworking of its themes, often highlighted by ironic variations of biblical quotations now fit to a world without Zionism and Israel, a world in which refuge and not return—*miklat Zion,* not *shivat Zion*—is the modern Jewish collective call. The three parts are not wholly separate but uncanny repetitions of the same encounters and events in new clothes, reading like a sestina in prose. The novel also has its limitations and flaws. Some characters are drawn either as ciphers or as stereotypes: Native American themes in particular, being so central to the novel, are sometimes deployed with delightful surprise but sometimes with stale convention. Little Dove of part 2, for example, is a recycled Pocahontas, the melancholy but dutiful princess of the dying tribe. And, perhaps intentionally, there is no overt consideration of American Jewry as having positive value or culture in its own right. Instead, American motifs circle around Indians; New York City; Ararat / Grand Island / Iyisrael; and the legacies of oppression, racism, and slavery. If Iyisrael is an opportunity for Semel to consider the absence of Israel, it does not seem to require a consideration of the absence of an American Jewry as we know it today.[11]

11. Interestingly, Semel relates that her career as a fiction writer began when, as a girl, she had the responsibility for accompanying her blind grandfather on walks. Her grandfather, an inveterate anti-Zionist who would have preferred to live in the United States, constantly denigrated anything in Tel Aviv his granddaughter described to him, declaring it less impressive than what he had known in New York City. In response, the young Semel began

Semel's novel is very evidently intended as an imaginative provocation to the Zionist narrative and the Arab-Israeli conflict, a reimagining of what Jewish life might be had the Native (here the American Indian, but acting to some extent as a stand-in for the Palestinian Arab) and the Jew come to more peaceful terms—that is, had the yearning for homeland and refuge been a source not of division but of fusion. Nevertheless, *Iyisrael* implicitly reaffirms the positive significance of Zionism and its achievements. The stakes of the novel rest on how we read the conclusion to the third part, which involves a replay of the 9/11 attack that heartbreakingly closes the first part. Neither ending reduces to ideological allegory, yet both operate through the poignant juxtaposition of individual loss and collective fate. As we leave the grieving lover of the first part in lower Manhattan, adding another "Have you seen . . . ?" flyer to those tragic collages, the surviving member of the couple in part 3 wanders "the shoreline between Jaffa and Gaza" (273)—that is, the space of Israel's absence. This latter *shivah* is Semel's final unraveling of the State of Israel, the elimination of the collective and the national, its territory entirely individual: even the Arab woman who joins in the bereaved lover's Kaddish prayer is absent in the final line. The Land of Israel is now a random shoreline, given meaning only momentarily through the mourning gesture of the character, and—for the reader—the ironic knowledge of what is missing. It may be that I am reimposing on the book precisely the Zionist narrative that Semel has sought to set aside, yet I do not think it accidental that the main difference between the conclusion of part 3 and part 1 in this regard is that part 1 (like part 2) ends with a child in the picture. However hopeful and moving, part 3 offers no such procreative continuation. The alternate reality of part 3, of Noah's Iyisrael, is therefore reflected in this final reduction to the individual without nation, without peoplehood, and without future. And yet this is the nature of alternate histories, which are inherently sad. They posit the stillbirth of the reality we know and haunt us with the extinction of lives that might have been.

---

to embellish and exaggerate the urban wonders of Tel Aviv to her blind grandfather so that what she described might compare more favorably to America. See Lurie (2005).

One evening not long after the establishment of the State of Israel, Harry Sackler recounts in his quirky little story "Major Noah Breaks Out of His Frame," Mordecai Manuel Noah stepped out of the portrait hanging in Sackler's study and began to complain to his fellow dramatist and Jewish activist. Now that the Jewish state had become a reality, Noah felt slighted that his role in launching modern Jewish nationalism was being ignored. Should not this American visionary get some credit for the State of Israel? And Sackler, accused Noah, had helped to undermine Noah's reputation with his play, which focused with excessive levity entirely on the Ararat plan, to the exclusion of Noah's later espousal of a thoroughly Palestino-centric proto-Zionism. He now demanded that Sackler make atonement by writing a new play, rehabilitating Noah in the history of modern Jewish nationalism and producing it in Israel so that all would know "that the seed of political Zionism was sown in New York" (Sackler 1966a, 96).

It would seem that so long as the meaning of the Jewish state, of America and its promise for the Jews, and of Jewish identity itself are in question, Noah will from time to time break out of his frame, rediscovered and reimagined for new times and contexts by new writers. We have seen Howells's Noah, an emblem of the ambivalent power of American romanticism; Zangwill's Noah, a doubtful Herzl and object of desperate Zionist hope; Lewis's Noah, exemplar of the patriotism and excellence of American Jewry. We have seen, in works by Sackler and Twersky, the contradictory impulses of acceptance and rejection exhibited by the American Hebraists toward the Jewish place in the United States. And, in recent years, we have seen Noah and his Ararat plan smoldering among the embers of ethnic consciousness in Katchor's graphic novel and resurrected in Semel's imaginative dismantling of modern Jewish history in order to find the *Ding an sich* of Jewishness and to reaffirm Israel's connection with Jewish and human destiny. Like other Jewish messiah figures from Jesus to Shabbetai Zvi, Noah compels the imagination, yet he does so in an American context all his own.

For Sackler, however, this was not the time to take Noah on the road and thrust him again into Jewish consciousness. Now that the Jewish State was a reality, disappointingly imperfect and unpredictably alive, Sackler decided to remain in the United States. America, he indicated, was indeed a refuge: a refuge for utopians and romantics who preferred to dream of Zion rather than contend with its reality. "Here in America," he replies to Noah, "it is still possible for old Zionists who are not men of action to sit in a quiet corner and preserve the romantic spark hidden in their heart" (97). And with that, Noah resumed his place in the picture on the wall.

6

Coffee and Snowflakes

SHIMON HALKIN AND GABRIEL PREIL
IN THE UNITED STATES

This is America! If it weren't for Jews and Judaism, you couldn't find a
nicer place in the world.

—Shimon Halkin, *Ad mashber* (Until the crash)

IN THE COURSE of the twentieth century, the American refuge provided
a home—sometimes temporary, sometimes permanent—for more than a
dozen significant Hebrew authors, with a number of first-rate talents among
them by any standards. Of them all, Shimon Halkin and Gabriel Preil remain
the two indisputably major figures, and certainly the best known to Hebrew
readers today. And yet in many ways these writers were two of the least typical members of an already quite diverse group. Indeed, in certain respects
their careers constitute a kind of repudiation—in one case ideological, in the
other poetic—of the ethos and project of American Hebraism.

Halkin, though it may surprise readers of my analysis of his role in the
Americanness debate to say so, ultimately rejected the possibility of any significant Hebrew cultural life outside of Israel, taking a fiercely anti-Diaspora
position that flew in the face of the aims and ambitions of the American
Hebraists. For all the pessimism of the Hebraists toward Jewish life in the
United States, Halkin's was perhaps the most extremely negative view of
the future prospects of American Jewry as a whole. Gabriel Preil, on the
other hand, was the poetic rather than the ideological anomaly among the
American Hebraists. He developed a wry, antirhetorical lyric that was quite
at odds with the prevailing literary expectations of his fellow Hebrew poets,

186

who tended to look upon him as a kind of poetic changeling, a modernist imp-child mysteriously placed in the cradle of their traditionalist literature.

Halkin and Preil were as different from each other as they were from the other American Hebraists. Though both were immigrants from Eastern Europe, Halkin grew up in a household in White Russia where the influences of both Haskalah and Habad Hasidism were felt, and Preil spent his childhood in the culturally distinct milieu of Jewish Lithuania. Halkin, the elder by a dozen years, immigrated to America in 1914 at the age of sixteen. Preil arrived in 1922 at the even more impressionable age of eleven. Furthermore, although one would never confuse Halkin's poetry, with its rich lexicon, demanding syntax, Romantic-mystical intensities, and shifting layers of philosophical abstraction and earthly concreteness with that of any of the other American Hebraists, his poetry does remain within the orbit, if in a deeper and more cosmopolitan mode, of literary romanticism. Halkin was a modern, but unlike Preil, as a poet he was not a modernist, confining his avant-gardism to prose fiction. Another quite glaring difference in these two careers is the almost total absence in Preil's output of significant writing in genres other than poetry. Preil produced little criticism, no prose fiction of which I am aware, and relatively little translation outside of his self-translation between Hebrew and Yiddish. At the other end of the spectrum is Halkin's oeuvre, which includes novels, stories, and volumes of criticism—though nothing in Yiddish, which is another significant difference. Indeed, one of Halkin's most enduring literary legacies is the influence he had as a professor of literature at the Hebrew University in Jerusalem, where he trained and inspired a generation of ardently devoted students, including some who would become pivotal figures in Israeli literature and literary criticism, such as A. B. Yehoshua and Dan Miron—all this in contrast to the personal privacy and marginality cultivated by Preil. Finally, whereas Halkin found life as a Jew in America ideologically untenable, Preil lived in the United States for almost half a century before he even visited Israel, and even then he never relocated but continued to think of himself as profoundly American.[1]

---

1. For information on Halkin, see Laor (1978) and Shahevitch and Peri (1975). For information on Preil, see Miron (1993).

Yet in spite of these differences, Halkin and Preil enjoyed an excellent, lifelong relationship. Halkin was the first to read and encourage the younger man's Hebrew poetry. (The great Yiddish writer Jacob Glatshteyn advised Preil on his first efforts in Yiddish.) Preil even credits the critical interest in his poetry to Halkin's professorial influence on his students in Israel. In this chapter I therefore want to offer not only an examination of these two poets, exploring some of the distinctive features of each, but also to pay homage to the friendship between them.

AN UNCONDITIONAL ZIONIST

In his seventy-first year, Shimon Halkin looked back on his dissimilarity to the other American Hebrew poets. "If I was different from them," he reflected, "it was in this one thing: my Zionism was a crueller Zionism than theirs" (S. Halkin 1985, 206). Halkin explains that he realized long before the other American Hebraists that Jews could not "exist as a historical people except in one place, in the Land of Israel" (207). The turning point in his assessment of the future of Judaism in America came, he recalled, as a result of his experiences in the years 1928–29. In 1928 he took a sabbatical from his teaching in the United States and traveled in France and Central and Eastern Europe. He recalled his depression at the widespread assimilation he encountered among the Jews there and claimed he could already sense "the beginning of the physical and spiritual destruction of the people in both Lithuania and Poland" (206). Then, in November of that year, he began his first stay in Israel, which lasted until his return to America in October 1929. "I came, I saw, I was conquered" (207), he said of that first visit. "I could no longer believe at all in the naïve dream of our Hebrew-cultural renaissance in the exile," he said, "above all in America." Halkin became an "unconditional Zionist," as he put it in the title of a late collection of essays drawn from a lifetime's engagement in such issues. His extreme pessimism about Hebrew and Judaism in America made him "unique among [his] fellow writers and educators in the United States" (207).

What Halkin describes as a turning point in the late 1920s was really more of a way station on a road that led, during the 1930s and 1940s, to the complete extinguishing of his hopes for Jewish life in America. This process, consummated with his final emigration from the United States in 1949, was influenced as much by Halkin's consciousness of the horrific fate of European Jewry as it was by his perception of conditions in the United States. In an essay written during his 1929 sojourn in Israel, for example, Halkin still sounds quite positive about the future of American Jewry and, in particular, about the quality of its youth. "Something new and healthy in a national sense has begun to shape itself into being in America these last 10–15 years," he writes, noting the great strides in Jewish education, and even a kind of Jewish revival among young American Jews, that "will bear fruit in the coming years" (14). He offers no guarantees of success, worrying that the minority of active, searching young Jews, while growing, will still be swallowed up in the indifferent, assimilating mass. Yet he does not believe that America should simply be perceived as "the land of Jewish assimilation par excellence" (15) at most "only a warning and an object lesson" of what Jews elsewhere should not do. American Jewry, or part of it, may very well be part of the reawakening of Jewish national consciousness. As late as 1937 Halkin speaks with high regard for the possibilities of Hebrew culture in the United States, offering a generally admiring review of *Niv,* a journal for new Hebrew writing in America that included some of Preil's earliest poems (S. Halkin 1985, 29–31).

On the other hand, we see examples of Halkin's "crueller Zionism" even before his 1928–29 travels. Even in his most positive assessments, Halkin often describes America as cultureless, spiritless, contentless—a possible location for the national revival of the Jewish people, but not a worthwhile influence in and of itself. In 1926 he published a blistering attack on the state of Hebrew culture in America, accusing his fellow Hebraists of lacking national sentiment and complaining that they were becoming coarse, ignorant, self-centered, and possessed by "American ghetto materialism" (S. Halkin 1926b, 115). More damning was the 1933 essay—written, ironically, for the occasion of the anniversary of the founding of *Hadoar*—in which he argued that American Hebraism was based on a "complete lie" (1985, 27). Inasmuch as a national Jewish culture in the Diaspora is successfully inculcated, he wrote, it generates by its very nature a desire to leave Diaspora and go to Israel. Therefore

American Hebrew culture founders on a fatal and insurmountable contradiction: "[t]he paradox of the Hebrew idea in the exile" is that "the
planting hand uproots the plants."

Halkin wrote these words in Israel, where he spent the period from
1932 to 1939 writing, editing, and supporting himself by teaching. During
this time he gave expression to the ambivalent emotions swirling around his
relationship to America and to Israel in one of his finest and better-known
poems, "Tarshisha" (To Tarshish [1935]).[2] In the poem, Halkin compares
himself to the prophet Jonah, who "rose up to flee to Tarshish from the presence of the Lord" (Jonah 1:3). Halkin's Tarshish is a figure for America—
identified with its rustic northern landscapes—and for the forces pulling
Halkin there. It is a casting off of responsibilities both familial (the speaker
imagines leaving behind his wife and daughter) and national (the speaker
turns from the difficult clarities of Jewish-national ideological commitment
to the seductive ambiguities of the world of nature and the senses). The
poem, the initial setting of which is the Mediterranean shoreline at Jaffa,
describes the land of Israel in terms of the harsh and unforgiving brightness
of its light and heat—that is, the searing noonday truths of Zionism and the
historical demands of the Jewish nation. The land beneath its sun is perpetually "exposed" (S. Halkin 1977, 262): bare, stripped, awesomely clear. The
poet even complains at one point that the "glassy light" (265) of Israel acts
as a "screen" between him and the place. In contrast, "my Tarshish" (262),
as he calls the America of his yearnings, is a place of cool, moist, inviting
forests. It is a sweet oblivion, a shedding of commitment and discipline, a
surrender of the self to the flowing transience of nature.[3]

The speaker describes his experience of the American environment as
an almost ecstatic reduction to animal desire and biological instinct. "Oh,
that I might immerse myself again, alive and unthinking, / within your
mournful light," he writes, "and like a drunken mole press my face / into

2. My translations of the poem in the discussion that follows are based on that of Ruth
Finer Mintz in her *Modern Hebrew Poetry: A Bilingual Anthology* (1966, 144–57).

3. Halkin also refers to Jonah fleeing from the Jewish national demands of the Land of
Israel in his 1929 poem, "Be'erets zot" (S. Halkin 1977, 217–19).

your tangled grass" (263). Merging with the panorama of mating insects and animals, the poet finds that even God seems to disintegrate within this abundance of life-urge and eros, reforming in new, natural unities. Halkin is conquered by a biological determinism in which he is merely a product of the urgings of his forebears: "The river of my blood is but a vat aflow with ancient wines" (264). Tarshish-America, though, is a dissolution of self ultimately beyond eros. "My heart belongs to the black, wet clods of the field" (267), he declares at the poem's end, and he imagines the flickering out of his own memory, only hazily aware of his young daughter still wandering the shoreline in Israel, unaware of "her father's twisted paths." America in this poem is not a solution, but a temptation. Jonah was wrong to flee Jaffa, of course, and Halkin recognizes in the poem's first section that America cannot ultimately sustain the soul of the Jew: during the "black-winged winter" (262), the "lean wolf"—one of the many animal figures for the poet—will be "too desperate to howl." Yet Halkin gives expression to his dark and highly conflicted desires, and even in the land of his fulfillment he confesses his attractions to oblivion, to the memory-dulling charms of nature and the body, to the possibilities of his Tarshish-America.

This mixture of attraction and repulsion regarding the United States also characterizes Halkin's Great American Novel, *Ad mashber*, published in 1945 but mostly written in the 1930s. Because of its dizzying stream-of-consciousness technique, its immersion in the metropolitan landscape, and its psychological and psychosexual probings, this work is justly considered by some critics to be one of the most significant novelistic ventures in Hebrew between the world wars.[4] Comparable to David Fogel's *Married Life* (and a more daring if not as satisfyingly complete achievement) in its exploration of interwar Diasporic sexual-national dysfunction, it seems a precursor to the novels of Yehoshua and Yaakov Shabtai, with their indirect discourse and interior monologues representing various unhappy voices within the larger society. As the novel's subtitle—"Book 1: Winter

---

4. See especially the discussion of the novel in Shaked (1988, 3:4). Katz briefly considers the representation of African Americans in the novel (2009, 163–66).

1929"—hints, Halkin had intended this to be the first of three parts, but although he worked and reworked the material, he never managed to arrive at a satisfactory continuation, and only this first section was released in book form. More than a decade after the publication of book 1, Halkin confessed that his inability to finish the work "lies upon me like a stifling yoke and keeps me from setting myself to something new" (qtd. Yardeni 1961, 82), a paralysis that may in part reflect his ambivalence about the novel's subject: the condition and destiny of the Jews in America. Nevertheless, although Halkin never completed its sequels, the novel we have stands easily with the best of Reuven Wallenrod's work as the finest achievements of American Hebrew fiction.

Critics, particularly American ones, have tended to read the novel as a celebration of Jewish life in New York City, pointing especially to the third chapter, a high-flown paean to the city and its Jewish population.[5] On the contrary, however, the prose poem of chapter 3, while often movingly lyrical, displays a forced ebullience, as if the speaker had to convince himself of the unalloyed worth of his subject, and the novel as a whole is deeply ambivalent about Jewish life in America. The novel's title is a biblical allusion to Isaiah 37:3 and II Kings 19:3—"This day is a day of trouble and rebuke and blasphemy, for the children are brought to the point of crisis [ad mashber] but there is no strength to birth them"—though given the date in the subtitle it might be best translated as "Until the Crash." Either way, Halkin intended to portray a world stumbling aimlessly on the brink of a precipice. The chronicles of his Jewish protagonists and their Jewish and non-Jewish colleagues and lovers are united by the psychological malaise of the characters, a spiritual sickness that can extend, as in the meditations of one character, even to inanimate objects:

> Chairs and tables, simple wooden objects whose legs wrapped in damp fibre casings resembled the moist hair on the limbs of a slaughtered beast, were heaped up in stacks in a fearful weariness, strengthening in her . . .

5. Robert Alter, for instance, calls the novel an expression of "the passionate romance of the East European Jewish immigrants with New York" (1994, 85).

the sad, wretched impression, a reflection of the sluggish, insipid licentiousness of her whole generation's way of life. (S. Halkin 1945, 35)

The scene depicted here is that of a nightclub called the Black Pony—probably a reference to the White Horse in Greenwich Village where Dylan
Thomas drank himself to death. The novel being set during Prohibition,
alcohol is indeed a persistent prop throughout the book, although the characters are more likely to drug themselves with their own sad yearnings.

The real touchstone of the novel is found in chapter 7, in which the
immigrant businessman Lazar Luskin muses to himself, "[t]his is America!
If it weren't for Jews and Judaism, you couldn't find a nicer place in the
world than this great wide land, eager to live and in love with life" (275).
The United States, in Halkin's view, is an extraordinary and blessed country but one that proves sweetly and beguilingly corrosive to Jewish identity. The novel is therefore not devoid of positive, even celebratory views of
America. Luskin's reveries in particular contain the novel's most unambig-
uously generous appraisal of America, whose refreshing "sense of humor"
and "cheerfulness" are juxtaposed with the grim, ideological extremism
of interwar Europe, where ruthless dictators "poison their own lives and
the rest of the world too." In his imagination, Luskin counsels President
Herbert Hoover to bring Stalin, Mussolini, and the leaders of Europe to
the United States so that they can learn a characteristically American levity
and appreciation for life: "Teach them a bit about baseball, about diving
into a cool lake—and perhaps they will wake up from their vain, seductive
phantasms!"(275).

Nevertheless, Luskin views the situation of the younger, American-
born generation of Jews in the United States with deep apprehension. A
traditional-maskilic Jew of Hasidic background—he arrived in New York
with his tefillin and a copy of the Haskalah classic, Mapu's *The Guilt of
Samaria*—Luskin has tried to give his children a Jewish education and passion for their people and tradition. And yet his son Tully is a communist
with no interest in matters Jewish. Although the prose poem of chapter 3
culminates in the scene of a young Jewish couple talking revolutionary politics in an automat, and although their dreams of refashioning society are
described as a new "Torah" bestowed by these young Jews to the non-Jews

around them, in Luskin's anxious meditations we see young Jewish radicals such as Tully not as Jewish lawgivers but as unmoored individuals losing themselves amidst American society as a whole.

Luskin's attempts to synthesize Jewishness and Americanness in his imagination are tellingly problematic. His reveries of chapter 7, for instance, conclude with a nostalgic recollection of the Jewish restaurant on Canton Street where, as a poor new immigrant, he once came to listen to and engage in the intellectual, political, and spiritual debates brought by the Russian Jews with them from the Pale of Settlement. In this little toast to the immigrant *batlanim* (intellectuals and idlers), Luskin goes so far as to exalt them as the true exemplars of America, in contrast to the more established "German" Jews who sought to Americanize these supposedly uncouth newcomers. "America is the land of freedom," he thinks, "and not you [the German Jews] but rather your poor immigrant coreligionists, who have shed neither their greenness nor their language, they and not you are the true testament to human liberty," carrying the spirit of "Belinsky and Kropotkin and Tolstoy" across the Atlantic where it unites with the spirit of "Franklin and Jefferson and Lincoln" (283). How arrogant for the German Jews to presume to Americanize their brethren, he thinks indignantly:

> Yet who reads Buckle and delves into the thought of Emerson—you [the German Jews] or they [the Russian Jewish immigrant intellectuals]? Or are you familiar with the history of English parliamentarianism and the American Revolution? Are you experts in the details of the abolition of slavery in the United States? You are not the ones who know America, but rather these *batlanim*, whom you are embarrassed by, and who insist on speaking their own languages, a Russian that is Yiddish and a Yiddish that is Russian . . . they and not you are the Americans!" (S. Halkin 1945, 283–84)

In this internal monologue, an imaginary defense of precisely the Yiddish intelligentsia that seemed so alien to America, Luskin attempts to argue that these people who do not know English or the U.S. Constitution are nevertheless "the Americans," preserving an American yet transnational essence of intellectual and human freedom via their lively knish-fueled debates in this Canton Street hole-in-the-wall.

And yet such an ironic argument is difficult to sustain, designating as most "American" precisely the immigrant circles that seem least ready—except in their own minds—to break out of the world of the Lower East Side and into the language, culture, and contemporary life of the rest of the United States. What is at stake in chapter 7, as throughout the novel, is in any case not the immigrant but the American-born generation. And here Luskin finds himself perpetually uneasy about the younger generation in general and his own son in particular. Luskin's tender memories of the Canton Street restaurant are poignant and momentarily soothing, but they do not function as an adequate answer to the generational crisis at the center of the novel.

Instead, Luskin pins his hopes for American Jewry on Reuven B. Fuller, a rabbi and professor at the Jewish Theological Seminary whose philosophy of modern Jewish life bears more than a passing resemblance to Mordecai Kaplan's Reconstructionism. Like Kaplan, Fuller conceives of Judaism as a civilization that "discards and takes on new forms in the course of its ongoing vital development" (235), and his public assessment of the Jewish future in the United States is fundamentally if not assuredly optimistic. America, according Fuller, "will strengthen and support the civilization of the Jews . . . on the condition of course that Jewish civilization truly desires to live and strives to continue its development in the bosom of this great and promising land" (236). Luskin is convinced that American Jewry can be "redeemed" (253) through Fuller and his teachings. And yet Fuller is an improbable redeemer, being one of the many Jewish characters in the novel suffering himself from some sort of psychic crisis. Whether psychosexual neurosis or breakdown of identity, the erotic and psychological dysfunctions of Halkin's characters are clearly meant to reflect an ideological crisis, the psychically unstable position of Jews in the United States. Luskin's comment that America would be wonderful "[i]f it weren't for Jews and Judaism" is manifest in the negations, distortions, and dissolutions of Jewish selves in the novel.

In Fuller's case, he is both unable to achieve sexual and emotional intimacy with his wife Newta—who herself exhibits a classically Freudian set of neurotic symptoms—and unable to find a purpose in American Jewish life. The psychic impotence from which he suffers is indicated when we first encounter him on a gray winter's dawn, unnerved in his morning prayers by his sudden inability to understand the traditional praise to God "Who makes firm the footsteps of a man." This uncertainty, an unraveling of both his faith and his masculinity, is linked in the same chapter with his timorousness before his beautiful wife, whose sexual and emotional inaccessibility all but bars him from her bedroom. This impotence is further expressed in the same chapter as writer's block: Fuller is soon to deliver an as yet unwritten major address to a convocation at the seminary in which he will distill his vision for American Jewry, but he cannot seem to compose this credo. All these paralyses—as man and husband, as writer and Jew—are reflections of each other and of the condition of American Jewry as a whole. "And just as it is beyond one's ability to explain to oneself what one's connection is to another individual, that is, to Newta," Fuller thinks in his abstracted way, "one is similarly unable to explain to the upcoming convocation what its connection is to its God. That is, what is the connection between the Jewish community and its God here on American soil" (208). Luskin's hope in Fuller and his ideology is therefore presented as ironically misplaced from the start.

Undergoing a similar psychic collapse is Leon Akst, a young Jewish intellectual who plays Stephen Daedelus to Fuller and Newta's Leopold Bloom and Molly. The object of almost hysterical fascination and near worship by the other young bohemians and radicals in the novel, Akst is nevertheless as paralyzed and tormented by doubt as Fuller. He is in the midst of an existential crisis that threatens his very sense of identity: when he looks in the mirror each morning, he is surprised to see his face still there. Meanwhile, he treats the women around him with chivalrous but misogynistic ambivalence, torn between his desire for them and his fear of and contempt for such attractions. He is, for instance, aroused by the physical charms of the voluptuous Mary at a New Year's Eve party, but he is dismissive of what he sees as her simpleminded femininity and the superficial biological imperatives that he believes determine her actions. Sex, for Akst, is both powerful and contemptible, profound and superficial. He is moved by it, yet he cannot find in it the meaning he seeks. Like the other characters in the novel, Akst's erotic sorrows are displacements of neglected or stifled spiritual quests. This is particularly explicit in his case as this character, like Halkin, was brought up in the orbit of Hasidism—itself exhibiting a complex interpenetration of the religious and the erotic—and finds himself wrestling simultaneously with the loss and persistence of Jewish tradition as he makes his way among the sexually permissive circles of young New York bohemians. (It may be relevant to note here that photographs of Halkin during this time, with his high brow, sensual mouth, and profound if slightly disapproving gaze, display a considerable glamour and attractiveness.) Akst's meditations on sex and women are shot through with references to the Hasidic text the *Tanya,* and his depression is as kabbalistic as it is Freudian—even his sense of psychic insubstantiality is described as a *bitul hayesh,* playing on the Hasidic term for the obliteration of mere material reality before the true reality of the divine. His charisma affects characters of both sexes—Tully Luskin describes Akst's influence as a kind of bisexual spiritual-erotic aphrodisiac: "You make a man fruitful, you activate his seminal glands" (192)—but nothing creative seems to result from this influence, and Akst himself is cast adrift in a haze of self-contempt. He functions in the novel as a kind of failed messiah, a redeemer figure who cannot, as the novel's title indicates, bring his people beyond their crisis to a creative-redemptive fulfillment.

Despite the novel's evident ideological pessimism about the state of Jewish life in the United States, its strength and complexity rest not a little on the extent to which it simultaneously conveys the genuine exhilaration offered by American life, whether the metropolitan seductions of New York City or the attractions of rural Montana and Arkansas. Even the very psychic instability and dissolution that the novel would otherwise seem to lament are often portrayed as intensely enjoyable possibilities. Luskin, for instance, experiences a hypnotic pleasure in his anonymity and loss of self in the great city. Sitting in his car in a Manhattan traffic jam, he muses:

One attains a feeling of being without will or sentience, carried along despite oneself like all the others enclosed in their automobiles, moving like an ant in a colony as long as all the rest are moving, and similarly stopping as long as the rest stop and are not uprooted from their spot. That is to say: an unknown person controls the traffic and decrees when it halts, and one enjoys not being responsible for it. (S. Halkin 1945, 270)

New York affords an insectlike freedom from choice and consciousness, a pleasurable self-abandonment quite similar to Halkin's experience of American nature in the poem "Tarshisha."

In a similar vein, the character of Lena Fuller, Newta's daughter and Fuller's stepdaughter, appears as a contrast to the male characters who struggle lugubriously with their psychic crises and loss of identity. One of the most compelling figures in the novel, Lena is the perfect young urban ego, "all a network of receptive nerves, unceasing stimuli, receiving constantly to the point of trembling" (59). Unlike Akst and Fuller, who suffer from their lack of identity, Lena possesses an unflappable conviction of her inner self, which paradoxically allows her to revel in theatricality, pretense, and multiple identities. She passes herself off in the speakeasies of Greenwich Village, for instance, as a non-Jew of Russian descent. Largely indifferent to the concerns of Jewish identity, her sure sense of selfhood rests upon her conviction of her own purity, sexual and emotional, in contrast to the promiscuities and superficialities of the bohemian milieu in which she moves. Although she is a virgin who remains surprisingly untouched by the dissolute environments she visits, she is at the same time the character most attuned to the play of sexual desire, particularly and de-idealizingly perceptive about the compulsions and foibles of the male characters around her. Halkin's realization of Lena's complex sexual imagination is one of the real achievements of the novel.

Lena is one of several Jewish characters in the novel who are romantically involved with non-Jews. Indeed, because the novel expresses the national predicament of American Jewry as psychosexual dysfunction, a major theme throughout is the erotics of strangeness and difference, the ways in which Jews and non-Jews are attracted to and repelled by each other. One non-Jewish character reflects that it was the "external foreignness" of her immigrant Jewish husband, "that un-Americanness in his face and in all his manners, so hateful to her parents and her siblings" that "drew her near to him" (124). Leon Akst is aroused by one young woman's "strange, Gentile presence" (127). Lazar Luskin, in another instance of the Hebraist journey into rural, Christian America, displays an almost erotic fascination with a non-Jewish ranch owner he meets while exploring the possibilities for Jewish agrarian settlement in Montana.

The ironies surrounding these Jewish and non-Jewish attractions are particularly evident in the scene in which Lena meets her Protestant boy-friend, Walter Hendricks, in the Black Pony tavern. Edna Kenan, the Texan waitress who dotes upon Lena (whom Edna believes to be a non-Jew named Elaine), announces Walter's arrival by telling Lena/Elaine that a "dark, *but American*" (70, my emphasis) man has come to see her. Lena, who is herself passing as a non-Jew, understands that Edna means to indicate by this "that the swarthy visitor is not a Jew," and enjoys pretending that she does not understand Edna's insinuation, forcing the waitress to explain further. Edna, who does not want to admit her prejudice overtly, stammers: "I meant to say that he isn't a New Yorker." Hence, the Jew is linked with New York City, in contrast to "America," which for the southerner Edna is as distinct from the metropolis as Jews are from Americans. Ironically, however, the non-Jewish Walter proves to be absolutely smitten with New York, precisely because of its Jewish ambience, and especially its young Jewish intellectuals—"students of Dostoevsky" (74), as he calls them—who strike him as being more European or Russian than American. In a passage that also points up the stylistic pitfalls of the novel's reliance on indirect discourse—the need to insert exposition can sometimes turn both dialogue and internal monologue into heavily artificial and contrived broadcasts of information—Walter moons over Leon Akst and the other Jewish intellectuals he associates with:

> "Oh, stop with the paradoxes, Walter! A little longer and even you will be nothing but one of those . . . those . . ."
>
> "Those students of Dostoevsky?" offered Walter Hendricks, still savoring the complaint she bore against him. "Those wonderful children of 'Jew York'? But what can I do, Lena, when they really are amazing, these young New York Jews of yours! It was no accident that I was led astray after Leon Akst, for example, when he formed a favorable impres-sion of me in his wanderings in the Adirondacks when I was still a real naïf, a village boy in every way. It was no accident that some time later Walter Hendricks rebelled against his father, the Presbyterian minister, in his lecture room whose windows were always darkened by the fernery outside, and went out himself to roam around the country like Leon Akst, to wander according to his spirit like that eternal traveller. There are no

men like those young Jews, Lena! . . . There are no men in the world like
Leon Akst!" (S. Halkin 1945, 74)

For Walter, the slur against "Jew York" is actually a badge of honor with
which he is delighted to be associated, as this proves that he has successfully escaped his father's provincial, Christian world and become truly cosmopolitan, intellectual—and "Jewish." The irony is increased by Walter's
evident infatuation with Leon Akst. Although we are meant to be witness-
ing a romantic rendezvous between Lena and Walter, he is more excited by
Akst than by Lena, who is for him mainly an entrée into the Jewish world
of New York.

The novel is thus to a great extent a comedy of errors: a series of characters in love with the wrong thing, or with something other than that which
they think they love. And the major example of this comedy is American
Jewry itself, in love with America yet somehow embracing not America but
its distant cousin, New York City. Walter's gushing admiration for Leon
Akst is the complementary flip side of the cultural dynamic described in
chapter 3 of the novel, in which New York City is defined as a love affair
between the Jews and Wasp culture. "Go and see," says the speaker. "You
enter a theater, for example, where there is a production of that pinnacle of
your Anglo-Saxon culture, New York, to wit: a play of Shakespeare—and
whom do you find filling up the seats of the theater? That is to say: Jews,
the youth of Israel, with non-Jews merely an inconsequential minority"
(107). In proving their superlative love for Anglo-Saxon culture—represented here by the jewel in the canon's crown, Shakespeare—the Jews only
reinforce their own conspicuousness, their national genius all too evident
even as it pursues the genius of a different nation. In fact, the Hebraists in
particular made no small contribution to this Jewish bardolatry, American
Hebrew writers having translated over a dozen of Shakespeare's plays into
Hebrew (Spicehandler 1993, 103-4). We recall that Izzy's Hebraist roommates in the story by Bernard Isaacs we discussed in chapter 4 spend much
of their time translating Shakespeare into Hebrew. Of course, as Shlomo
Grodzensky noted, the "devotion to and proficiency in Shakespeare"
(Grodzensky 1978, 46) found among the Hebraists represented their dis-
tance from American culture as much as their participation in it. As in the

Isaacs story, the Hebraist passion for Shakespeare was often at the expense of a more contemporary, noncanonical relationship with America. Halkin's New York City is, then, a national bedroom farce—Jews pursuing England, non-Jews pursuing Russia, and everyone colliding in New York.

The novel adds a further and quite poignant dimension to these anxious shiftings of Jewish national identity in America when it turns to the subject of race, drawing parallels between blacks and Jews. As we have already seen, Halkin adopted this comparison in his pseudonymous poem from the 1920s, "To a Negress," which linked Jews and blacks as racial comrades languishing in the oppressive "northern" culture of Wasp America and only masquerading when they purport to leave their innate racial characteristics behind. The idea of race is of course an attractive one to those anxious about cultural assimilation because it would seem to guarantee the inability of the minority in question to assimilate: their culture will always be hardwired into their genetic make-up. So long as they do not miscegenate, their culture will never die. Like most of the Hebraists, however, Halkin seems to have been generally suspicious of this notion, despite his grotesque embrace of it in the (perhaps tellingly) pseudonymous poem we have mentioned. As we observed in chapter 1, the nationalism of the Hebraists rested too much upon culture and language to have allowed them comfortably to define Jewishness as an automatic racial inheritance. As we saw in Reuven Wallenrod's story "Refuge," discussed in the previous chapter, it is not the Hebraist but his cultural archenemy, the self-satisfied American allrightnik, who leans upon an intrinsic or genetic meter of Jewishness. In Wallenrod's story this anodyne notion is embodied by the vice-principal of Dubin's school, who opines that the "Jewish soul, the Jewish spark will not disappear: they are passed down from generation to generation" (Wallenrod 1937, 90). Similarly, although several Jewish characters in *Ad mashber* link Jews with blacks in racial terms, Halkin's novel ultimately suggests that Jewishness is not racial and that the black-Jewish analogy is not only false but a product of the distorting transformations of Jewish existence in America.

The novel contains two important scenes concerning race, and in each one a female Jewish character sorts out her own perplexities by meditating on a nonwhite character. That is, in both cases Jews try to understand themselves through blacks. The first case occurs in the Black Pony, while Lena is waiting for Walter. The stream of consciousness of her reveries is momentarily interrupted by the entrance of the janitor, Bottomly Logan, who briefly wrests the novelistic perspective away from Lena as his consciousness imprints itself upon the voice of the narrative. Bottomly's name is clearly meant to connect him with the character Bottom in Shakespeare's *A Midsummer Night's Dream,* a play in which Lena acted in high school when she played Titania—thus making Halkin's novel another example of the New York Jewish love of Shakespeare he describes in chapter 3. But more than Bottomly's name, it is his racial indeterminacy—he is referred to as "perhaps Cuban, perhaps mulatto" (35)—that links him with Shakespeare's comic hybrid, the very embodiment of erotic border-crossings: half-human, half-beast; a human who dallies with faeries, a commoner who shares a tryst with a queen. Bottomly is foul-mouthed and sexually hungry, mentally stripping away the niceties of social interaction in order to focus on the sexual dynamic underneath, as when he describes Lena speaking with Edna "as if the two of them were on a movie screen and were about to start licking each others' strawberry lips" (39). When Lena's consciousness recovers the narrative, this erotic interest is mentally reciprocated by Lena, who imagines kissing Logan, pondering the "sweetness" in "the surprising question of the taste of a kiss from the equine mouth of this shoot of the Negro stock" (59–60). Lena becomes, then, a Titania gazing on Bottom, savoring the taboo of cross-racial erotics. It seems significant, moreover, that she does so by fixing Bottomly as "Negro," reducing his initial ethnic indeterminacy to a single and clear category by focusing on him as a representative of "the Negro stock." Race, instinctive and clear, therefore becomes an antidote to the ambiguity of identity, and yet also as another of the novel's instances of Jewish/non-Jewish erotic attraction.

It also functions as a model of lost or repressed Jewish masculinity. In her meditations, Lena not only identifies Professor Fuller as "Negroid," but she also posits that it was precisely his "blackness" that had attracted her mother, Newta, to him. Musing on Bottomly's allure, Lena supposes that her "occasional attraction . . . toward a Negroid face is perhaps an inheritance from her mother, whose heart Professor Fuller had surely set afire somehow with a Negro-like flame in those long-gone days. . . . [I]t was the black blood, so to speak, of Professor Fuller that had enchanted [Newta]" (60). Yet now Newta is presented as a Sleeping Beauty figure, imprisoned in her "marmoreal slumber" because Professor Fuller will not act with the "powerful masculinity" that would awaken his wife from her neurotic symptoms and emotional isolation. "Blackness" is thus imagined here as a missing or blocked virility that, if restored, would break through the paralysis and alienation of the novel's characters.

On the other hand, this racial Jewishness is undermined in the novel's penultimate chapter, in which we finally hear the interior monologue of Newta herself, who has for so long been presented to us only through the thoughts and theories of the other characters. On her own terms she emerges as a complex and fragile character, her infidelities peripheral to her gnawing desire to be truly understood by those around her and thus known to herself as well. As with all of the other characters, the tenuousness of her identity is an issue. Yet in Newta's case, there is in fact another who does truly understand her and in whose eyes she "is always as she is" (290). This is Martha, her black maid and mother substitute, source of her identity. Newta's own mother died giving birth to her, and her father is a nonpresence. Martha became for her the perfect mother-figure, always caring and available, a source of love, understanding, and acceptance she has found nowhere else in her life. But in addition to this, Newta early began to understand her own Jewish identity through Martha's otherness. Having moved from Mississippi to New York, Newta was sent to a Catholic private school where the other girls were cruel to her, attacking her as "the Negro Jew" (301), a racial attack that merges Jewishness and blackness. Surprisingly, Newta accepts this charge, accepts that she is in some fundamental sense the daughter of Martha, a little black girl turning the taunt of her classmates into a proud sense of identity as the persecuted racial other. Her understanding of her own Jewishness is linked to her ostracism by the other girls and to her deep emotional identification with Martha.

Thus, the Jewish identification with blacks is not essential but rather the reflection of a national identity crisis. Newta's biography makes clear that her identification of Jewishness with Martha's blackness is an alluring—and here maternally comforting—image of identity stability, in which the denigration of white American society (the Hebraists make little distinction between Catholics and Protestants in this case) is accepted as a badge of honor. The Jew as Negro may be hated but is at least determinate. Newta's assimilated upbringing propels her into the arms of a female, motherly figure, herself an ur-stereotype: Martha even makes pancakes, à la Aunt Jemima. With Martha, Newta feels that she is herself, "always as she is"—and yet this identity is itself a product of trauma and loss, another deception. The juxtaposition of blacks and Jews in the novel thus functions on two levels. On the first, it functions as a warning that Jews, like blacks, don't really belong in the United States. As in Lena's meditations, both are essentially other. As we see in Newta's chapter, however, the deeper warning is that Jews are not blacks: that such an identification is mistaken and results from the confusion due to a lack of Jewish national identity.

This, then, is Halkin's portrayal of the ultimately neurotic condition of Jews in the United States. And although he does not draw an explicit lesson in the novel, he increasingly matched this condition with its Zionist solution. The year after he published *Ad mashber,* he published the polemic "To the Hebrews in America" (1985, 32–43) and the sociopolitical monograph *Jews and Judaism in America,* both of which predicted that American Jews would be snuffed out, through assimilation if not something akin to the physical annihilation seen in Europe. The significant achievements of American-Jewish culture, including Hebrew literature, had been merely a result of immigration, Halkin argued, and were now reaching their end. Bewildered by their increasing insubstantiality, the Jews of *Ad mashber,* Halkin seems to say, must make the leap to *hagshamah,* to the Jewish concretization and commitment that is only possible in Israel.

Halkin made this leap in 1949. He had returned to the United States in 1939, having been invited by Mordecai Kaplan to teach for a year at the Jewish Theological Seminary, and was forced to remain after the outbreak of the Second World War. When he returned to Israel for good it was to assume a chaired professorship at the Hebrew University of Jerusalem. This move was the final realization of his unconditional Zionism. And almost at the same time, he delivered his final verdict on Hebrew literature in America, a verdict that took the form of a caustic silence. In 1950 Halkin published *Modern Hebrew Literature from the Enlightenment to the Birth of the State of Israel: Trends and Values,* his one work in English and for decades the most widely used critical study of modern Hebrew literature in English. This study, which includes meditations on writers from Bialik and Tchernikhovsky to Shlonsky and Goldberg, is characterized by the near-total absence of any treatment of Hebrew literature in the United States apart from a reference to the "hopeless drivel" (80) of Dolitzky, brought in to illustrate the shortcomings of late nineteenth-century sentimental Hibat Tsion poetry. Halkin later wrote at various points about this or that American Hebrew writer. But it is surely significant that here, in his major work on Hebrew literature for an American audience (and again in its 1970 reprinting), he does not tell his audience the news that there are Hebrew poets living among them.

A CAFÉ GUARD

In one of his rare forays into criticism, Gabriel Preil penned an understandably ambivalent review of Halkin's book, criticizing him for not including Hebrew writers in America and for his exclusive emphasis on Israel. Preil also questioned what he saw as Halkin's social-collectivist approach to literature, in which Hebrew literature is seen primarily as an expression of the national-historical experience and will of the Jewish people. Preil felt that this did not give sufficient attention to the writer as individual. Moreover, he chided Halkin for eliding poets such as David Fogel and Berl Pomerantz, leaving a gap where these understated modernists writing in Diaspora should have been. This dissent of course reflects on Preil's own quiet, Diasporic modernism. The title of Preil's review, "In the Margins of Sh. Halkin's English Book on Modern Hebrew Literature," refers not only to the act of his commentary upon Halkin's text but also to his sense of the place of his own poetry on the margins of the literary canons of his day.

Preil had earlier responded to Halkin's unconditional Zionism in the form of a poem that appeared in the March 24, 1944, issue of *Hadoar,* which was later incorporated into Preil's enchanting sequence "Shirim mibeit hakafeh" (Poems from a café). The latter title recalls Halkin's own "Café Royal," as if to remind Halkin of his brief dalliance with modernism.

The specific poem in question, "Mishmeret eragon" (The watch of yearning), is dedicated to Halkin. Responding to Halkin's insistence on Israel, Preil offered a personal demurral—not as an argument against Halkin's Zionism (Preil was not at all opposed to Zionism and, according to Dan Miron, was even close to right-wing Revisionist circles when he was young), but as an apologia, both whimsical and poignant, for his own unwillingness to make aliyah. Preil presents his ideological delinquency as an ironic version of the heroic Jewish *shomer* (guard) of the kibbutzim in prestate Israel. He writes that he too will be "on duty" (Preil 1954, 33), but that his post is a "watch of yearning" in a New York café. Rather than enter the Israeli present, which Preil fears will be "alien" or "pretentious" and might betray him "as this hour betrays me in its sweep of blinding light," he prefers instead to cultivate "the shadows of the years" (34). The juxtaposition of threatening light and soothing shade recalls Halkin's language of ambivalence in "Tarshisha," the difference being that Halkin wrote his poem in Jaffa, yearning for the shadowy pleasures of immanence, whereas Preil writes from New York, praising the shadows of deferment. Preil does not want to risk being disappointed by the real Land of Israel and the national struggle happening there, for it might displace his love affair with memory (what once was) and desire (what might be), and with the imagination's vivid life on the margins of the actual. Indeed, the poem's wariness at the flinty impermeability of the present applies not only to Israel but to the present moment anywhere. The Eden of the "now is a sealed gate," he writes, whose keys are found only "in the lap of the past" (34), a Proustian sentiment that marks much of Preil's poetry. From early in his career, Preil sought not the dawn of Jewish-national resurrection in Israel, but the "sad, electric sunset" (33) of his New York café, in which the mind is immersed in the exercises of nostalgia and longing, and the "blooming garden" it inhabits is always alive because it is "recall[ed]," not real.

Indeed, Preil was a coffee poet. The medievals had their wine, the Romantics their opium; for Preil, the cafés of New York were the launching pad for his reclusive sensibility, their windows his eyes on the world. His poems proliferate with images of steaming cups, meditations on the life glimpsed within and from his beloved *conditorias*. Even a poem dealing with Cold War fears of atomic destruction ("Hamtanah lamahar ha'atomi"

[Waiting for the atomic tomorrow], also part of the "Poems from a Café" series) turns on a paean to the coffee bean which, in implicit contrast to the atom, can be split to release a "wise energy" (36). Moreover, for Preil, the activity of poetry is precisely mirrored in the experience of drinking coffee. Consider: one is tired and listless and the world gray. Then one drinks from a warm and fragrant cup, and soon the world and the self, which had both seemed so exhausted, are infused with new significance. Perhaps nothing has actually changed, yet colors become vivid, people seem more precious, possibilities stir. Just so with the poem, which in its moment of small exaltation wins a sharpening of vision, a recommitment to the sense that the world and the self are meaningful. Again and again, Preil's poems enact this modest blossoming. Yet they also insist on documenting the passing of this rush, the cooling of the cup, the world and the self's return to grayness and torpor. Like the effect of caffeine, Preil's enthusiasm is always ephemeral.

This ephemerality stems in part from what Dan Miron, in his superb monograph on Preil, has called the "accidental man" (Miron 1993, 326) at the core of Preil's poetry. In contrast to the psychic strength of the great Romantic poets, convinced of their own visionary power and of the harmonious reflection of the universe in their souls, Preil's poetic ego is ever conscious of its own arbitrariness, of its incommensurateness with and disconnection from the cosmos around it. Although Miron's characterization of romanticism may be questioned—he elides here the dejection and melancholy, the self-consciousness and doubt that mark the most famous representatives of romanticism in poetry, from Wordsworth in English to Bialik in Hebrew—his characterization of Preil is accurate. Preil does at times depict moments of visionary wholeness and transcendence, but these moments are always brief and partial. His is a poetics of equilibrium, inhabiting a moderate midpoint between two extremes, twin poles characterized throughout his work in terms of temperature: the crushing heat of ideology and inspiration on the one hand, the paralyzing cold of logic and death on the other. Preil's allegiance is to the truth of the temperate poem.

This does not make for thunder—there is little of the demonic or celestial in his work. It does account, though, for the strange attraction of his best poems, as they move along their tightrope with careful integrity. Preil's word for this commitment to balance is *pikahon* (sobriety). In his earliest collections, this sobriety is expressed less as a balance between heat and cold than as an embrace of cold in defense against heat. We see this in the poem "Nehamat pikahon" (The comfort of sobriety) from the 1954 collection *Ner mul kokhavim* (A candle facing stars). Watching someone kindle a fire amidst the snow of a winter's day, Preil muses that by contrast, he himself finds a "comfort of sobriety" in "the snow's light alone" (Preil 1954, 29), a confession that reflects Preil's temperamental distance from the sweeping passions that have animated so much of modern Hebrew poetry. Such contrasts are handled with a certain dialectical touch, as Preil concludes the poem by linking the snow's sober light with a fire "hotter than the burning summers." By the time Preil writes the poems collected in *Ha'esh vehademamah* (The fire and the silence; 1968), however, we see sobriety not as a privileging of snow over fire, but as a balance, an aesthetic and ascetic refusal of either extreme. "After the heat and cold," he writes in the poem "Izun umikreh" (Balance and happenstance), "the vessels will summon / a balanced season" (1968, 45). Unlike Wallace Stevens, to whom Preil has often been compared, Preil is no snow man. Stevens, working in a more sublime vein, sought to "unite the extremes of ice and fire" (Preil 1954, 29)—as Preil describes the man attempting in "Nehamat pikahon"—in a vision beyond either. Preil's already defeated poetry carves out the minor key between the two, his temperate band. At times this can be a highly narcissistic, overly precious register, as Preil seems to forfeit the psychic struggle toward poetic greatness, insulating himself from responsibility and competition in order to meditate upon the minor movements of his own ego. At its best, however, his is a poignant poetics of "between," of "meanwhile," words repeated often in his work. As we learn in the beautiful poem "Onesh venes" (Punishment and miracle): "The poem never reaches its fulfillment"; it "refuses the conclusion" (1968, 84). This inconclusiveness is both torment and promise.

Much of Preil's poetry is about the difficulty of being fully present in any one place or time. He writes about the imaginative claims of one's past, one's forebears, the immigrant's sense of being elsewhere, the Hebrew poet's gravitational pull toward the Zion of his imaginings. At the same time, he was more at home in the United States than any other American Hebrew poet. "America has entered me very deeply" (1991, 14), Preil said in an interview he gave a couple of years before his death. Unlike so many of his colleagues, he was not hostile to the urban environments of America. As Miron points out, the New York of Preil's poems is not "a satanic city," and life therein is "neither tragic nor grotesque, but ordinary, mundane, human existence" (Miron 1999, 331). Indeed, Preil's restrained melancholy and intimacy with solitude at times recalls that most American of artists Edward Hopper and his images of lonely people in diners and office buildings. Preil's poem "Mis'adah avtomatit" (The automat) resembles the scene of the Hopper painting of the same name. (It also reminds us of the near-religious blessing that was air conditioning on a sweltering summer night in New York City in the 1950s.) Also Hopperesque is the uncanny poem "Hat-siur hameharher" (The pensive painting) and its anonymous, transient hotel guests. In this poem, a painting in a hotel room becomes a figure both for the "devouring fire" of an obsolete romanticism and for the dumb, visionary anguish of the poet, who will die like one of Ben Katchor's businessmen "in a lonely, indifferent room, / his face to the wall" (Preil 1954, 43).

Despite such affinities, however, Preil's poetry is not significantly more shaped by American literary influences than that of any of the other immigrant Hebraists. "I wanted to make my Hebrew into an English Hebrew," he said in a 1972 interview (Preil 1993b). Yet this "English Hebrew" is a product of atmosphere and personal temperament, as well as literary influences from the Hebrew and Yiddish, but not English, worlds. Yael Feldman, in her groundbreaking study of Preil, describes his poetry as oscillating dialectically between the twin influences of Hebrew literary romanticism and American Yiddish imagism. Miron follows Feldman in seeing Preil's romanticism as dialectical rather than absent. However, he prefers to locate Preil not between Hebrew and Yiddish literature, but in a constellation of Hebrew modernist writers such as David Fogel, Berl Pomerantz, and Haim Lensky, who emerged in the interwar period and who were based for the most part outside of the Land of Israel. Miron defines these modernist poets, including Preil, not by style or technique (they differ quite widely), but by a shared temperament: their distance from ideological fervor, their focus on individual and everyday experience, their often self-deprecating sense of humor, their intentional cultivation of peripherality. In contrast to early reviewers of Preil who attempted to account for his modernist approach, so different from most of the other Hebraists, by attributing it to American literary influences, both Feldman and Miron correctly caution against such approaches (Feldman 1986, 32–36; Miron 1993, 285–99; Miron 1999, 330–38). Preil had a certain respect for Robert Frost and Wallace Stevens, particularly as he became aware later in his career of the similarities between himself and the latter. These similarities should not be overstated, but they consist of an overlapping vocabulary (autumns and sunsets and weathers and abstractions), a seasonal structuring of the dialectic of reality and the imagination, and a need to test the flames of poetic vision in the icy ordinariness of ordinary American cities. Yet there was no direct influence, only a recognition on Preil's part that the English-language poet had mapped some of the territory in which he had been moving, a recognition that leads to the references to Stevens in Preil's later collections, and perhaps to an increase in the use of a tellingly Stevensian lexicon. (Robert Friend's fine translations of Preil in *Sunset Possibilities* sometimes exaggerate the Stevensian quality.) Indeed, the American literary presences in Preil's poetry are usually more iconic than nuanced: Whitman the amiable wanderer, Frost the hardscrabble New Englander, Stevens the aesthete-poet of peacocks. Preil himself warns us about this in a late poem:

> Likewise after many years
> when some know-it-all mumbled gravely:
>
> "At the beginning he had in him a bit
> of Whitmanism, but in his later work
> one is more sensible of a Stevensian polish"—
> I was convinced that there was no comparison whatsoever.
> Each of these poets is peripheral
> (at most) to the game of sleep I play.
> (Preil 1987, 37)

ATONING FOR POETRY

As Miron reminds us, Preil began his poetic career during the mounting horrors of the 1930s: the Great Depression, the Spanish Civil War, the Moscow Show Trials, the Nazi persecution of the Jews. In Miron's estimation,

Preil's poetry was overwhelmed at the start by these dark events. Indeed, in his first collection, published in 1944, Preil gives voice to the deep pessimism he felt concerning the significance of poetry in the face of the catastrophes of his day. In such ghastly times, poetry is only "a meager, narrow shelter" (Preil 1972, 235) and likely not even that. In a later poem, the traditional figure for Romantic poetry is shown to be utterly useless in the face of the Nazi atrocities:

> The birds didn't capture the killers' hearts,
> didn't even know how to sweeten an answer to the demanding
>   questioners
> who were taken from the blind world,
> on the verge of some sort of blossoming.
> (Preil 1961, 72)

Preil can only hope that God will offer a "song of comfort" to the murdered children, while the living sit in mute silence. The same bitter stance toward the aspirations of the Romantic poet mark poems such as "Hameah hatsha-esreh" (The nineteenth century), wherein Preil yearns for the innocence of earlier times but can be "only a chronicler of hard facts on a fragile table" (1954, 100). In another poem, written in 1952, Preil compares the knowledge of the death camps to Whitman's experience of the Civil War, telling the American poet that "my wounds are more fatal than those of any of the soldiers you loved" (1961, 100). For Preil, the enormity of the Holocaust nullified the basic assumptions of literary romanticism. In a number of his longer poems from the 1940s (e.g., "Birches," "Maine Landscapes," "A Little Wreath of Poems for Aviah"), he goes out to the pristine landscapes of rural New England only to find that any moments of solitary forgetfulness or communion with beauty are quickly swallowed up by the fear, rage, and guilt stemming from his awareness of the war against the Jews.

Nor was he the only Hebrew writer in America to view his pursuit of aesthetic or sensual pleasure as somehow constituting a sin against his people. The main character of Reuven Wallenrod's novel *Ki fanah yom* (*Dusk in the Catskills*) is a Catskills resort owner haunted by the obscene incommensurateness between his American existence and his knowledge of what is occurring in Europe: "You had here wide peaceful spaces and blue skies and green trees, while over there old men, women and children were pressed into filthy box cars with black fear hovering over them and cruel eyes peering from every corner" (Wallenrod 1957, 6).[6] Avraham Zvi Halevy's poem "Va'ani bevigdei tsava hamudot" (And I am in my dashing uniform) describes the poet's guilt while serving as a U.S. solider in the Second World War regarding the conflict between his sensual desires for the world and its beauty, on the one hand, and his awareness of what his people are suffering. After depicting a beautiful autumn landscape and girls walking by, "their lovely budding breasts moistening the eye and weakening the knee" (Halevy 1948, 38), he concludes with the judgment: "And I am guilty, for my soul longs for the world and its charms / And I am guilty, my heart goes out to fields and to poems" (39).[7]

Halkin, too, grappled with the conflict between the vocation of the Romantic poet who seeks, in the experience of natural beauty, intimations of the divine, and the searing knowledge of the modern Jew overwhelmed by the nightmare of the Holocaust and the desperate struggles of his people in the Land of Israel. Yet while Preil responded by further suppressing the Romantic registers in his poetry, Halkin's major long poems of the 1940s— we will discuss "Beharerei-haholot beMishigen" ("At the Sand Dunes of Michigan") and "Mar'ot beNovah Skotyah" ("Visions in Nova Scotia")— attempt to hold fast to the project of Romantic nature poetry and so are both more acutely and more openly conflicted, and more grand and unpredictable, in their results.

The sonnet cycle "Beharerei-haholot beMishigen" was written in 1943–44, against the background of the glacier-carved, wind-sculpted, still-shifting landscape that had inspired much of the Indian folklore that found its way, via the ethnological reports of Henry Rowe Schoolcraft, into English poetry in the form of Longfellow's *Hiawatha*. When Halkin visited the dunes they were already a popular resort area, but they still could have

6. In his superb story "Arba'ah hadarim beViliamsburg" (Four rooms in Williamsburg), Wallenrod offers a poignant study of the way that family strife and human limitations inevitably persist even in the shadow of destruction.

7. This translation leans on Wallenrod's in his *The Literature of Modern Israel* (1956, 242).

been expected to provide the solitude and sublimity necessary for a poet seeking transcendence in nature. In these sonnets, Halkin wants to hold on to a Wordsworthian belief in the saving power of nature. He wants to believe that God's goodness is manifest in nature's beauty. This is what, in sonnet 5, he calls the "blessing of the eye" (1977, 281): the Romantic experience of beauty that, though transient, points toward God's presence in creation. Through the eye, the poet discovers "the possibility of redemption in this ephemeral view." When, in the first sonnet, "the eye of man . . . awakens" to a tremulously radiant, rain-cleansed landscape, then "man's heart is overcome" (279). The heart, here the organ of memory, conscience, duty, and guilt, is quieted by the eye. Beauty overcomes history. But only momentarily, for the consciousness of the Holocaust undoes the Romantic apprehension of natural beauty, turning it into sin and guilt. In the final lines of the first sonnet, dead Jews suddenly appear in the sunny, blue skies. In the fourth sonnet, Halkin asks:

> Who then will pardon the heart, broken and guilty,
> as it clings to a mushroom, to a bug on a twig, to a raspberry's
> sheen,
> as it clings to the sight of a storm-swept tree, a thundercloud?
> (S. Halkin 1977, 281)

In the face of his people's torment, every appreciation of natural beauty becomes a transgression. "Never will the shame of my poem be erased," he writes, "the poem of one who lives upon blood." By sonnet 11, the American landscape blurs into the forests of Europe: not a site of beauty or transcendence but of mass murder, of innocent Jews whispering psalms "before the death squads, the demons swinging their clubs / among the birch trees" (285). In the same sonnet, Halkin cites tropes from the books of Daniel and Ezekiel of redemption after suffering, only to break off disgustedly: "Let this search for God, this game of hide-and-seek, end." There can be no redemption given the murder of the victims, and to expect one is sinful: "Let the sin of my life without you be cleansed. Erase the sin / of expecting a day of redemption, a day of salvation, without you" (285). If there can be no redemption, then nature promises nothing, and Romantic and traditional metaphysics alike are shattered.

Halkin considers this possibility, yet he ultimately refuses it, preserving his damaged, besieged romanticism. "Beharerei-haholot beMishigen" concludes by affirming, if ever so tentatively, the hint of redemption within beauty. A "leaf on a tree," Halkin writes, "[s]till alludes to something eternal, without ever atoning for its sin" (287). Although the poet's guilt cannot be dispelled, he chooses to emphasize the continuing evidence of redemption he sees in the world. To appreciate beauty during catastrophe is sin. Yet beauty still promises the redemption of sin.

This fragile optimism is absent in "Mar'ot beNovah Skotyah," a sequence of poems begun in 1948 during Halkin's final quest for peace and tranquility in the North American landscape. Here too the poet seeks in nature a deliverance from the horrors of history, and here too he is pursued by guilt and fear. Yet there are fundamental differences between his Nova Scotia and Michigan poems, indicated first of all by their form. The latter poem is a (partial) corona, a series of sonnets in which the fifteenth and final sonnet is composed of the first lines of all fourteen preceding sonnets. (In Hebrew literary history, this form is indissolubly linked with Saul Tchernikhovsky, a poet to whom Halkin was drawn and whose major coronas meditate on the possible redemption in poetic structure of the chaos and barbarity of modern war.) The Michigan sonnets do not make a true corona, in which the last line of each sonnet is the first line of the next, an imperfection that suggests that Halkin was not fully able to connect the contradictory impulses of his experience. Yet the corona, with its integrated final sonnet, does suit the poem's ultimate affirmation of a redemptive, Romantic metaphysics. The Nova Scotia series, on the other hand, includes a range of different forms, from rhymed quatrains to unrhymed hexameters to a nine-line stanza. Both more formally and thematically varied, the sections of "Mar'ot beNovah Skotyah"—a greater poem, I think, than the Michigan sonnets—interrelate but do not at first glance comprise anything like a seamless whole. The poem's unity derives instead from the larger symmetry with which Halkin has arranged the separate sections of his poem, which can be mapped roughly as shown in table 1. This mirrored tableau gives the disparate poems a loose, dramatic structure, placing the emphasis on the crisis at the poem's center without necessarily implying the sort of resolution inherent in, for instance, the sonnet and sonnet cycle.

TABLE 1. STRUCTURE OF "MAR'OT BENOVAH SKOTYAH" BY SECTION

1–3	4	5–9	10	11–13
Arrival	Interlude	Crisis	Interlude	Departure
tension between		night of		tension between
guilt and beauty		terror		guilt and beauty

In "At the Sand Dunes of Michigan" Halkin is trying to find God. In "Visions in Nova Scotia" he is first of all trying to lose himself. This shift is indicated by the role of the eye, of sight, which is just as central (as the title would indicate) in the Nova Scotia poems as in the Michigan sonnets. In the Michigan sonnets, the eye affords the possibility of transcendence because it can perceive, in the world's beauty, intimations of the divine. In the Nova Scotia poems, nature has a far more ambiguous relation to God. Vision therefore affords not hints of salvation, but a nullification of the self in the sweet facticity of the visual. The poet wants to shed all fear and grief, all memory and obligation, all connection with the human race, all sense of self, until "there is nothing now but the faculty of sight" (S. Halkin 1977, 307). This is a seeing that obliterates the self, a seeing of such perfect plenitude that, paradoxically, it is often indistinguishable from a kind of blindness. The vistas of sky and sea upon which "the eye sates its thirst" (310) merge in misty radiance, a visual counterpart to the silence toward which these poems also strive. Seeing is an escape from history, consciousness, and conscience into the serene immanence of the seen.

This loss of self through sight also exists in the Michigan poems, but not for the poet. Instead, it is God who, in the third Michigan sonnet, "dive[s] into the light of day" (280). His is "the only eye" looking calmly out on a world redeemed through sight. Like a grizzled fisherman, God squats on the rocky shore, "in His eyes no trace of sorrow" while "His gaze caresses that sandy, sinless vale, / as if the sight of the world's fullness had washed it of blood and wickedness" (280). To see, to drink in the world through the eyes, and not to grieve, is to be as God. In "Visions in Nova Scotia," the poet attempts to be like God in the Michigan poems, beyond grief and shame, experiencing a purity in vision, entirely, supremely alone ("as if mankind had ceased to exist"). The poetic mode here is still Romantic, but it is not the cheerful romanticism of the self in harmony with God through nature, but the dark and wild sublime in which the self is obliterated in nature. As Emerson famously wrote of a walk in the woods:

> There I feel that nothing can befall me in life,—no disgrace, no calamity (leaving me my eyes), which nature cannot repair. Standing on the bare ground,—my head bathed by the blithe air and uplifted into infinite space,—all mean egotism vanishes. I become a transparent eyeball; I am nothing; I see all. (Emerson 1981, 11)

As in the rest of Halkin's oeuvre, such Romantic paradigms are difficult to separate from those he derived from Hasidism: the dissolution of the self in order to apprehend true, pure reality; the clinging to the world through sight, with its kabbalistic overtones of adhesion to God; the brokenhearted poet seeking solace alone in nature. All these—*bitul hayesh, devekut, hitbodedut,* to use their Hasidic terms—were familiar to Halkin before he had ever read the Hebrew, Russian, German, or English Romantics.

Halkin's solitude is momentarily interrupted in section 4, as he watches a local farmer at work in the fields. However, the encounter serves only to increase the poet's sense of disconnection from his surroundings. The section juxtaposes, on the one hand, the North American man of the soil, "surrounded and secure" (S. Halkin 1977, 310) in his environment, and who partakes of the same unthinking, "humble animal gladness" as the ox harnessed before him; on the other hand, the Jewish wanderer, embarrassed by his longing for human connection, embarrassed by his lack of belonging to the splendid vistas around him ("the expanse of the earth, the space of the heavens so vast— / and how narrow the steps of the traveller"), embarrassed by his self-consciousness and "sad strangeness." There is a faintly homoerotic, quasi-Whitmanian element in Halkin's mournful gazing at the farmer's "sweaty coat, swelling / around his hips," the poet's sadness at his unreturned greeting which, because of "the reaper's refusal of his silent love bundled like a sheaf," will not touch "him, his sweaty coat, and the power / of man within it" (310). Yet this solitary reaper is primarily an image of the immanence and tranquility Halkin yearns for, another instance of the American Hebraist attraction to the rural, non-Jewish world, as discussed in chapter 4.

The poem reaches a crisis in the middle sequence (the sixth through ninth poems). At first Halkin watches the "sunset, / terrible in its bronze conflagrations" (311) and sees the sky turn to a majestic "purple gauze cut by the half moon" (312). As night falls, however, he is thrown back into his own fear, his ravenous need for God. Halkin should feel a sense of benign marvel at the beauty of the night, he should experience the night as a refuge, "a tower ever safe, ever closed." But natural beauty cannot speak to human dread. Rather than the sublime loss of self he had hoped to achieve, he finds himself stamped irrevocably with his insufficiency, locked into his own human finitude. Nature cannot absorb or console him; it merely is. The "world's beauty" (313) and "man's orphanhood" both persist, side by side, the second unassuaged by the first. The extrahuman "night of splendor" (312) is simultaneously an all-too-human "night of terror" (313). Without God, nature is "the hopeless void" in which the poet stumbles, "like a child" (312) mad with fear.

At the poem's midpoint, Halkin's father, who had died in 1933, appears with echoes of *Hamlet* and *Don Giovanni:*

> My father comes tonight, alive in death,
> tonight in the third watch:
> in pity and in mournful silence
> he points noiselessly
>
> to the window, in which a band of sky
> is inlaid with the seven stars of the Big Dipper,
> frozen in the palpable black of the horizon,
> huge enough to rend the eyes.
> (S. Halkin 1977, 313)

The father's gesture underscores that nature is not the sufficiency of sight but the engulfing, indifferent void, "huge enough to rend the eyes." "My father is no more," writes Halkin. "Only death and I stand before the amazed stars . . . and there is no strength to scream, O God!" (313). Halkin is no longer the Romantic poet, but the Jewish son yearning desperately for his absent father and beloved God.

Halkin does not resolve this crisis. Whereas section 9 finds him tearfully pleading for his father to take him to penitential prayers where he might relearn how "to pray to the unremembered, unforgotten God" (314), section 10 is a lovely, placid sonnet, unrelated to what has gone before. Night here is benign, a happy return to childhood's "exalted riddle" (315). This is not an answer to the previous sections but an interpolation, an interlude. Nor does Halkin return to his night of terror in the three concluding sections of the poem. Instead, he connects the existential guilt and shame before God, which he describes in the middle sections, to his sense of guilt before his people. The season is Indian summer, as in "Tarshisha" a figure for the entrancing plenitude of America, yet more emphasized here is the sense of Indian summer as a time of glorious twilight finality, a liminal season "between fecundity and death" (316). The poet, a "survivor" and a "wanderer," addresses a lone, lame bird who, like the poet, seems to have remained apart from his "people." This is the bird that has cast off "the yoke of life and fate," choosing to die alone in the deepening cold rather than join his fellows in a warm and far-off land. A reversal of Bialik's famous bird who bears tidings of national revival in the Land of Israel to the poet in Diaspora, Halkin's bird, like the poet "a living-dying creature" (317), stays in North America, preferring the solitude, the beauty, and the oblivion of nature ("without demands or commands") to the anguish of national history.

Yet, as in the Michigan sonnets, this is a sin for which Halkin must atone. In section twelve, imitating the Yom Kippur liturgy, Halkin asks for forgiveness:

> for the sin I committed by hinting at salvation in sunrises and
>   sunsets,
> when my people's salvation howled as children were hung on
>   the gallows,
>
> and for the sin I committed by trembling falsely over the
>   miracle of light in a tree,

> when my people trembled at the survivors bringing their ruined
> land to life . . .
>
> (S. Halkin 1977, 317–18)

In this *al het,* Halkin beseeches not God but the Jewish people ("Forgive me, pardon and redeem me, my people of great forgiveness" [318]), martyred in the Holocaust and struggling desperately for life in the Land of Israel. To seek release from history in natural beauty, to write as a solitary poet in nature rather than as a member of the nation in its agony, to linger in the North American landscape while the fate of the Jewish people is being decided in Israel—Halkin experiences these as rending sins. If the existential predicament of his own human fragility and finitude, his unanswered quest for God in his night of terror cannot be solved, he can nevertheless atone for his historical sins by joining his people in the Land of Israel.

This seems to me to be the context for the final poem of the series, a sorrowful love poem to and leave-taking of his "northern landscape." "[W]ith no expectation ever again to drink of your abundance with quiet eye," Halkin is bidding farewell not merely to the landscape of Nova Scotia but, more fundamentally, to his Diaspora existence in North America as a whole. He refers to his love for the landscape as "the sin of Tarshish" (319), a passion that he will not be able to excise from his yearning heart. Not long before his final departure, he again confesses the powerful and painful hold Tarshish-America has on his soul. "[T]ied to you by a curse," even when he is far away and never to return, "the swish of your birches [is] sealed within him," "the sin of your cool, fine fragrances wafts within him," and his prayer for Tarshish persists "like lingering perfume." The primary sense shifts from sight to sound and scent as Halkin concludes his difficult and tender goodbye to America.

GHOST WRITERS

That same summer in Nova Scotia, Halkin saw a ghost. Yaakov Rabinowitz, the great Hebrew man of letters whose simultaneously encouraging and stern criticism of American Hebrew literature had prompted Halkin's entry into the Americanness debate, and whom Halkin had greatly admired as a writer and trusted as a mentor and friend, was hit by a truck and killed in April 1948 at the age of seventy-two. The accident occurred in Tel Aviv in the midst of the agonizing struggle that would determine the survival of the nascent Jewish state. Yet according to the author's note preceding Halkin's long poem, "Yaakov Rabinovits beYarmut" (Yaakov Rabinowitz in Yarmouth):

> While I was staying for a time in the town of Yarmouth in Nova Scotia, at the end of the summer of 1948, I was accompanied for over two days of meanderings, as if in a vision, by the late Yaakov Rabinowitz of blessed memory, who had died in a road accident in the spring of that year. He conversed with me at length, in his own voice and in his particular manner, about a number of different matters, and immediately upon my return to my hotel I wrote down his words, as my heart was pounding all that night after our leave-taking. (S. Halkin 1977, 376)

To the end of his life, Halkin insisted that the deceased Rabinowitz had indeed appeared to him that summer in Canada. The record of his vision is both one of Halkin's major poems and perhaps the most curious elegy in modern Hebrew poetry. Like Milton's "Lycidas," "Yaakov Rabinowitz in Yarmouth" honors a dead writer and companion in a series of meditations that end with dawn. Yet in Halkin's poem the speaker is the dead writer. If this conceit—or, according to Halkin, event—has a literary cousin, it may be the American poet James Merrill's communions with departed writers in his Ouija board poems. Perhaps there is also a faint echo of the kabbalistic custom of the *ushpizin* (guests), in which the patriarchs (in this case, Jacob) are thought to pay a visit during the holiday of Sukkot.[8]

"Yaakov Rabinowitz in Yarmouth" is a poem of thresholds, not only between life and death, but also between past and future, between the new Jewish state that is coming into being in the travails of an unwanted war, and the Diasporic and prestate Jewish experience that has gone

---

8. While I would like to believe Halkin's account of Rabinowitz's visitation, the fact that the first section of the poem was not published until 1952 and that subsequent sections did not begin to appear until the 1960s suggests that the 1948 date of composition is doubtful.

before. The poignant quality of the poem—Halkin granted a final night with his dead friend—is increased by the tangled net of associations woven by Rabinowitz's speeches, a net that seems to catch up prestate Jewish history and literature, old and departed Zionist visionaries and writers, the lost world of Eastern Europe, the nineteenth century, and to bid all this a fond but unavoidable farewell. As the State of Israel comes into being, Rabinowitz meditates on Ahad Ha'am, Hibat Tsion, and the Haskalah, jumping amongst nineteenth-century figures from the Jewish and non-Jewish worlds: Nahman Krochmal and Solomon Rubin, Burckhardt and Taine.

Halkin's claim to be a scribe recording the monologues of his dead friend is given support by the significant stylistic shift constituted by the poem. Unlike his syntactically dense signature style with its high literary-philosophical register, "Yaakov Rabinowitz in Yarmouth" is written in straightforward and conversational iambic hexameters, Rabinowitz holding forth to his friend, whom he addresses by his nickname, *tsadik* (holy man, an ironic reference to Halkin's Hasidic background and influences). This stylistic shift moves the poem closer to everyday spoken Hebrew than anything seen before in Halkin's poetry and even has something of a Yiddish ambience in its cadence and syntax, its conversational, associative, and colorful quality. Indeed, in its associativeness, the poem depicts a kind of placelessness, the mental geography of the immigrant and the exile, in which the actual landscape becomes ghostly as it continually conjures the memories of other places. (This geographical overflow, a simultaneous being everywhere and nowhere, at times resembles Preil's poetry.) Rabinowitz, who appreciates the strangeness of meeting up with Halkin in Nova Scotia "of all places" (376) and, as he puts it in a delicious understatement, "not necessarily alive," immediately muses on the name of Yarmouth—how it reminds him of a place named in the books of Joshua and Nehemiah (both, significantly, narratives of *shivat Zion*—return to Zion), and how he remembers reading about Nova Scotia forty years ago (also a significant number) when he was a Zionist activist traveling in southern Russia. We move from Canada to biblical Israel to Bessarabia, and the poem has only just commenced. The poem even ends its first canto (the first of four) on a sudden associative swerve as Rabinowitz anticipates the arrival of evening in Yarmouth: "And there'll be stars too, pale ones, just a few, / And a scent of flowers like in Copenhagen" (385).[9]

Yet it emerges in the poem that Rabinowitz is less of a ghost than Halkin is. It is Halkin, wandering around in Nova Scotia while the yishuv in the Land of Israel is fighting for its life, who is the real ghost—disconnected, floating outside of the Jewish world. There is a growing and sharpening rejection, throughout the poem, of this Diasporic ghostliness, although in the first half of the poem there is still an occasional embrace of this unworldliness—the pattern, again, of Halkin's struggle with the sin of Tarshish. The poem's second section ends with a blurring, a merging of opposites—light and dark, literature and reality, life and death, Diaspora and Israel—into one chiaroscuro unity. Rabinowitz observes with a mixture of wistfulness and irony that he and Halkin could as easily be in Tel Aviv as in Yarmouth: "No, only the jackals are missing here—but instead there are / the howling voices of ships in the night. / So what's the big difference, tell me, *tsadik*, really?" (395).

In the remainder of the poem, however, Rabinowitz answers his own question unmistakably: the difference between Tel Aviv and Yarmouth is as decisive as the difference between life and death, and no man can long hover between the two. The third section commences with the hard reality of war: "the whole yishuv one besieged city / without bulwark or rampart" (396). It should be remembered that a horrifying 1 percent of the entire Jewish population of Israel was killed in the 1948 war, and many of the slain were survivors of the death camps of Europe who had only just arrived in their new home before they were killed in combat with invading Arab armies intending to expunge the Jewish state. In the final section, especially, the poem gives voice to guilt at not being in Israel and anger at Diaspora Jews who can go about their lives untouched by the devastations of their people. Commenting at one point on what he sees as the complacence of American Jews regarding Israel's dire existential situation, Rabinowitz says:

9. I have used here Hillel Halkin's translation of the poem's first canto (H. Halkin 1988). The writer and translator Hillel Halkin is Shimon Halkin's nephew and has written a remembrance of his uncle in "My Uncle Simon" (H. Halkin 2005).

it was hard for me to imagine how a Jew
in the Land of Israel continued to live
from day to day after the destruction of the Temple.
But it wasn't difficult for me then to imagine
how a Jew in Alexandria or Tarsus
received the news of the destruction:
it's certain he came home from the market sighing,
perhaps weeping bitterly in his wife's presence—
and she is silent a moment and nods her head
and barely restrains herself from asking right away
if he's hungry.

                    (S. Halkin 1977, 412–13)

By the end of the poem, the difference between life and death, so apparently blurred in the conversation of shades in Nova Scotia, is marked out in terms of the values of Jewish national existence, then as now under threat. If death has value for Rabinowitz it is the solace of not having to witness the grieving parents of the Jewish partisans fallen in battle for their country. And if life has value, it is in being able to be a part of that country. Rabinowitz admits he is jealous of the living, "for they—if they so desire—can go there" to the Land of Israel. "If I were in your place," he tells Halkin, "I would be there again tomorrow" (423).

After "Yaakov Rabinowitz in Yarmouth" Halkin continued to fuse the demanding syntax and high Romantic register of his earlier poetry with elements of colloquial speech, and this went hand in hand with a shift in tone and perspective, a greater willingness to include wry humor, and a slow relinquishing of his anguished metaphysical questing. And like Preil, Halkin continued in his later years to add to the richness of his poetic output. Some of Halkin's most beautiful and affecting poems were written in his seventies. One of these is the poem "Jerusalem, New York?" a poem Halkin dedicated "To Gabriel Preil with love."[10] The poem might even be

10. This is the dedication attached to the poem in its first appearance in the May 1974 issue of the journal *Siman kriah*. The poem's later reprinting in Halkin 1977 shortens the dedication to "For Gabriel Preil."

taken at first for a Preil poem because of its meditation on snow, its dissolution of the present in memory, and the combination of long lines and short sentence fragments. In the poem, a heavy snowfall in Jerusalem—which really is an amazing experience—intensifies Halkin's sense of Jerusalem's vivid uniqueness: "Only in Jerusalem," a phrase the poem repeats three times, does the sight of doves atop a snow-covered tree "astonish like a revelation at life's end" (442–43). At the same time, however, Jerusalem dissolves into memories of Dubsk (where Halkin was born) and New York, becoming, in its startling whiteness, a "city that is never singular." The disorienting snow allows Halkin to give himself over to a wistful imagining of his own death. "Only in Jerusalem is it also good to die," he writes with a curious echo of the Trumpeldor line, "as in a sudden kiss / on a morning of snow." Most strikingly, Halkin's death, and his serene, almost childlike acceptance of it, is portrayed in the terms of Preil's café guard: an inviting café, an attractive waitress, a bottomless cup of coffee, an always renewable dream of love. Yet this is no vindication of Preil's café existence. The sweet detachment of Preil's ethereal, Proustian café guard is an image for Halkin's death, not his ideal life.

Preil had by this time made his first visits to Israel, beginning in 1968. Asked why he took so long to visit Israel, Preil had difficulty explaining his reluctance. "I wanted to sit by myself on this island called the United States and write my poetry" (1993b), he said, intentionally or unintentionally echoing the title of Halkin's first collection of poems, *Al ha'i* (On the island). When Preil finally did encounter the reality of Israel, the result was a profound and exciting shock to his poetry. Prior to this encounter, his poems had tended to link Israel with the imagination and America with reality. Certainly, in the earlier poems, America is the cold to counter the heat of an imaginary Israel. These categories spin vertiginously when Preil visits Israel and the terrain of the imagination is suddenly transformed into the real. The results consist in a new set of highly Stevensian possibilities and conundrums. Will the collision of imagination and reality allow Preil a barer, more penetrating apprehension of reality? Can such a reality, perceived in such bareness, sustain the imagination? Or will Israel, with its text-drenched geography, overwhelm the imagination with a welter of poetic tropes so that reality is lost?

In "Levanah yerushalmit" (Jerusalem moon), one of the first poems Preil wrote in Israel, he observes (in Robert Friend's translation) that the moon "is not now a silver vessel on an azure sea, / nor any other metaphor that drops / from rhetoric's tired trees" (Preil 1985, 77). (Or as Wallace Stevens put it in "The Man on the Dump": "Everything is shed; and the moon comes up as the moon" [Stevens 1990, 202].) Yet Preil still does require metaphor, calling this barer, trope-stripped moon "the single slice of bread / to feed my hunger," an image that suggests his anxiety that mere reality may not be enough to sustain his poetry. On the other hand, it may be significant that in this poem Preil refers to the moon with the more poetic Hebrew term *levanah*, rather than the more prosaic and masculine *yare'ah*—perhaps indicating the impossibility of detaching words from rhetoric's concealing foliage. In a much later poem, "Panim bemar'ah yerushalmit" (A face in a Jerusalem mirror), Preil experiences a snowstorm in Jerusalem as a kind of liberation from the trope-heavy landscape of Israel. In the dislocating whiteness, he imagines he is back in America, with its purer, barer reality: "I'm stuck, it seems to me, / in Maine, in Montana, / perfect in their winter" (Preil 1993a, 214). Suddenly, Preil looks up and sees "the Church of the Dormition / unsheath its bold majestic height," an undeniably Freudian moment that Preil experiences as a threatening return from American blankness to the overdetermined Israeli terrain:

> and I am trapped
> among the rugged peaks of a pale text,
> chapters of the plain resting
> among the chain of hills,
> a competition of interpretations
> in this erudite view.
>   (Preil 1993a, 214–15)

Yet while Israel could be threatening to Preil, trapping the poet in its interpretations, Preil's return to the United States was rendered more difficult by his encounters with the richness of the Hebrew country. Like Paul Celan returning to Paris from Jerusalem, Preil seems to have felt a greater paucity in his Diaspora existence, though he alleviated it with his sardonic and self-deprecating humor, as in the poem "Adiv le'atsmi" (Courteous to myself):

"I disregarded in Jerusalem / my title to nobility. / In New York I am a threadbare jacket / hanging on an old clothes-hanger" (1985, 25).

Ultimately, the impact of Israel on Preil's poetry was to sharpen the collisions between reality and the imagination, not to end them. Preil incorporated his visits to the Jewish state into the poetic dialectics he had always grappled with. Increasingly, the central instance of the unsettling disjuncture between reality and the imagination in Preil's poetry was not Israel but the experience of old age, which Preil expressed so poignantly in his later poetry, and especially the widening rift between one's private image of oneself, shaped by memory, and the contradictory images thrust upon one by the unforgiving, indifferent mirrors of the present. Preil's longevity increased his sense of alienated whimsy. Having long outlived the brief heyday of Hebrew poetry in America, and most of the poets themselves, he came to embody American Hebrew poetry as its last representative.

Which brings us to Preil's final conversation with Halkin, a conversation that never took place but could only be hoped for in a poem. Preil had first dedicated a poem to Halkin in 1944, "The Watch of Yearning" that we discussed earlier, depicting a poet conjuring up memories in a New York café. As we have seen, Halkin's reply came several decades later in his "Jerusalem, New York?" in which a café on a winter's day becomes an image of memory, friendship, and death. Finally, in 1988, Preil published "Meser lididi Sh. Halkin" (A message to my friend S. Halkin"), a mournful response to Halkin's death in November of the preceding year. In this poem, Preil recalls his strolls with Halkin "in the New York we loved so much" (Preil 1988, 12), their beloved cafés and the pretty waitresses therein, their conversations about literature, the "elegiac poem" ("Jerusalem, New York?") Halkin had dedicated to Preil, Halkin's encouragement of the younger poet's work, and the touching inscription Halkin wrote in a booklet of poems just before he died. Preil wants to be able to continue their conversation, to return the dedication, but this is now impossible. And so he ends their exchange:

> And it's sad, so sad I could cry,
> that I can't give you in return
> an expansive, trembling elegy

or a shortish harvest line
dear Halkin mine.

(12)

Preil himself died in 1993. With his death, the story of the immigrant Hebraists and the literature they created in America came to an end. Perhaps Halkin would have appreciated the fact that his friend died while on a visit to Jerusalem—although, it being June, there was no snow.

7

The Last Mohicans

"I myself am an Indian astonished before a darkening glass."
—Gabriel Preil, *Adiv le'atsmi*

"A zoo for defeated languages. Come on, kids, let's visit the Hebrew cage."
—Nava Semel, *Iyisrael*

BY THE END OF THE 1960S, much of the literary culture built by the Hebraists in America had disappeared—transferred to the State of Israel or to the more mysterious territory of the world beyond. The concentration of Hebrew literature almost exclusively in the State of Israel was, as we have seen, already well underway in the interwar period. Yet it was not until the postwar period that American Hebraism was increasingly stripped of its major writers and activists, left as a graying movement struggling for membership and financial support despite the strenuous efforts of its partisans. In the late 1940s and 1950s, major figures in American Hebrew literature such as Shimon Halkin, Israel Efros, Avraham Regelson, and Yohanan Twersky moved to the State of Israel. The 1960s would deal a further series of blows to the community of Hebrew writers in the United States with the deaths of Hillel Bavli, Reuven Wallenrod, Ephraim Lisitzky, and Avraham Tzvi Halevi, among others.

This is not to say that Hebraism did not achieve significant successes after its interwar heyday. In the 1940s, for instance, Camp Masad was founded, the first of a series of Hebrew-speaking summer camps affiliated with or inspired by the Hebraist movement, and which for at least part of the year created a total Hebrew environment for their participants. The 1940s was also a time of considerable activity in the youth wing of the

Hebraist movement, some of whose members (such as Gerson Cohen, later the chancellor of the Jewish Theological Seminary of America, and Abraham Foxman, later the director of the Anti-Defamation League of B'nai Brith) would go on to assume influential roles in Jewish communal life. The postwar period saw successful educational initiatives and new publications. Led by new generations of capable editors, *Hadoar,* the central publication of American Hebraism and one of the longest-existing Hebrew periodicals in the world, continued to publish into the twenty-first century. Hebrew literature of high quality continued to be produced.

Nevertheless, it is indisputable that, overall, the postwar decades were characterized by developments that slowly strangled American Hebraism. The extreme extent of linguistic and cultural assimilation among American Jews; the exciting and hard-won novum of the State of Israel as a Hebrew-speaking nation; the post-Holocaust turn among American Jewry to nostalgic conceptions of Eastern Europe that left little room for an appreciation of the diverse ideological and cultural experiments tried in that laboratory: these developments relegated even the existence of American Hebraism to the dimmest part of the American Jewish cultural memory. Without readers, without new writers, the waters of possibility for an American Hebrew literature all but dried up, leaving the remaining writers of significance moored upon lonely islands separated one from the next, rather than as parts of an active cultural movement.[1]

In the early 1950s, Gabriel Preil had already reflected in a poem on the immanent disappearance of this culture. In "Hamtanah lamahar ha'atomi" (Waiting for the atomic tomorrow, part of Preil's "Poems from a Café" series), the speaker ponders with a mixture of sardonic understatement and resigned serenity what will happen "in the future, after our little world is blown up" (Preil 1954, 36). In his surmise of how extraterrestrial academics might one day reflect on a defunct humanity's archeological remains, we see that the poem is not only an expression of Cold War fears of atomic destruction. It is, above all, a proleptic elegy for American Hebrew

---

1. For the most complete treatment of the condition of the Hebraist movement in postwar America, see Pelli (1998).

literature. In words that I have tried to keep before me throughout the writing of this book, as they caution humility to the academic who approaches American Hebraism from the outside, Preil depicts his future—i.e., our detached present:

> Sipping lukewarm coffee in a time of conflagration,
> a time of waiting for the atomic tomorrow,
> will perhaps be considered one of the strangest of our customs,
> in the future, after our little world is blown up.
> Then, on a neighboring planet, a scholar will discuss us, an
>   historian will analyze us:
> we will seem to them like faceless Indians, like anonymous
>   Aztecs,
> we will seem to them like the tribes that were scattered and
>   lost.

The Indian motif signals that the poem is to a great extent about the American Hebrew literary culture that claimed such lost tribes as its central and self-prophesying image. Preil issues a message of instructive caution to academics like myself who would one day discuss and analyze the apparently failed project of American Hebraism from a cultural and temporal distance that places us practically on another planet.

For an American reader, Preil's poem calls to mind Wallace Stevens's similarly self-archeologizing poem "A Postcard from the Volcano," in which the speaker tells of "Children picking up our bones," never guessing, in their confident and oblivious future, "that these were once / As quick as foxes on the hill" (Stevens 1990, 158–59). The difference, though, is that Stevens's poem affirms the enduring impact of the bygone generation upon the language of the living who, he writes, will "speak our speech and never know." Preil's poem presents the American Hebraists as "faceless Indians" and "anonymous Aztecs"—foreign and inscrutable, metaphors for precisely the vanished civilizations that have not bequeathed their culture to us (although the reference to the Lost Tribes of Israel perhaps hints vaguely at the possibility of future redemption). Preil puts us today in the position not even of the ignorant descendants of this shattered culture but of an alien species living on another world entirely.

The poem indicates other referents as well. The imagining of abso-
lute devastation and the poem's opening thought—how future researchers might look upon the practice of "sipping lukewarm coffee in a time
of conflagration" as "one of the strangest of our customs"—conjures the
shadow of the Holocaust, as the detachment of the New York café during the Korean War is made both more understandable and more dire by
the tacit gesture toward Jews sitting in the coffeehouses of Europe during
the rise of Nazism. The dry "nearby planet" and its alien researchers perhaps allude to Israel, imagined as ready to perform its autopsy of American
Hebraism, indeed, of American Judaism as a whole. Preil does not claim
this is wrong, does not claim Hebrew culture in America will thrive and
endure. Yet he also wants to speak up for the internal, lived experience of
that culture. He wants to assert, as Stevens puts it, "that with our bones /
We left much more. . . . left what we felt / At what we saw." Preil continues
with his celebratory testament to the power of coffee:

> a wise energy is hidden in the coffee bean,
> its brown thought is sharp and serious, its quickening is
> > pleasant,
> and so my daily view is infinitely greener.
> > (1954, 36–37)

The academic or archeologist, holding up the hard brown seed, will not
understand the experience of coffee (or culture) itself, unless its warmth is
unlocked and brewed. "Wise energy," indeed, for those who respond to the
idea of Hebrew in America as quixotic or absurd.

Preil's poem accepts the demise of Hebrew culture in the United States.
Nevertheless, the years following the appearance of this poem saw the
publication of many significant works of American Hebrew literature, from
prose fiction by Sackler and Wallenrod to poetry by Hebraist transplants
to Israel such as Halkin, Regelson, and Efros.[2] Preil, of course, remained

2. Although writers such as Halkin, Regelson, and Efros exerted varying degrees of
influence on Israeli cultural life, as poets they continued to be identified by literary historians as American Hebrew writers by virtue of their decades of work and publication in the
United States.

active for decades more in the United States, as did another excellent Hebrew poet, Eisig Silberschlag (1903–88), who expressed his combination of isolation and persistent hope in one of his last poems, "Meshorer shel yisrael velo b'erets yisrael" (A poet of Israel, but not in the land of Israel), which appeared in 1981. This poem begins with Silberschlag's acerbic regret at his situation as a Diasporic Hebrew poet:

> If I were in Israel, I would be
> a poet of Israel,
> published by state presses
> and not at my own expense,
> paid a reasonable writers' wage,
> read by the public,
> quoted by officials
> at the inaugurations of cultural institutions funded
> by non-Israelis.
>
> (Silberschlag 1981, 93)

The wry jibe here may indicate Silberschlag's bitterness at American Jews ("non-Israelis") who fund Israeli cultural institutions while letting Hebrew culture in their own country wither away. Yet the poem continues more philosophically:

> A poet of Israel but not in the Land of Israel:
> a strange creature. Yet before Joshua's conquest
> there were already others like him, laying the paths of the
> Hebrew poem
> by the sea, but not entering the water.
>
> (93)

Silberschlag here claims a venerable lineage for the Diasporic Hebrew poet, one even older than the Israelite nation in its land, since it predates Joshua's conquest of Canaan. Indeed, the phrase "by the sea" alludes to an even earlier work of "Diasporic" Hebrew literature: the biblical "Song at the Sea," sung before the Israelites had entered the Promised Land and recognized by scholars as one of the oldest units in the Bible. The poem then turns from the past to the future, concluding with perhaps surprising confidence in the future of Hebrew poetry in the United States:

There were others like him, and there will be more,
laying the paths of the Hebrew poem
outside of the place of their people.
(93)

"There were others like him, and there will be more": when Silber-schlag published this poem he was living in Texas, a perhaps unlikely place in which to anticipate the appearance of future Hebrew poets, although, as we will see further on, such hope was not at all misplaced. After four decades at Hebrew College in Boston, where he both taught and served as dean and president, Silberschlag was invited to Austin in 1973 to take up a visiting professorship at the University of Texas. There he remained for the last fifteen years of his life, during which he published his final two collections of poetry—sharp ruminations written with his typical musicality and stoic sensibility. Throughout these late works, Silberschlag develops his lifelong themes of isolation and otherworldliness, an isolation of which, his former student Arnold Band notes, he was quite proud.[3] Confronting the urban violence and cultural crassness of 1970s America, in these poems Silberschlag turns to the past for fellowship, identifying with the proud elitism and acerbic wisdom he finds in the figure of the medieval Hebrew poet Solomon ibn Gabirol, whom he addresses as a comrade in cultural arms:

> Much wounded you were by those slick alchemists
> who turned the fair into filth, the lofty to low.
> Yet you also knew how to give as good as you got,
> to shut up their mouths befouled as a chamberpot.
> (Silberschlag 1981, 19)

Another kindred spirit is Proust, whom Silberschlag presents meditating on the biblical Noah, both sealed off from the world beyond their interior spaces. "Like Noah, my spirit half-dozes in the ark of my room," thinks

---

3. See Band (1988). In one poem, Silberschlag describes his main vocations—poetry and teaching—not as affirmations of human communion but rather as a "double isolation" (Silberschlag 1976, 17).

Silberschlag's Proust, "walled off with cork from the city noise" (1976, 21), much like Silberschlag himself.

These late poems with their meditations on human vanity and violence are written under the sign of Ecclesiastes, yet the younger Solomon of the Song of Songs is not absent either. In the 1920s and 1930s, Silberschlag's poetry was already marked by a sensitivity to the erotic quite in contrast to the main developments of Hebrew poetry taking place in the Land of Israel. This was due in part to his early immersion in classical Greek studies, which combined potently with the Jewish Nietzcheanism he had absorbed from his Zionist youth movement as a teenager in Austria. He translated the erotic poetry of the sixth-century Byzantine poet Paulus Silentiarius as well as the plays of Aristophanes and Menander, and his cultural ideal remained to the end of his days a utopian fusion of Jewish and Greek culture perhaps achievable only in the imagination of a Central European intellectual. In his penultimate collection, the muse of desire returns in a series inspired by Persian poetry, in which the male speaker, simultaneously jealous and aroused, asks his beloved:

> Of your legion of lovers, who sucks from your breasts
> a dizzying intoxication at this moment?
> Who presses the incomparable grapes of your body
> to make wine of sensuality?
> Who pounds at your hips, who soars in your heavens
> with you in dizziness, in a spasm of delight?
> (Silberschlag 1976, 82)

Silberschlag was, apart from Preil, the last active poet among the immigrant Hebraists in America, and like Preil he too was ultimately gathered to the Jewish state. When he died in 1988, the "poet of Israel" was finally brought to "the place of his people," as his body was flown for burial on the Mount of Olives in Jerusalem.

And today? What remains of Hebrew literature in the United States? One answer can be found in the traces Hebrew has left upon American Jewish literature in English. Such traces do not necessarily indicate the influence of Hebrew itself—most American Jewish writers are largely illiterate in the language—but rather of an idea of Hebrew, the presence of an absence, a haunting of sorts. Such provocations are felt especially in poetry, where language itself is most intensely felt. Hebrew often functions as a metaphor for a lost or elusive Jewish identity and authenticity, mourned over or sought after by the poet. Charles Reznikoff, in an oft-cited poem from his 1927 sequence *Five Groups of Verse,* writes:

> How difficult for me is Hebrew:
> even the Hebrew for *mother,* for *bread,* for *sun*
> is foreign. How far have I been exiled, Zion.
> (Reznikoff 1989, 72)

Similarly, in his poem "Work Song" the contemporary poet Stanley Moss confesses his surprise that he cannot understand Hebrew when he hears people speak it. He writes that he "expects to understand [Hebrew] / without the least effort," simply because he is Jewish. This sentimental, somewhat biologistic notion that the Hebrew language is a natural patrimony for Jews and therefore requires no effort to learn it, as well as the vague sense of guilt for not doing so, is widespread among Jewish American writers. As we see in these examples, a linguistic exile, the absence of Hebrew, becomes a central symbol for Jewish assimilation in America.[4]

In American Jewish fiction we may in a few cases detect the actual footprints of the immigrant Hebraists themselves. We have already seen this in Abraham Cahan's inclusion of the Hebraist poet Tevkin in his novel *The Rise of David Levinsky.* A more complicated instance is Cynthia Ozick's famous story "Envy, or Yiddish in America." Ozick's story, about aging Yiddish writers in New York, and in particular about one poet's envy of the single Yiddish writer to break out of obscurity via English translation and

---

4. See Weingrad (2003) for reflections on the way in which American Jewish poetry in English, from Emma Lazarus to the present, has been shaped by the absence and opacity of Hebrew for these writers. For a more positive assessment of the traces of Hebrew and Yiddish in American Jewish literature in English, see Hana Wirth-Nesher's excellent study *Call It English,* in which she describes Hebrew and Yiddish as "languages that [these English-language writers] evade, repress, transgress, mourn, deny, translate, romanticize, or reify" (2006, 3).

become famous (the latter a figure generally agreed to be based upon Isaac Bashevis Singer), generated a great deal of controversy for its less than flattering, if still quite moving, portrayal of these Yiddishists, when it was first published in *Commentary* magazine in 1969. "There were articles in the Yiddish press and in periodicals, there were telephone calls, and unpleasant anonymous letters," Ozick later recalled, "and out of the blue I found myself and the magazine which had published my story branded as enemies of Yiddish and Yiddishkeyt." Yet, she explained, her motives in writing the story had been misunderstood. It was not to defame but rather to utter a plea for the treasure of Yiddish culture, murdered in Europe and forgotten in America, that she had written the story. "I wrote it as an elegy, a lamentation, a celebration, because six million Yiddish tongues were under the earth of Europe, and because here under American liberty and spaciousness my own generation, in its foolishness, stupidity, and self-disregard had, in an act tantamount to autolobotomy, disposed of the literature of its fathers" (1972, 60).[5]

More significant for our purposes is that Ozick also explained that her portrayal of the Yiddish writers that had caused such offense (especially to the great Yiddish poet Jacob Glatshteyn, who assumed he was the model for the story's desperate protagonist) was not even based on the Yiddishists. It was, she said, based instead on the immigrant Hebraist writers, whom Ozick knew through her uncle Avraham Regelson (1896–81), one of the major Hebrew poets in the United States. This striking fact makes of Ozick's story an even more intricate American Jewish cultural puzzle: a lament, written in English, for the erasure of Yiddish, modeled on the Hebraists.

The importance of Ozick's family connection with the Hebraists is not to be underestimated. Regelson was a key contributor to Hebrew literature in America (and secondarily to American Yiddish literature as well), the author of volumes of poetry, translations, essays, and children's literature, and the recipient of prestigious literary prizes in Israel, to which he moved in 1949 after living for most of four decades in the United States. Ozick has

5. For a discussion of this episode, see Klingenstein (1997).

said that her uncle was for her "a kind of spiritual model" (qtd. Friedman 1991, 2). As one critic summarizes, Ozick "feels that, somehow, he paved the way for her to embark on such a 'strange' career [i.e., that of a writer]. Because of him, she says, 'it seemed quite natural to belong to the secular world of literature'" (Lowin 1988, 4).[6]

Certainly, Regelson would have been one of Ozick's earliest models for the possibility of a profoundly Jewish cultural seriousness in America, a seriousness that Ozick herself has subsequently exemplified and advocated. In her essay "Towards a New Yiddish," she famously rendered the culturally serious mode of Jewish discourse she wished to see in the United States through the metaphor of Yiddish. Yet the essay also makes clear that it is Hebrew, again as a metaphor for Jewish cultural and moral intensity, that allows this "new Yiddish" to come into being. Like all languages, she posits, English has, as it were, a "Hebrew-speaking capacity" that is engendered by pouring "the genius of Abraham and Moses and the Prophets [that] runs like mother milk through the lips of Hebrew" into the "vessel" of this non-Jewish tongue (Ozick 1984, 152).

Regelson's passion for Hebrew is seen above all in the long poem he published in 1946. "Hakukot otiotayikh" (Engraved are your letters) has been called a "poetic tour-de-force" and "the most comprehensive, brilliant, and unusual attempt" in modern Hebrew literature "to attribute supreme metaphysical status to the Hebrew language" (Miron 2005, 90). It is a mystical love poem whose various sections praise all aspects of Hebrew—its letters, conjugations, tenses, compound words, gender, history, connection to the Jewish people and Land of Israel, etc.—in each instance making skillful use of the linguistic element being praised.[7] In the glorious opening sec-

6. As of this writing, Regelson's daughter Sharona maintains a Web site devoted to her father's work: http://www.abrahamregelson.org/. In English, see Hudson (1988), which includes an extensive critical bibliographical essay.

7. Dan Miron remarks that it was "no accident" (2005, 90) that such a poem was written in the United States. The almost religious passion of the American Hebraists for their language, which in some sense had to function as the national territory they lacked, often resembles the traditional Jewish and kabbalistic apprehension of the holy tongue as more

tions of the poem, Regelson identifies Hebrew with the creation of the cosmos, with the botanical and zoological proliferation of life on earth, and with the entire Jewish conception of cosmic history as creation, exile, and redemption. As he anatomizes his beloved language, Regelson describes himself as "a lover, enumerating the praises of his lady, though his expression falls short of his emotion" (Regelson 1964, 8):

> and who can seek the secrets of your letters' shapes, the sculpt-
> ing of their bodies and the crafting of their hollows,
> and who can ascend to the height of your vowels, those plan-
> etary bodies that guide the letters,
> and like the planets in the firmament are so tiny to the eye,
> even as their power is supreme?
> And who can trek to the secret place of your accentuations and
> intonations,
> the animating souls of the vowels, the melodies of the stars?
> (8–9)

This impulse to praise Hebrew, given such extraordinary force in Regelson's poem, finds expression in another of Ozick's stories, in which the protagonist admires the mathematic-mystic beauty of the Hebrew root structure:

> The Hebrew verb, a stunning mechanism: three letters, whichever fated three, could command all possibility simply by a change in their pronunciation, or the addition of a wing-letter fore and aft. Every conceivable utterance blossomed from this trinity. It seemed to her not so much a language for expression as a code for the world's design, indissoluble, predetermined, translucent. (Ozick 1997, 5)

The place of Hebrew in "Envy, or Yiddish in America," however, is less glorious, although the story does testify in various subtle ways to the fading world of the American Hebrew writers. The periodical published by the aging Yiddish poets in the story is funded through the bequest of a laxative manufacturer, a minor detail unless we know that Israel Metz, one

---

than instrumental. Alan Mintz's forthcoming book contains a brilliant and crucial discussion of this poem.

of the only major financial supporters of Hebrew literature in the United States and who helped, for instance, to support the journal *Hatoren* in the 1920s, was the owner of the Ex-Lax company.[8] The journal's title is likely the basis for another in-joke, as Ozick names the fictional Yiddish periodical in her story *Bitterer Yam* (Bitter sea): it would seem that the Mast (*Hatoren*) has finally sunk beneath the waves. I have also speculated that the character of Ostrover, long presumed to be a stand-in for and send-up of Isaac Bashevis Singer, may owe something to the figure of Gabriel Preil as well. Although Preil obviously never attained anything remotely like the fame of Singer, he did have, compared with the other American Hebraists, far more luck with English translators—a central concern of the story—and an impish personal quality not altogether dissimilar to Singer to boot. Another touch: Ozick's story first appeared in *Commentary*, and in the collection *The Pagan Rabbi and Other Stories*, in which "Envy" was subsequently published, Ozick includes the dedication "to Norman Podhoretz: *ba'al hanifla'ot*," referring to the editor of *Commentary* (himself a former student of the Hebraists at the Jewish Theological Seminary, where he received a B.A. in Hebrew literature) as a "wonderworker"—and not in Yiddish, as she might have done, but in Hebrew. Finally, the characters in "Envy" give little voice to the often nasty rivalry between Yiddishists and Hebraists that—although this rivalry was never particularly sharp in the United States as compared with Russia or Palestine—still might have marked the story. Indeed, the protagonist, Edelshtein, is clearly very fond of Hebrew.

And yet, for all this, the Hebraists upon whom Ozick based the characters in her story remain hidden here, only revealed by the author in later interviews. The work of the story, Ozick has explained, is to mourn the demise of Yiddish. A story mourning the demise of Hebrew in the United States would be even more ambivalent, as, unlike Yiddish, the language thrives elsewhere, in Israel. More than once, Edelshtein juxtaposes their two fates:

---

8. See Alan Mintz (1993, 35–36). For a portrait of Metz, see Scharfstein (1956, 225–33).

In Israel they give the language of Solomon to machinists. Rejoice—in Solomon's time what else did mechanics speak? Yet whoever forgets Yiddish courts amnesia of history. Mourn—the forgetting has already happened. (Ozick 1983, 74)

American Jewish ignorance is ignorance of Yiddish. Hebrew, on the other hand, cannot be mourned because it is a success—only not in America.[9]

In another instance, Philip Roth gives us, in one of his most intriguing short works, an obscure and lonely immigrant Hebrew teacher who is very much like the sorely put-upon Hebraists whose often unhappy tenure in the afternoon Hebrew schools ("this hell," in Y. D. Berkowitz's phrase) was dramatized in their fiction and recorded in their memoirs. Roth admits of the nine-year-old self he places in the story and his coconspirators: "we vent on [our Hebrew teacher] our resentment at having to learn an ancient calligraphy at the very hour we should be out screaming our heads off on the ball field" (Roth 1975, 258), a well-known (because so true) motif in which baseball trumps Hebrew in the *goldine medine*.

And yet, Roth's teacher is hardly an idolater of the Hebrew language. He gives his students the quite odd assignment, for a Hebrew school, of inventing their own alphabet "out of straight lines and curved lines and dots" (259). He explains: "That is all an alphabet is. . . . That is all Hebrew is. That is all English is. Straight lines and curved lines and dots." In this view, the diametrical opposite of Regelson's, there is nothing special about Hebrew—or any language for that matter—and therefore there can be no linguistic fall from a supposed Hebraic grace, a view that has implications for Roth's own status as a Jewish writer, as well as for his fictional Hebrew teacher, who is none other than Franz Kafka, audaciously reimagined as having immigrated to the United States and taken up Hebrew teaching in Newark, New Jersey. Both Roth and Kafka can be fellows, as there is nothing inherent in language that predetermines literary affinity. Yet even while Roth undoes any notion that Hebrew possesses an intrinsically exalted

---

9. Wirth-Nesher speculates that "Ozick's translation" of the Hebraists into Yiddishists might "be understood as her reluctance to associate Hebrew with the barrenness, aridity, and pettiness that she depicts" (2006, 147–48).

status, his story clearly acknowledges the real Kafka's well-documented interest in Hebrew, which he was intently learning at the end of his life and which he enjoyed speaking in public because he could savor the surprised reaction of passersby who inquired what unfamiliar language they were hearing. Roth seems here to have no interest in a metaphysical dimension to language, yet he does exhibit an abiding and incisive interest in the twists and turns of modern Jewish culture, Hebrew included.[10]

Mark Helprin, too rarely acknowledged as one of the great American Jewish fiction writers, gives us in the title story from his collection *Ellis Island* an immigration narrative whose hero is no unlettered tailor, but rather a cosmopolitan maskil who often emphasizes his Hebrew skills—not quite a Hebraist, but a close cousin. Yet it seems telling that Helprin's immigrant story is squarely in the realm of mythology: outsized and apotheosized, intentionally loosed from the conventions of history or literary realism. The result is moving, magnificent, often riotously funny—but still myth, the central aspect of this myth being that the transition from Old World to New World entails no loss but only fantastic gain. The lesson here may be that an American Hebraist can be a hero with a happy ending only in a mythical portrayal that elides the tension between Jewish and American national identity. And even then he apparently needs to go to work at the Yiddish *Forward* to make a living.

Such appearances by the immigrant Hebraists and their kin are, however, few and far between in American Jewish literature. Instead, more often than not Hebrew is no cultural proposal, no living American possibility. It is talismanic and funerary—scraps from long-abandoned religious practice, letters and phrases whose very unintelligibility and foreignness contributes to their nostalgic power—or it is Israeli and distant.[11]

In considering the state of American Hebraism today, it is worth noting that there have been several American immigrants to Israel who have made the transition into Hebrew literature, in some cases to quite spectacular

---

10. One wonders if it is only coincidence that the name of the vile Merry Levov in Roth's novel *American Pastoral* means "rebellious heart" in Hebrew.

11. Again, for a more affirmative estimation, see Wirth-Nesher (2006).

effect. This small group includes the first-rate poets T. Carmi, who grew up in a Hebraist household in the United States and so in some sense did not have to undergo a major linguistic upheaval; Reuven Ben-Yosef, whose rich career, cut short by cancer in 2001, I hope to explore at a future time; and (*yebadel lehayim arukim,* may he enjoy long life) Harold Schimmel, whose playful New York School poetics, influenced by such poets as Frank O'Hara and George Oppen and so refreshing to the Israeli poetic tradition, do not prevent him from writing a paean to Hebrew such as "Ha'alfabeta hamevorekhet," Regelsonian in its pious praise of "every Hebrew book" and "each mark and point" in them (Schimmel 1974, 7). In prose there is Jacob Jeffrey Green, more distinguished as a translator than as a fiction writer, though his 1998 novel *Sof-shavua amerikani* (American weekend), set in Western Massachusetts in the 1970s, is an affecting cultural snapshot with a Zionist force stronger for being so carefully implicit and unstated. Nevertheless, except through their work as translators, none of these writers' careers has significantly impacted the development of Hebrew culture in the United States. They have all been American-Israeli contributors to Israeli culture, not to American Jewish culture, which does not seem to recognize them as its own.[12]

What, then, happened to the Hebraist dream of raising American-born readers and, especially, writers? In fact, there have been several American-born writers who reside in America, poets all, educated by the Hebraists, who published volumes of Hebrew belles lettres. Interestingly, this short list includes two women, in notable contrast to the almost exclusively male provenance of the American Hebraists. This may reflect the frequently egalitarian tendencies of Hebraist and Jewish nationalist educators in the United States, as well as the general neglect of Jewish education in the United States, which ironically left the field more open to girls.

12. Reuven Avinoam (1905–74), raised in a Hebrew-speaking household in Chicago, was probably the first American-born Hebrew writer to publish significant volumes of belles lettres in Hebrew. He moved to Palestine early in his career. Another American Israeli Hebrew writer active today is the poet Shira Twersky-Kassel, who grew up in a Hasidic household.

Chana (Anne) Kleiman, the daughter of Russian Jewish immigrants, received an extensive Hebrew education in the 1920s at the excellent Talmud Torah in St. Joseph, Missouri, a five-day-a-week supplemental school. The St. Joseph program was one of the many achievements of the Hebraist educators who fanned out across the Mississippi Valley in the first half of the twentieth century, creating high-quality Talmud Torahs in cities such as Minneapolis; St. Paul; Indianapolis; Detroit; and Superior, Wisconsin. Moses Zalesky, a prominent Hebraist teacher at the Talmud Torah and later the head of Cincinnati's Bureau of Jewish Education for a quarter century, became Kleiman's first husband and encouraged her literary gifts. Kleiman went on to study at the University of Chicago while continuing in advanced Hebrew and Jewish studies courses at the Chicago College of Jewish Studies (today the Spertus College of Judaica), an institution that published her 1947 collection of poems, *Netafim* (Droplets).[13]

The modest title of her collection indicates the minor key in which many early twentieth-century female Hebrew poets were expected to write, even as their literary activity was also seen as a positive coming-of-age for modern Hebrew literature. Most of Kleiman's poems are indeed short, imagistic poems in the mode of the poet Rachel.[14] This in no way precludes a considerable storminess that occasionally carries over in her work into the more conventionally "masculine" register of ideological exhortations,

13. For the story of Hebraist activity in the Midwest and Mississippi Valley, see Elazar (1993). Among the teachers at the St. Joseph Talmud Torah was the accomplished fiction writer L. A. Arieli (see Hollander 2004). For biographical information about Chana Kleiman, I am indebted to her daughter, Adina Kleiman, and to Professor Shachar Pinsker of the University of Michigan. A volume of translations of Kleiman's poetry is being prepared by the poet and translator Yosefa Raz, with an introduction by Pinsker.

14. See Zierler (2004) on the ambivalent position of the early women writers in modern Hebrew literature. One of the very few books of Hebrew literature published by a woman in the United States was a 1941 volume of poetry, *Kisufim*, by the Grodno-born writer Claire Levy. Kleiman herself was particularly enamored of the Hebrew poet Anda Amir-Pinkerfeld, whom Kleiman met during a visit to Palestine in 1937 and corresponded with afterward. Also, Kleiman's active involvement in Hebraist circles should not discount the possible influence on her poetry of local, American modernist influences in English—i.e., the Chicago of *Poetry* magazine.

such as the untitled poem addressed "to the Hebraist youth" (Kleiman 1947, 14). Impatient with the dead weight of assimilated Jews, the speaker of the poem attacks them with some ruthlessness as they "sit *shivah* / for half-dead children" and "rot in their grief." Unlike those impotent parents and their children who "abandon the hall of God," the young Hebraists by contrast "hold in our hands the clay of the future" (15). Kleiman declares:

> We'll expel the corpses from our midst,
> and we'll know:
> who is with us
> and how to seize the reins.
>
> (15)

A second American-born Chana published two collections of Hebrew verse in the early 1960s. Like Kleiman, Chana (Annabelle) Farmelant was encouraged and inspired by Hebraist teachers, especially Silberschlag, with whom she studied in Boston.[15] (Her first collection, *Iyim bodedim* [Desert islands; 1960], echoes in its title Silberschlag's first collection, *Bashvilim bodedim.*) Farmelant's is, however, a decidedly postwar sensibility, restless and often acerbic. Her short, mainly free-verse poems often seek and do not find a basis for idealism and stable values in a post-Holocaust world. In poems such as "The Moon is Renewed" and "Skyscraper" we find a disgust with technology and its misuses, a sense that humankind is divesting itself of its humanity. This reaches its fullest development in the major poem of the collection, "B'mot Europa" (With the death of Europe), a bitter résumé of civilizational collapse. Farmelant indicts the murderousness and amorality of European culture and thought, from European anti-Semitism and assimilated Jewish self-hatred to the Holocaust. She then meditates on the continuing reign of brutal materialism behind the Iron Curtain, faced ineffectually by a still callow America and an existentialist France that follows along stupidly in the ongoing philosophical fire sale of essence and meaning. Against the background of Sputnik and the space race, Farmelant finds the West ready

---

15. I am indebted to Ms. Farmelant for our correspondence about her work, which deserves further consideration by literary scholars.

once again to rip out the secret of divinity
and turn man into a machine.
They already make progress, rape the moon,
they will rip apart the cosmos soon.
Do not ask America
why it competes,
the babe in the golden cradle
has not yet grown,
and do not ask the French
existentialists who sacrifice the essence of creation
upon the altar of being.
All is dissected, disinterred,
and what remains is indeed absurd.
                    (Farmelant 1960, 18–19)

In the wake of the general moral collapse of the West, the poet reflects on her own patrimony and situation as a rootless remnant who nevertheless must strive for some sort of expression as a poet:

I had a grandfather, owner of dense woods
an intellectual, a lord of trees,
but he did not see that Europe is mad,
the tree rotten, the trunk fell
and the wind scattered the seed
insoluble to America
and commanded me to sing.
                    (19)

Neither America nor Israel provides Farmelant with a sure basis for her values as a poet. *Iyim bodedim* contains critiques of both. The most acid is the satire "American Tour," a verse play that lashes out against American Jewish ignorance, superficiality, and suburban decadence. The characters, a wealthy American Jewish family, spit out their idiotic weltanschauung like robots. "Have them make you a recording," the father advises his son, who has to learn a bit of Torah for his bar mitzvah, "[i]t will save you from having to think." "What an amazing age we live in," says his wife admiringly, "There's no need for books" (21). The short exercise ends with a tableau of the wife in tears because her husband did not buy her the mink coat she expected to show off to her friends, the son turning on the hi-fi to listen to rock and roll, the daughter turning on the television, and the father refusing to give any more money to his synagogue unless they make him temple president. More forgiving is the critique of Israel in poems such as "The Israeli Parrot," which chastises Israel for not being different from America and Europe, for its materialistic and technological ambitions: "I want I want / a satellite, jet plane, rocket," just like "every country, even America" (32).

Although softer and more reflective, this uncertainty continues into her stronger second collection, *Pirhei zehut* (Flowers of identity), as the title would indicate. The poem "Hahoma" (The wall) uses the Western Wall in Jerusalem as the anchor for a decidedly inconclusive search for Jewish identity in the modern State of Israel. "I sought my people and did not / know from which well / to draw my future" (1961, 10). In many ways the evocative and Celan-esque poem that opens the collection most poignantly expresses Farmelant's uneasy search for roots, the relationship between the buried and the living, while also hinting at the bloody and creative processes of the female body:

Sad Roots

Rain falls
earth's womb
    blooms.
Let all who are hungry
be rinsed,
earth-diggers
among the strata
something scratches
something leads astray
underneath a blood river
    flows
a silent skeleton
    and the flower above it.
      (5)

Other students of the Hebraists include Arnold (Avraham) Band, the dean of Hebrew literary studies in America, who published his collection of poems *Hare'i bo'er ba'esh* (The mirror burns with fire) in 1963. His background in classics figures strongly in the collection, a trait he shares with Silberschlag, who was Band's teacher and then colleague before Band left Hebrew College to take up a position at UCLA where he would found the university's comparative literature program. Band's subjects tend to be literary and historical—he precedes Silberschlag, for instance, in comparing Proust with the biblical Noah. Nevertheless, a poem such as "Efer" (Ashes), a monologue by a first-century survivor of the destruction of Pompeii, likely inspired by Pliny the Younger's description of the eruption of Vesuvius, also resonates unsettlingly with twentieth-century themes of survivor's guilt and the persistence of trauma. The poem begins: "By chance I wasn't there. Only by chance" (24). And, years after the decimation of his town, the speaker confesses:

> That boy I was is now a man, a father too,
> Yet every morning, when the sun's blood
> blooms on the eastern horizon, I witness
> flocks of ravens lashing the sky,
> and I smell the acrid clouds of ash . . .
> (Band 1963, 26)

As a young man, Robert Alter, today perhaps the most influential scholar of Hebrew literature in the United States, also contributed poems to American Hebrew literary publications.[16]

Yet both Band and Alter are critics and scholars first, not poets. Band's first collection, like Kleiman's, was his last, whereas Farmelant, after publishing two books in the early 1960s, turned to writing plays in English and never again published a book in Hebrew. And so, when Gabriel Preil

---

16. For a discussion of Alter's career as an interpreter of Hebrew literature for an American audience, with some attention to his connection with American Hebraism, see Klingenstein (1998).

concluded his late-life survey of Hebrew literature in America, he understandably referred to himself as "the last of the Mohicans."

Still, there remains today a Mohican whom Preil missed. Born in 1947 in North Carolina, Robert Whitehill moved as a child to Lubbock, Texas, where he stayed through his college years. His parents, both of them children of Jewish immigrants, were themselves very much assimilated. Along with a few childhood years in the Sunday school of a local Reform synagogue, Whitehill grew up with a tree in his house at Christmastime and no bar mitzvah. Yet at thirteen, he was spurred both by curiosity and the relentless Christian proselytizing of his peers to begin reading about Judaism in the local library. He soon became entranced with Israel and its Zionist heroes. More decisively, in 1962 he purchased the *Berlitz Hebrew Self-Teacher,* quickly graduating to the "Living Language" teach-yourself-Hebrew program on vinyl records. In this solitary and determined way, he learned the language.[17]

As an undergraduate at Texas Tech in Lubbock, Whitehill found his first Hebrew conversational partner in an Israeli Arab fellow student. At the age of twenty-one, he took his first trip to Israel and spent two months in an ulpan in Netanya before returning home again to begin law school at the University of Texas in Austin. While working toward his law degree, he also sat in on Hebrew classes and completed an M.A. in English literature. A few years later, to relieve the tedium of an appellate hearing—by now he was working in a civil court—he picked up a pen and wrote his first Hebrew poem. It was accepted for publication by *Hadoar.*

Although *Hadoar* turned down subsequent poems, finding them overly vague, Whitehill had meanwhile entered into correspondence with the Israeli writer Aharon Megged, whose novels he was translating. Megged asked to see Whitehill's work, and as a result, the verse that was being rejected by *Hadoar* in America began to appear in the literary supplements

---

17. Biographical information about Whitehill comes from the author's interviews with Whitehill undertaken in March 2004, as well as Whitehill's unpublished eleven-page "Autobiographical Sketch" (in author's possession). See also Frumer (2006).

of the newspapers *Ha'aretz* and *Davar* in Israel. In 1977, thanks to the combined enthusiasm of Megged, the lyricist Yossi Gamzu, and Shimon Halkin, Whitehill's first collection, *Orvim humim* (Brown crows), was published in Israel, an occasion marked by a reception in Tel Aviv that was attended by a number of well-known Israeli literary and artistic figures as well as by the author, who at that point had still not spend more than a few months total in Israel.

In 1981, Whitehill's second collection, *Efes makom* (No place), appeared in Israel to generally positive reviews, although in some places he was treated mainly as a curiosity—the "Hebrew poet from Texas." Understandably, Whitehill was and remains concerned not to be seen as the proverbial dog walking on hind legs; still, one cannot ignore the fact that he is probably the only non-Israeli publishing fine Hebrew poetry today. And it is ironic, to say the least, that after all the efforts of the immigrant Hebraists to raise native-born American Hebrew writers, the career of America's only active Hebrew poet should have been launched more or less ex nihilo from Texas. Silberschlag was right after all: there will be more.[18]

If Hebrew poets of Whitehill's ability do not normally spring forth from assimilated families in the far reaches of the Diaspora, his emergence does owe something, I believe, to a very American tradition: the self-educated and self-trained writer. Even more ironically, it also owes something to the same Southern atmosphere that the young Whitehill found so importuning—an atmosphere characterized by an unmediated immersion in Scripture. In these respects, his act of self-invention is at once supremely American and uncannily Christian.

But a darker psychic engine also drives much of Whitehill's early work. In the most haunting sequence in *Efes makom,* a series of fifteen poems entitled "Bein tsiurei hashemen shel avi" (Among my father's oil paintings), Whitehill shifts between realistic, acerbic commentary and cryptic

---

18. Whitehill met Silberschlag while in Austin, although in what is perhaps a further irony, the latter was in Whitehill's view extremely unencouraging about his writing. According to others this lack of encouragement of younger writers was typical of Silberschlag, although Farmelant ascribes this to Silberschlag's wish not to unduly inflate the expectations of as yet unproven writers (letter from Farmelant to the author, July 6, 2007).

yet revealing meditations on the dissonances of his family relationships. In the former mode, for example, he discusses his parents' ambivalent expectations both toward their son and toward their own Jewishness: "Before I found [my wife] Susan," he writes,

> they certainly wanted me to find a woman.
> Perhaps Jewish, perhaps not.
> In any case not too much so either way.
> All religions are the same, and Jewish is just a religion, they
>   said.
> Or he said, and she said, echoing him.
> In any case it went without saying that I wouldn't marry a
>   Catholic,
> or a Protestant from one of the more extreme sects:
>   snake-handlers
> or poison-swallowers,
> and not a Mexican
> and not a black.
> Perhaps in their dreams they envisioned me standing under a
>   *huppah*
> next to Princess Anne in Westminster Cathedral
> but how to approach her?
> They certainly wanted me to find happiness
> but not too much lest I become spoiled
> to be fruitful and multiply, but not too much
> to be a man of distinction under his fig tree
> awake in dreamed America
> in any case.
>   (Whitehill 1981, 16)

In the other poems in this series, however, the ironic distance is gone, and we seem to wander with Whitehill as a boy among the strange and disturbing imagery of his father's art—by profession a psychiatrist, the elder Whitehill was also an amateur painter. Both endeavors are seen by the son as implicitly linked to the individual psyche, and both need to be transcended in favor of a more communal vision:

My father delivers me to a remote island, to a realm of horizons
with no mountains or fields around it
no produce of years but only unfathomable ocean.
                    (14)

From this perspective, Hebrew was both a means for Whitehill to express the tensions and sorrows of his family, and a form of protection against them. The first poem in the series ends: "My father passes before me, silent in another language" (13).[19]

Not long after the publication of *Efes makom,* the confidence that had allowed Whitehill to stake his claim as a Hebrew poet seemed to evaporate. The fault, as he himself has related it, was that of Saul Tchernikhovsky (1875–1943), one of the titans of modern Hebrew poetry. In the 1980s, reading Tchernikhovsky's complete works, Whitehill came to the conclusion that the worst of the classic Hebrew poet's juvenilia was better than his own best efforts. Thereupon he entered the business world—not an unreasonable decision for a family man—and though he continued reading and translating from Hebrew, he stopped publishing poems.[20]

It was over a decade later that, revisiting his own work, Whitehill decided he had been too hard on himself and actively resumed writing and publishing. He even put himself to the task of composing a sonnet cycle, just as Tchernikhovsky had done. The result of this new phase of activity has been an exciting and growing body of work, parts of which have appeared in Israeli literary journals, and forty poems of which have now been collected in Whitehill's 2007 collection *Aharei hashtikah* (After the silence), published by the Carmel Press in Israel. A second volume, *Kofim ra'im: Texas bamar'ah ha'ahorit* (Bad monkeys: Texas in the rearview mirror), is forthcoming.

---

19. By coincidence, Reuven Ben-Yosef, the only other significant Hebrew poet to emerge from an assimilated American Jewish family, also had a father who was an amateur painter.

20. Whitehill's translations of the Israeli author Yitzhak Ben-Ner's collection of stories, *Rustic Sunset*, appeared in 1998.

These new poems are impressive in their formal range, running from free-verse lyrics and prose poems to the sonnet garland. Indeed, even within the last few years Whitehill has revised many of his formerly free-verse poems in accordance with a new devotion to rhyme and formal metrics, something that has endeared him to the neoformalist group of Hebrew poets gathered around the Israeli avant-garde journal *Ho!* and its editor Dory Manor, and his work appears in other prominent Israeli literary journals such as *Iton 77*, *Keshet*, and *Shvo* as well. Moreover, Whitehill's distinctively un-Israeli style, sometimes criticized or treated with wariness by reviewers of his first two collections, now seems refreshing, even timely, in the postmodern Israeli literary scene.[21] Just as notable is Whitehill's idiosyncratic sensibility, alternately confessional and hermetic, flip and serious, pious and heretical. Some of his poems read like the stuttering loops of a psychoanalyst's malfunctioning tape recorder, others disgorge random bits of detritus like the slit-open bellies of captured sharks. They may end inconclusively, in an awkward or mischievous silence, or ascend tenaciously toward visionary horizons. They are as unpredictable as the career of their author.[22]

Several of the poems in *Aharei hashtikah* date back to the 1980s, though most are more recent. The poem "Metamorfozah," for instance, is haunted by the intensified terror-war conducted against Israel since 2000. In the poem a BBC interviewer flirts ecstatically with an aspiring suicide bomber—as if, Whitehill writes, on a blind date in the very café the bomber would destroy. Other poems offer more wide-ranging meditations on human cruelty and on the frail absurdity of the human position when faced with such cruelty. A poem composed of the poet's thoughts while exiting the Whitney Museum in New York ends with a sudden and horrifying swerve into an image of human sacrifice:

> And what passed through the soul of Hernando Cortez
> when he walked in the company of Montezuma

21. See Manor's comments in Frumer (2006).

22. My translations of Whitehill's poems reflect the revisions made by the poet since the appearance of my earlier essay on Whitehill (Weingrad 2004).

the king through the heavy stench
of the Pyramid of the Sun by dusty, turbid light,
when he choked in the reeking heat
as he raised his torch before the wall,
blanching before the dried blood
spattered there and the still wet blood
from that morning's offerings, and the massive
stone vat filled to the brim
with thousands of human hearts,
most rotting some still pulsing,
in the holy of holies. And the king said:
all is valid and binding.

(Whitehill-Bashan 2007, 10–11)

Lending unsettling force to this image in the original Hebrew is the final justificatory phrase of the king—*hakol sharir vekayam* (all is valid and binding)—familiar from the traditional Jewish marriage contract.

And indeed, part of what makes Whitehill's poetry so often surprising is its associative leaps, a kind of daydreaming. In an as yet unpublished sonnet sequence, Job, who in the Bible is from the land of Uz, becomes in one sonnet the Wizard of Uz, mourning the death of the good witch Glinda. Except that Whitehill, not content to let the reference alone, links Glinda with her wicked counterpart as two sides to the same personality, with Glinda's face turning green in death's decay and melting like water in Job's memory. The effect of these shifts and revisions is reinforced by Whitehill's language, slightly eccentric as compared with standard Israeli Hebrew, drawing opportunistically from multiple linguistic strata: Jewish liturgy, the Israeli media, the Bible, classic Hebrew literature, the classroom, and the marketplace.

Whitehill's poetry is enlivened as well by a heterodox religious imagination that often juxtaposes and fuses the sacred and the profane. These moves are not the predictable ironies of a secularist but the richer and more complicated impressions picked up by spiritual antennae that do not easily taxonomize along sacred versus secular lines. In one poem from *Aharei hashtikah,* the speaker chats with the false messiah Shabbetai Zvi in a Paris café; in another, the poet savors an image of the Lubavitcher rebbe on a billboard in Rockville, Maryland, through which peeks an older advertisement for a bygone Madonna concert. At its sharpest, Whitehill's heretical streak is expressed through the motif of biblical Judaism's arch-enemy, Baal worship, in Whitehill's hands a kind of American Canaanism. In the collection's title poem, he cites the psalmist: "I will dwell in the house of the Lord the length of my days," but then continues, "and the length of my nights I will lie in the fields / of Baal" (13). This theme is carried on at greatest length in "The Prophet of Baal Entertains Guests at His Home in Texas," a prose poem that is humorously surreal even as it reveals both Whitehill's lingering sense of alienation from Christian Texas and his somber isolation and self-deflation as a poet. Here it is, translated in its entirety:

> On the day I die, stick my corpse in a plastic bag and ship it by
> refrigerated truck to Houston. Can't waste time, it's sum-
> mer already, such heat.
> As for the ritual altars, maybe you can sell them at a garage sale.

> His embarrassed wife runs to the living room and showers the
> guests with excuses: he's been so tired lately, with all the
> sacrifices—how many showers can he take in one day?
> And the press conferences; being a prophet is hard, you
> understand, I hope, let alone a prophet of Baal, anywhere
> but particularly in Texas. Pe'or, Hadad, Zafon, Dallas, San
> Antonio, Ramat Aviv Gimel, Waco, Pardes Katz, Lubbock,
> it doesn't matter where.
> One of the guests says: Besides that, my back is killing me, I
> bumped into the edge of the dining-room table; I'm think-
> ing of calling my son, the chiropractor.
> The prophet of Baal waves his hand contemptuously and says:
> Don't bother. I went to a chiropractor and he screwed me.
> Then he excuses himself and steps into the bathroom. (Excuse
> me, I'm on a diuretic.)
> There he goes to the mirror and draws imaginary scribbles
> with his finger on the glass. He fantasizes: Thus sayeth
> Baal, And Baal said, And Baal spoke unto me saying, Thus
> speaketh Baal of Hosts, son of El, who abideth in Zafon,
> Ascribe to Baal honor and majesty. Then he flushes the
> toilet as if he had really used it, and returns to the guests.

In the living room, on the Sony color television with video and
DVD, Madonna chats with Bill Clinton about the doctrine of *tsimtsum* according to the system of the Tanya as
opposed to that of the Vilna Gaon, and they both tend to
side with the former, since (says the ex-president, biting
his lower lip as he does when he feels your pain) without
the constant presence of at least a residue of the eternal
light of the *eyn-sof*, be blessed, (now Madonna interrupts
him, caressing his hair as though they were an old married couple) neither the existent universe nor anything else
would exist.

President Clinton remarks that one clear night something odd
happened to him: he woke up to the sound of a pin falling
on a carpet. Hillary wasn't there.

Madonna adds: how strange, I dreamed the same thing, only in
my dream it wasn't a pin but a goose feather.

And another thing, says Mr. Clinton, I discovered a huge cock-
roach nesting in the bristles of my toothbrush. What does
that mean?

Madonna says: It means, Mr. President, that it's time for a message from our distinguished sponsors, our good friends at
Lone Star Beer.

Good night, O Bill.

Good night, sweetheart. Shalom, girlfriend.

Fade out.

The prophet of Baal goes to the refrigerator, fetches some cans
of Lone Star for himself and his guests.

Meanwhile, some of the guests start a game of Clue.

Who killed whom, how and where.

The losers have to jump out of the window into the front yard,
thank Baal that it's only a one-storey house.

Two-storey houses in Texas are extremely rare, even the houses
of prophets.

The prophet of Baal loses at Clue and is forced to jump from
the ground floor window to the front yard. After the jump
he gets up and shakes the dust from his clothes, and then

he sees something astonishing: Madonna and President
Clinton sitting in partial lotus style on the grass. And
they're both crying.
Why are you crying? he asks.
Weren't you paying attention? says Madonna.
I feel your pain, says the former president, and he points across
the walkway.
The prophet of Baal turns and sees that someone has stuck a
cardboard sign on a thin stick into his yard. Written on it
in sloppy handwriting are the words: FUCKING JEWS.
The prophet of Baal hesitates a moment, deliberating. And then
he laughs. Friends, please don't cry. Those stupid vandals
don't know the truth. Yes, my wife is a Jew, but I—I was a
Jew, but now I'm just a Caananite.
(57–59)

Whitehill's capacity for humor (sometimes mischievous, sometime dark) and surprise is never at the expense of humane warmth. The poem that opens *Aharei hashtikah,* for example, is a touching meditation on how a good marriage weathers life beyond the simplicities of youth. At their best, Whitehill's poems offer images of startling originality, love lyrics notable for their eroticism and vulnerability, and a personal-cultural chronicle unique in the annals of Hebrew literature. American Hebrew literature could do worse for its last Mohican.

Whitehill's literary activity is encouraging for those who care about the survival of Hebrew culture in the United States. And there are other positive signs as well. New Hebrew language programs continue to appear at American colleges and universities, and a small number of foundations work to promote Hebrew education on the early-childhood, grade-school, and high-school levels. Perhaps most significantly, in our globally and electronically connected world, Israeli literature, film, and media are readily available in America by way of DVD and the Internet to anyone who wants them.

However, such easy access to Israeli culture, wonderful as it is and unthinkable only a generation ago, may have the paradoxical effect of undermining the very possibility of a uniquely American Hebrew literary center, as Hebrew in America necessarily becomes an overseas subsidiary of Israeli culture. Air travel and the Internet today make the notion of an autonomous or distinctive Diaspora Hebrew culture highly improbable. In this regard, the few Israeli writers of promise today residing in the United States do not constitute a grouping distinguishable from the Israeli literary system.[23]

But even if this were not the case, it remains a fact that the level of fluency that would allow for the creation and appreciation of Hebrew belles lettres no more exists among American Jews today than it did in the early twentieth century when the Hebraist movement first began. More than one contemporary observer of the state of Hebrew culture in the United States has noted that although more Americans may be studying Hebrew than ever before, there are far fewer today than there were in the first half of the twentieth century who attain anything resembling the mastery of the language of a Kleiman or a Farmelant or a Band or a Whitehill, i.e., the degree of control and intimacy that might permit new creation. Whitehill's recent fecundity, fascinating as it is, cannot on its own constitute an American Hebrew renaissance, and the trajectory of his career continues to lead him again and again to Israel, where his real literary community exists.

The recent fate of *Hadoar*, the last great Hebrew publication in Diaspora, is emblematic. While the journal had always struggled, it continued to be published for over three quarters of a century. Yet in recent years the journal devolved into a biweekly and then, in a last attempt at securing a fresh lease on life, a quarterly published in partnership between the Histradrut and the Hebrew College of Boston. Finally, in 2004, the journal announced that it was no longer financially viable and, while there continue to be hopes for some new incarnation to rise from the ashes, the journal folded, bringing an end to the existence of one of the longest-running Hebrew periodicals in history, and the last forum for Hebrew belles lettres

---

23. The California-based writer Maya Arad, for instance, belongs entirely to Israeli literary culture. Similarly, English-language writers in Israel, rather than working in the isolation many such writers described twenty years ago, now compete in the same marketplace as, and share a literary community with, their Anglophone fellows in the United States, England, etc. See Alkalay-Gut (2002).

in the United States. As the immigrant Hebraists well knew, in America the situation of the Hebrew writer is, in the words of a Whitehill poem, that of "one who plays lullabies before a noisy audience / in an empty hall."[24]

And yet the relevance of the American Hebraists has not ended with their demise. Quite the opposite, in fact. This is not only because of their enduring, though insufficiently appreciated, accomplishments. Their significance derives also from the fact that, whatever may become of their literary work, their collective concerns—the fundamental questions of cultural survival in the United States—remain both urgent for Jews and universally relevant. How does a minority culture express itself as both distinct from and reflective of the larger society? How does American culture shape, challenge, and nourish the aspirations and outlook of the various populations that have made a new home here? And, of most pressing concern, what cultural and spiritual resources do American Jews today possess by which they might effectively articulate the substance, the vividness and new potentialities of their tradition to future generations in this other promised land? These are questions that the American Hebraists lived out and that in no way died with them. Along with their work, their writing, and their example, they bequeath to us the ongoing demand for answers. They can therefore say to us, as Gabriel Preil does at the end of the poem with which we began this chapter:

> From now on the responsibility no longer falls to me.
> The wise men will go about on their nearby planet, and they
> are the ones
> who will chase after a lone bird that vainly seeks a thin trickle
> of water
> in a cleft of the scorched rock.
> (Preil 1954, 36)

24. "Hadran" (Encore), unpublished poem in author's possession. The last editor of *Hadoar*, Lev Hakak, has since 2006 begun to publish an annual of American Hebrew writing entitled *Hador*.

References
——————
Index

References

Ackerman, Walter. 1993. "A World Apart: Hebrew Teachers Colleges and Hebrew-Speaking Camps." In *Hebrew in America: Perspectives and Prospects*, edited by Alan Mintz, 105–28. Detroit: Wayne State Univ. Press.

Aizenstein, Jill. 2008. "Engaging America: Immigrant Jews in American Hebrew Literature." Ph.D. diss., New York Univ.

Alkalay-Gut, Karen. 2002. "Double Diaspora: English Writers in Israel." *Judaism* 51, no. 4:457–68.

Alter, Robert. 1968. "Teaching Jewish Teachers." *Commentary* (July 1968): 60–65.

———. 1994. *Hebrew and Modernity*. Bloomington: Indiana Univ. Press.

Band, Arnold (Avraham). 1963. *Hare'i bo'er ba'esh* [The mirror burns with fire]. Jerusalem: Ogen and Ogdan.

———. 1988. "Shvilav habodedim shel Eisig Silberschlag" [The lonely paths of Eisig Silberschlag]. *Hadoar* 68, no. 8:13–16.

———. 1998. "Confluent Myths." In *Judaism and Education: Essays in Honor of Walter I. Ackerman*, edited by Haim Marantz, 1–19. Beer-Sheva: Ben-Gurion Univ. of the Negev Press.

Bavli, Hillel. 1917a. "Memories and Impressions of the Russian Revolution of 1905." *Canisius Monthly* 3, no. 8:398–405.

———. 1917b. "To Russia." *Canisius Monthly* 3, no. 9: n.p.

———. 1921/22. "Shirat Amerikah hatse'irah" [The new American poetry]. *Hatekufah* 12:433–53.

———. 1922. "Shirat Amerikah hatse'irah" [The new American poetry]. *Hatekufah* 14–15:672–92.

———. 1923. "Shirat Amerikah hatse'irah" [The new American poetry]. *Hatekufah* 19:435–53.

———. 1924. "Yashan vehadash besafrutenu" [Old and new in our literature]. *Hadoar* 4, no. 39:4–6.

———. 1937–38. *Shirim* [Poems]. 2 vols. Tel Aviv: Dvir.

———. 1955. *Aderet hashanim: Shirim* [The mantle of years: Poems]. Jerusalem: Mosad Bialik.

———. N.d. *Ruhot nifgashot: Divrei masa* [Kindred spirits: Essays]. Jerusalem: Ogen.

Ben-Or (Orinowsky), Aaron. 1965. *Toldot hasifrut ha'ivrit bedorenu* [History of contemporary Hebrew literature]. 2 vols. Tel Aviv: Yizrael.

Bialik, Haim Nahman. 1968. "As Bialik Saw America in 1926." Translated by Maurice Shudofsky. In *Modern Jewish Life in Literature*, vol. 2, edited by Azriel Eisenberg, 163–73. New York: United Synagogue of America.

———. 2004. *Hashirim* [The poems]. Edited by Avner Holtzman. Israel: Dvir.

Bourne, Randolph S. 1964. *War and the Intellectuals: Essays by Randolph S. Bourne, 1915–1919*. Edited by Carl Resek. New York: Harper and Row.

Brooks, Van Wyck. 1915. *America's Coming-of-Age*. New York: Huebsch.

———. 1968. *The Early Years: A Selection from His Works, 1908–1921*. Edited by Claire Sprague. New York: Harper and Row.

Bulletin of the New York Botanical Garden. 1909. Volume 7, no. 23.

Burstein, Andrew. 2003. *The Passions of Andrew Jackson*. New York: Knopf.

Buruma, Ian, and Avishai Margalit. 2004. *Occidentalism: The West in the Eyes of Its Enemies*. New York: Penguin.

Cahan, Abraham. 1929. "'Mayor Noakh,' a naye piese in Shvartz's teater" ['Major Noah,' a new play in Schwartz's theater]. *Forverts*. 19 Feb.

———. 1960. *The Rise of David Levinsky*. New York: Harper and Row.

Chametzky, Jules, John Felstiner, Hilene Flanzbaum, Kathryn Hellerstein, eds. 2001. *Jewish American Literature: A Norton Anthology*. New York: W. W. Norton.

Cox, James M. 1988. "Regionalism: A Diminished Thing." In *The Columbia Literary History of the United States*, edited by Emory Elliott, Martha Banta, et al., 761–84. New York: Columbia Univ. Press.

Donoghue, Denis. 1991. *Being Modern Together*. Atlanta: Scholars Press.

Dreiser, Theodore. 1987. *The Color of a Great City*. 1923. Reprint. New York: Howard Fertig.

Efros, Israel. 1933. *Vigvamim shotekim* [Silent wigwams]. Tel Aviv: Mitspah.

———. 1971. *Sefer hamasot: Histaklut besod haruah veharoshem* [Book of essays: Looking into the secret of spirit and impression]. Tel Aviv: Dvir.

Elazar, Daniel J. 1993. "The National-Cultural Movement in Hebrew Education in the Mississippi Valley." In *Hebrew in America: Perspectives and Prospects*, edited by Alan Mintz, 129–53. Detroit: Wayne State Univ. Press.

Emerson, Ralph Waldo. 1981. *The Portable Emerson*. Edited by Carl Bode and Malcolm Cowley. New York: Penguin.

Epstein, Avraham. 1952. *Sofrim ivri'im ba'Amerikah* [Hebrew writers in America]. 2 vols. Tel Aviv: Dvir.

Farmelant, Chana (Annabelle). 1960. *Iyim bodedim: Sefer shirim* [Desert islands: A book of poems]. Jerusalem: Kiryat Sefer.

———. 1961. *Pirhei zehut* [Flowers of identity]. Jerusalem: Kiryat Sefer.

Feldman, Yael. 1986. *Modernism and Cultural Transfer: Gabriel Preil and the Tradition of Jewish Literary Bilingualism*. Cincinnati: Hebrew Union College Press.

Friedman, Lawrence S. 1991. *Understanding Cynthia Ozick*. Columbia, S.C.: Univ. of South Carolina Press.

Frumer, Yoav. 2006. "Madonna veharebi meLubavich" [Madonna and the Lubavticher Rebbe]. *Maariv*. 14 April, weekend supplement.

Ginzburg, Shimon. 1913. "Bamigdal" [In the tower]. *Hashiloah* 29, no. 1:66–74; 29, no. 2:165–76.

———. 1918. "No-York" [New York]. *Luah Ahiever* 1:3–28.

———. 1920. "'Hakha' ve'hatam'" [Over here and over there]. *Miklat* 1, no. 1–3:158–60.

———. 1925. "Al shirat hashanah" [On the year's poetry]. *Hadoar* 5, no. 42:7–8.

———. 1931a. *The Life and Works of Moses Hayyim Luzzatto, Founder of Modern Hebrew Literature*. Philadelphia: Dropsie College.

———. 1931b. *Shirim ufo'emot* [Poetic works]. Tel Aviv: Dvir.

———. 1970. *Shirim ufo'emot* [Poetic works]. Jerusalem: M. Neuman.

Glants-Leyeles, Aaron. 1929. "H. Sekler's Mayor Noakh" [Hi Sackler's Major Noah] *Der tog*. 22 Feb.

Glenn, Menahem G. 1961. *Mordkhai Imanuel Noah*. N.p.: Jewish Education Committee of New York.

Gold, Michael. 1984. *Jews Without Money*. New York: Carroll and Graf.

Goldman, Shalom. 2004. *God's Sacred Tongue: Hebrew and the American Imagination*. Chapel Hill: Univ. of North Carolina Press.

Govrin, Nurit. 1986. "Bein olim lemehagrim: Kivunim menugdim behitpathut hamerkazim hasifruti'im ha'ivri'im be'Eretz-Yisrael uva'Arhab" [Homecoming or immigration: Opposite directions in the development of the Hebrew literary centers in Palestine and the U.S.A.]. *Bitsaron* 8, no. 31–32:26–33.

———. 1988. "Hateviyah la'amerikaniyut' vehagshamata basifrut ha'ivrit ba'Amerikah" [The call for "Americanness" and its realization in Hebrew literature in

America]. In *Migvan: Mehkarim basifrut ha'ivrit uvegiluyeha ha'amerikani'im* [Migvan: Studies in Hebrew literature and its American manifestations], edited by Stanley Nash, 81–97. Lod: Habermann Institute for Literary Research.

———. 2003. "'Amerikah—erets hamerets vehape'ilut: Shlomit Pflaum ba'Aratsot Habrit" [America—land of energy and activity: Shlomit Pflaum in the United States]. *Hadoar* 83, no. 1:35–41.

Greenberg, Uri Zvi. 1928. *Kelapei tish'im veteshah* [Against the ninety-nine]. Tel Aviv: Sadan.

Grodzensky, Shlomo. 1975. *Otobiografiah shel korei: Masot ureshimot al sifrut* [Autobiography of a reader: Essays and meditations on literature]. N.p.: Hakibuts hame'uhad.

———. 1978. "Shimon Halkin al i Manhatan" [Shimon Halkin on the island of Manhattan]. In *Shimon Halkin: Mivhar ma'amrei bikoret al yetsirato* [Shimon Halkin: A selection of critical essays on his writings], edited by Dan Laor, 45–56. Tel Aviv: Am Oved.

Halevy, Avraham Zvi. 1948. *Mitokh hasugar* [In the cage]. New York: Ohel.

———. 1968. *Nyu York: Shirim ve'iyunim basifrutenu hehadashah* [New York: Poems and studies in modern Hebrew literature]. Tel Aviv: Hamenora.

Halkin, Hillel. 2005. "My Uncle Simon." *Commentary* 119, no. 5:60–67.

Halkin, Shimon. 1920a. "Amerikah shelanu" [Our America]. *Miklat* 2, no. 4–6:306–9. (Signed "Ben Ha Ha.")

———. 1920b. "Amerika'iyut vesafrutenu" [Americanness and our literature]. *Miklat* 3, no. 7–9:477–80.

———. 1924. "Hashirah ha'ivrit ba'Amerikah" [Hebrew poetry in America]. *Hadoar* 4, no. 4 (28 November, 1924):10–12.

———. 1925. "Shkiah me'al ha'bos'" [Sunset over the bus]. *Hadoar* 6, no. 1:6–7.

———. 1926a. "El hakushit" [To the Negress]. *Hadoar* 6, no. 17:306.

———. 1926b. "Neged hahefkerut bamahanenu" [Against the corruption in our camp]. *Hadoar* 7, no. 8:115.

———. 1945. *Ad mashber* [Until the crash]. Tel Aviv: Am Oved.

———. 1946a. *Al ha'i: Shirim* [On the island: Poems]. Jerusalem: Mosad Bialik.

———. 1946b. *Yehudim veyahadut ba'Amerikah* [Jews and Judaism in America]. Jerusalem and Tel Aviv: Schocken.

———. 1969. *Derakhim vetsidei-derakhim basifrut* [Paths and side-paths in literature]. 3 vols. Jerusalem: Akademon.

———. 1970. *Modern Hebrew Literature, from the Enlightenment to the Birth of the State of Israel: Trends and Values.* New York: Schocken.

————. 1971. Interview. *Maariv.* 3 Sept.

————. 1972. *Nekhar: Sipurim* [Foreign land: Stories]. Jerusalem: Mosad Bialik.

————. 1977. *Shirim taraz-tashlag* [Poems 1917–1973]. Jerusalem: Mosad Bialik.

————. 1985. *Tsionut shelo-al-tenai: Masot ureshimot* [Unconditional Zionism: Essays and impressions]. Jerusalem: Hahistadrut hatsionut ha'olamit.

————. 1988. "Ya'akov Rabinovits in Yarmouth." Translated by Hillel Halkin. *Ariel* 73:4–20.

Halpern, Ben. 1996. "The Americanization of Zionism, 1880–1930." In *Essential Papers on Zionism,* edited by Jehuda Reinharz and Anita Shapira, 318–36. London: Cassell.

Handbook Number Ten: General Guide to the Museum Collections Exclusive of Paintings and Drawings. N.d., n.p.: Metropolitan Museum of Art.

Harshav, Benjamin, ed. 2000. *Shirat hatehiyah ha'ivrit: Antologyah historit-bikortit* [Hebrew renaissance poetry: A historical-critical anthology]. 2 vols. Jerusalem: Mosad Bialik.

Harshav, Benjamin, and Barbara Harshav. 1986. *American Yiddish Poetry: A Bilingual Anthology.* Berkeley: Univ. of California Press.

Helprin, Mark. 1982. *Ellis Island and Other Stories.* New York: Delta.

Hertzberg, Arthur. 1989. *The Jews in America: Four Centuries of an Uneasy Encounter.* New York: Simon and Schuster.

Higham, John. 1993. *Send These To Me: Immigrants in Urban America.* Rev. ed. Baltimore: Johns Hopkins Univ. Press.

Hollander, Philip. 2004. "Between decadence and rebirth: The fiction of Levi Aryeh Arieli." Ph.D. diss., Columbia Univ.

Holtz, Avraham. 1973. *Isaac Dov Berkowitz: Voice of the uprooted.* Ithaca: Cornell Univ. Press, 1973.

Howe, Irving. 1976. *World of Our Fathers.* New York: Simon and Schuster.

Howells, William Dean. 1968. *Their Wedding Journey.* Edited and with an introduction by John K. Reeves. Bloomington: Indiana Univ. Press.

Hudson, Steven P. 1988. *Fragmentation and Restoration: The Tikkun Ha-Olam Theme in the Metaphysical Poetry of Abraham Regelson.* Chicago: Adams Press.

Isaacs, Bernard. 1953. *Amos mokher tapuzim ve'od sipurim* [Amos the orange-seller and other stories]. Tel Aviv: M. Neuman.

Kabakoff, Jacob. 1974. "A quarter century of American Hebrew belles-lettres." In *Jewish-American Literature: An Anthology,* edited by Abraham Chapman, 607–17. New York: Signet.

———. 1978. *Shohrim vene'amanim: Masot umehkarim al hasifrut vehatarbut ha'ivrit ba'Amerikah* [Loyal and true: Essays and investigations on Hebrew literature and culture in America]. Jerusalem: Reuven Mass.

———. 1988. "Bein Shimon Halkin l'B. N. Silkiner ul'Avraham Regelson" [Shimon Halkin in connection with B. N. Silkiner and Avraham Regelson]. *Bitsaron* 9:55–59.

———. 1990. "B. N. Silkiner and His Circle: The Genesis of the New Hebrew Literature in America." *Judaism* 39:97–103.

Kaplan, Mordecai M. 2001. *Communings of the Spirit: The Journals of Mordecai M. Kaplan.* Vol. 1:1913–34. Edited by Mel Scult. Detroit: Wayne State Univ. Press.

Katchor, Ben. 1998. *The Jew of New York: A Historical Romance.* New York: Pantheon.

Katz, Stephen. 2003. "To Be As Others: E. E. Lisitzky's Re-presentation of Native Americans." *Hebrew Union College Annual* 73:249–97.

———. 2007. "Child's Play: Hillel Bavli's 'Mrs. Woods' and Indian Representation in American Hebrew Literature." *Modern Judaism* 27, no. 2:193–218.

———. 2009. *Red, Black and Jew: New Frontiers in Hebrew Literature.* Austin: Univ. of Texas Press.

Kleiman, Chana (Anne). 1947. *Netafim: Shirim* [Droplets: Poems]. Chicago: College of Jewish Studies.

Klingenstein, Susanne. 1997. "'In My Life I Am Not Free': The Writer Cynthia Ozick and Her Jewish Obligations." In *Daughters of Valor: Contemporary Jewish American Women Writers,* edited by Jay Halio and Ben Siegel, 48–79. Newark and London: Univ. of Delaware Press and Associated Univ. Presses.

———. 1998. *Enlarging America: The Cultural Work of Jewish Literary Scholars, 1930–1990.* Syracuse, N.Y.: Syracuse Univ. Press.

Lamdan, Yitzhak. 1925. "Hazit me'uhedet" [A united front]. *Hedim* 3, no. 6:89–93. (Signed Y. Labie.)

Laor, Dan, ed. 1978. *Shimon Halkin: Mivhar ma'amrei bikoret al yetsirato* [Shimon Halkin: A selection of critical essays on his writings]. Tel Aviv: Am Oved.

Lazarus, Emma. 1982. *Selections from Her Poetry and Prose.* Edited and with an introduction by Morris U. Schappes. New York: Emma Lazarus Federation of Jewish Women's Clubs.

Lederhendler, Eli. 1994. *Jewish Responses to Modernity: New Voices in America and Eastern Europe.* New York: New York Univ. Press.

Lewis, Alfred Henry. 1903. *Peggy O'Neal.* New York: Biddle, 1902. Reprint: American News Company, 1903.

Lewis, David Levering, ed. 1994. *The Portable Harlem Renaissance Reader.* New York: Penguin.

Lisitzky, Ephraim. 1937. *Medurot doakhot* [Dying campfires]. New York: Ogen.

———. 1953. *Be'ohalei khush: Shirim* [In the tents of Cush: Poems]. Jerusalem: Mosad Bialik.

———. 1959. *In the Grip of Cross-Currents.* Translated by Moshe Kohn and Jacob Sloan. New York: Bloch. Originally published as *Ele toldot adam.*

Longfellow, Henry Wadsworth. 1993. *Selected Poems.* London: Everyman.

Lowin, Joseph. 1988. *Cynthia Ozick.* Boston: Twayne.

Lurie, Aviva. 2005. "Yehudi haser manoah" [Restless Jew]. *Ha'aretz.* 30 Sept.

Malachi, A. R. 1961/62. "Latoldot Hillel Bavli" [Biographical study of Hillel Bavli]. *Bitsaron* 44, no. 7:166–73; 45, no. 2:67–75; 45, no. 3:137–48.

The Metropolitan Museum of Art: A Guide to the Collections. 1927. New York: n.p.

Michaels, Walter Benn. 1995. *Our America: Nativism, Modernism, and Pluralism.* Durham, N.C.: Duke Univ. Press.

Mintz, Alan. 1993. "A Sanctuary in the Wilderness: The Beginnings of the Hebrew Movement in America in *Hatoren.*" In *Hebrew in America: Perspectives and Prospects,* edited by Alan Mintz, 29–67. Detroit: Wayne State Univ. Press.

———. 2003. "Hebrew Literature in America." In *The Cambridge Companion to Jewish American Literature,* edited by Michael P. Kramer and Hana Wirth-Nesher, 92–109. Cambridge, U.K.: Cambridge Univ. Press.

Mintz, Ruth Finer. 1966. *Modern Hebrew Poetry: A Bilingual Anthology.* Berkeley: Univ. of California Press.

Miron, Dan. 1975. "Lareka hamevukhah basifrut ha'ivrit bareshit heme'ah ha'esrim" [On the uncertain background of Hebrew literature at the beginning of the twentieth century]. In *Sefer hayovel leShimon Halkin* [Jubilee volume for Shimon Halkin], edited by Boaz Shahevitch and Menahem Peri, 419–87. Jerusalem: Reuven Mas.

———. 1991. *Noge'a badavar: Masot al sifrut, tarbut, vehevrah* [Person concerned: Essays on literature, culture, and society]. Tel Aviv: Zmora-bitan.

———. 1993. "Ben haner lakokhavim" [Between the candle and the stars]. In Gabriel Preil, *Asfan stavim, shirim 1972–1992* [Collector of autumns, poems 1972–1992]. Jerusalem: Bialik.

———. 1999. *Ha'adam eino ela . . . , hulshat-hakoah, otzmat-hahulshah: Iyunim bashirah* [Man is nothing but . . . , the weakness of strength, the strength in weakness: Studies in poetry]. Tel Aviv: Zmora-Bitan.

———. 2005. *Harpayah letsorekh negiyah: Likrat hashivah hadashah al sifruyot hayehudim* [Moving away in order to touch: Towards a new theory of the literatures of the Jews]. Tel Aviv: Am Oved.

Moss, Stanley. 1998. *Asleep in the Garden.* N.p.: Seven Stories Press.

Nadell, Pamela S. 1998. *Women Who Would Be Rabbis: A History of Women's Ordination, 1889–1985.* Boston: Beacon.

Niger, Shmuel. 1929. "Moshiah—Amerikaner shtil" [Messiah—American style]. *Der tog.* 21 Feb.

Noah, Mordecai. 1999. *The Selected Writings of Mordecai Noah.* Edited by Michael Schuldiner and Daniel J. Kleinfeld. Westport, Conn.: Greenwood Press.

Ozick, Cyntha. 1972. "A Bintel Brief for Jacob Glatstein." *Jewish Heritage:*58–60.

———. 1983. *The Pagan Rabbi and Other Stories.* New York: Dutton.

———. 1984. *Art and Ardor: Essays.* New York: Dutton.

———. 1997. *The Puttermesser Papers.* New York: Knopf.

Parisi, Joseph, and Stephen Young, eds. 2002. *Dear Editor: A History of Poetry in Letters, The First Fifty Years, 1912-1962.* New York: Norton.

Pelli, Moshe. 1998. *Hatarbut ha'ivrit ba'Amerikah: Shmonim shnot hatenuah ha'ivrit ba'Aratsot-Habrit (1916–1995)* [Hebrew culture in America: Eighty years of the Hebraist movement in the United States (1916–1995)]. Tel Aviv: Reshafim.

Preil, Gabriel. 1950–51. "Bashulei sifro ha'angli shel Sh. Halkin al hasifrut ha'ivrit hamodernit" [In the Margins of Sh. Halkin's English Book on Modern Hebrew Literature]. *Bitsaron* 23, no. 3:196–200.

———. 1954. *Ner mul kokhavim* [A candle facing stars]. Jerusalem: Mosad Bialik.

———. 1961. *Mapat erev* [Map of evening]. Tel Aviv: Dvir.

———. 1968. *Ha'esh vehademamah* [The fire and the silence]. N.p.: Masada.

———. 1972. *Mitokh zeman vanof: Shirim mekubatsim* [From a time and a place: Collected poems]. Jerusalem: Mosad Bialik.

———. 1980. *Adiv le'atsmi: Shirim 1976–1979* [Courteous to myself: Poems 1976–1979]. Tel Aviv: Hakibuts hame'uhad.

———. 1985. *Sunset Possibilities and Other Poems.* Translated and with an introduction by Robert Friend. Philadelphia: Jewish Publication Society.

———. 1987. *Hamishim shir bamidbar* [Fifty poems in the wilderness]. Tel Aviv: Hakibuts hame'uhad.

———. 1988. "Meser lididi Sh. Halkin" [A message to my friend S. Halkin]. *Hadoar* 67, no. 19:12.

————. 1991. Interview with Ester Dotan. *Hadoar* 71, no. 3:13–16

————. 1993a. *Asfan stavim, shirim 1972–1992* [Collector of autumns, poems 1972–1992]. Edited and with essay by Dan Miron. Jerusalem: Mosad Bialik.

————. 1993b. "Re'ayon im Gavriel Preil" [interview with Gabriel Preil]. 1972. Audio recording. Jerusalem: Kol Yisrael. Harvard catalogue JCKY 353.

Rabinowitz, Yaakov. 1920. "Amerika'iyut" [Americanness]. *Miklat* 2, no. 4–6:463–65.

————. 1924. "Amerika'iyut" [Americanness]. *Hadoar* 4, no. 34:9–11.

————. 1927. "Bli rogez" [Without anger]. In *Sefer hayovel shel Hadoar* [*Hadoar* jubilee volume], edited by Menachem Ribalow, 46–50. New York: Hahistadrut ha'ivrit ba'Amerikah.

————. 1934. "Hamafkid ha'aharon" [The last of the faithful]. In *Sefer zikaron le'B. N. Silkiner* [Memorial volume for B. N. Silkiner], edited by Menahem Ribalow, 72–73. N.p.: Ogen.

Raisin, Zalman, ed. 1927–29. *Leksikon fun der Yidisher Literatur Prese un Filologie* [The Lexicon of Yiddish literature, journalism, and philology]. 4 vols. Vilna: Kletzkin.

Ravitz, Abe C. 1978. *Alfred Henry Lewis.* Boise State University Western Writers Series, no. 32. Boise, Idaho: Boise State Univ.

Regelson, Avraham. 1945. *El ha'ayin venivka: Shirim* [To the nothingness which split: Poems]. Tel Aviv: Am Oved.

————. 1964. *Hakukot otiotayikh: Shirim* [Engraved are your letters: Poems]. N.p.: Mahbarot lesifrut.

Reznikoff, Charles. 1989. *Poems 1918–1975: The Complete Poems of Charles Reznikoff.* Edited by Seamus Cooney. Santa Rosa, Calif.: Black Sparrow Press.

Ribalow, Menachem. 1924. "Safrut bimevukhah" [Literature in confusion]. *Hadoar* 4, no. 4:5–6.

————, ed. 1934. *Sefer zikaron le'B. N. Silkiner* [Memorial volume for B. N. Silkiner]. N.p.: Ogen.

————, ed. 1938. *Antologiyah shel hashirah ha'ivrit ba'Amerikah* [Anthology of Hebrew poetry in America]. New York: Ogen.

Rosenberg, Bernard, and Ernest Goldstein, eds. 1982. *Creators and Disturbers: Reminiscences by Jewish Intellectuals of New York.* New York: Columbia Univ. Press.

Roskies, David G. 2003. "Coney Island, U.S.A.: America in the Yiddish literary imagination." In *The Cambridge Companion to Jewish American Literature,* edited by Michael P. Kramer and Hana Wirth-Nesher, 70–91. Cambridge: Cambridge Univ. Press.

Roth, Philip. 1975. *Reading Myself and Others*. New York: Farrar, Straus and Giroux.

Ryskind, Morrie, with John H. M. Roberts. 1994. *I Shot an Elephant in My Pajamas*. Lafayette, La.: Huntington House.

Sackler, Harry. 1943. *Sefer hamahazot* [Book of plays]. New York: Ogen.

———. 1964. *Bein erets veshamayim: Roman* [Between heaven and earth: A novel]. Tel Aviv: Yavneh.

———. 1966a. *Olelot* [Gleanings]. Tel Aviv: Yavneh.

———. 1966b. *Sof pasuk: Simanim vesamemanim le'otobiografiah* [Full stop: Notes and ingredients for an autobiography]. Tel Aviv: Yavneh.

Samuel, Maurice. 1977. *The Worlds of Maurice Samuel: Selected Writings*. Edited by Milton Hindus. Philadelphia: Jewish Publication Society of America.

Sarna, Jonathan. 1981. *Jacksonian Jew: The Two Worlds of Mordecai Noah*. New York: Holmes and Meier.

Scharfstein, Zvi. 1956. *Arba'im shanah ba'Amerikah* [Forty years in America]. Tel Aviv: Masada.

Schimmel, Harold. 1974. *Shirei melon Tsion* [Hotel Zion poems]. N.p.: Hakibuts hame'uhad.

Semel, Nava. 2005. *Iyisrael* [Isra-island]. Tel Aviv: Yediot Ahronot.

Shahevitch, Boaz, and Menahem Peri, eds. 1975. *Sefer hayovel leShimon Halkin* [Jubilee volume for Shimon Halkin]. Jerusalem: Reuven Mas.

Shaked, Gershon. 1988. *Hasiporet ha'ivrit, 1880–1990* [Hebrew fiction, 1880–1980]. Vol. 3, *Hamodernah ben shtei milhamot, mavo la-"dorot ba'arets"* [Literary modernism between the wars, introduction to the "generation in the land"]. Tel Aviv: Keter and Hakibuts hame'uhad.

Shavit, Uzi. 1992. "The New Hebrew Poetry of the Twenties: Palestine and America." *Prooftexts* 12:213–30.

Shavit, Zohar. 1988. "Hanisayon hakoshel lehakim merkaz shel sifrut ivrit ba'Amerikah" [On the failure of the attempt to constitute a Hebrew cultural center in America]. In *Migvan: Mehkarim basifrut ha'ivrit uvegiluyeha ha'amerikani'im* [Migvan: Studies in Hebrew literature and its American manifestations], edited by Stanley Nash, 433–49. Lod: Habermann Institute for Literary Research.

Shneur, Zalman. 1934. "Shir-mizmor la'Amerikah" [A psalm for America]. *Gilyonot* 1, no. 6:486–87.

Silberschlag, Eisig. 1958. "Zionism and Hebraism in America (1897–1921)." In *Early History of Zionism in America: Papers Presented at the Conference on*

Early History of Zionism in America, edited by Isidore Meyer, 326–40. New York: American Jewish Historical Society and Theodor Herzl Foundation.

———. 1972. "Sackler, Harry." In *Encyclopaedia Judaica*, edited by Cecil Roth, vol. 14, 598. Jerusalem: Keter.

———. 1973. *From Renaissance to Renaissance*. 2 vols. New York: Ktav.

———. 1976. *Yesh reshit lekhol aharit* [Each end has a beginning]. Jerusalem: Kiryat sefer.

———. 1981. *Bein alimut uvein adishut* [Between violence and indifference]. Jerusalem: Reuven Mass.

Silkiner, Benjamin N. 1910. *Mul ohel Timurah: Shivrei poemah (mizman shilton hasfaradim ba'Amerikah)* [Before the tent of Timmurah: Fragments of a narrative poem (from the time of the Spanish rule of America)]. Jerusalem: Asaf.

———. 1927. *Shirim* [Poems]. Israel: Dvir.

Sollors, Werner. 1986. *Beyond Ethnicity: Consent and Descent in American Culture*. New York: Oxford Univ. Press.

Spicehandler, Ezra. 1993. "*Amerika'iyut* in American Hebrew Literature." In *Hebrew in America: Perspectives and Prospects*, edited by Alan Mintz, 68–104. Detroit: Wayne State Univ. Press.

Stern, Noah. 1974. *Bein arfilim: Shirim, tirgumim, reshimot* [Between fogs: Poems, translations, impressions]. Tel Aviv: Hakibuts hame'uhad.

Stevens, Wallace. 1990. *The Collected Poems*. New York: Vintage.

Trachtenberg, Alan. 2004. *Shades of Hiawatha: Staging Indians, Making Americans, 1880–1930*. New York: Hill and Wang.

Twain, Mark. 1966. *The Innocents Abroad*. New York: Signet.

Twersky, Yohanan. 1954. *Eifo eretz Ararat? Roman mehayei Mordekai Emanuel Noah* [Where is the land of Ararat? A novel based on the life of Mordecai Emanuel Noah]. Tel Aviv: Ayanot.

Udelson, Joseph H. 1990. *Dreamer of the Ghetto: The Life and Works of Israel Zangwill*. Tuscaloosa: Univ. of Alabama Press.

Untermeyer, Louis. 1919. *The New Era in American Poetry*. New York: Henry Holt.

———. 1923. *American Poetry Since 1900*. New York: Henry Holt.

Wallenrod, Reuven. 1937. *Badyotah hashlishit: Sipurim* [On the third floor: Stories]. Tel Aviv: Dvir.

———. 1952. *Bein homot Nyu York* [Within the walls of New York]. Jerusalem: Mosad Bialik.

———. 1956. *The Literature of Modern Israel*. New York: Abelard Schuman.

———. 1957. *Dusk in the Catskills*. New York: Reconstructionist Press.

Waxman, Meyer. *A History of Jewish Literature*. 1941. Vol. 4, *From Eighteen-Eighty to Nineteen-Thirty-Five*. New York: Bloch.

Wechsler, Lawrence. 1993. "A Wanderer in the Perfect City." *The New Yorker* 69, no. 25:58–66.

Weingrad, Michael. 2003. "Jewish Identity and Poetic Form in 'By the Waters of Babylon: Little Poems in Prose.'" *Jewish Social Studies* 9, no. 3:107–20.

———. 2004. "Lost Tribes: The Indian in American Hebrew Poetry." *Prooftexts* 24, no. 3:291–319.

———. 2006. "The Last of the (Hebrew) Mohicans." *Commentary* 121, no. 3:45–50.

Whitehill, Robert. N.d. *Orvim humim: Shirim* [Brown crows: Poems]. N.p.: Eked.

———. 1981. *Efes makom: Shirim* [No place: Poems]. Jerusalem: Dvir.

———. (Whitehill-Bashan). 2007. *Aharei hashtikah* [After the silence]. Jerusalem: Carmel.

Wiener, Haim. 1929. "Bate'atron, 'Mayor Noah'" [At the theater: Review of "Major Noah"]. *Hadoar* 9, no. 17:292.

Wirth-Nesher, Hana. 2006. *Call It English: The Languages of Jewish American Literature*. Princeton, N.J.: Princeton Univ. Press.

Yardeni, Galya. 1961. *16 sihot im sofrim* [16 conversations with writers]. Tel Aviv: Hakibuts hame'uhad.

Zangwill, Israel. 1938. *Selected Works*. Philadelphia: Jewish Publication Society, 1938.

Zierler, Wendy. 2004. *And Rachel Stole The Idols: The Emergence of Modern Hebrew Women's Writing*. Detroit: Wayne State Univ. Press.

Zylbercwaig, Zalmen, and Jacob Mestel, eds. 1934. *Leksikon fun Yidishn Teater* [The Yiddish theater lexicon]. Vol. 2. Warsaw: Farlag Elisheva.

Index

273